I Need a Smoke

Leianne McNair
I Need a Smoke

Published by BooxAi

ISBN 978-965-578-033-8

I Need a Smoke

A MEMOIR

LEIANNE MCNAIR

Contents

I want to dedicate this to my four children, without whom this book would not have been possible. I know you have all been through hell, and I respect you for not wanting to read this book—it is your story too and with that story, I know, comes a lot of pain. You believed in me, did not give up on me, supported me through some very rough times, over and over again and gave me a reason to live, and for that, I shall be forever grateful.

I love you.

About The Author

Leianne McNair, mother of four and grandmother of three, managed to handle the cards that were dealt to her with grace and acceptance. Throughout her life, she experienced what it was like to be impoverished and then was lucky enough to encounter the wealth that Oil and Gas Companies can provide before falling back into financial struggle. She never questioned why, and always did her best to *fix* things, until the year that her mother became gravely ill, and her mother-in-law was diagnosed with stage-four lung cancer—things that were out of her control and beyond her ability to fix. All at once, many unfortunate, very stressful incidents happened and Leianne found herself overwhelmed with grief and to the point that she knew something was terribly wrong. She learned things about grief that she did not know, and how it can rear its ugly head in many different ways.

Not only did her journey become extremely overwhelming, but it also affected her children deeply and the definition of 'family' took on a greater meaning. This is a story of that journey, which nobody wants to take, but for those who have, may this book help you realize that you are not alone and somewhere out there is the help that you desperately seek.

Part One

Chapter One

I have no self-esteem, I never have, and that is not a good thing. I'm always wishing I could be someone else. I don't like myself and I know that's wrong. I am embarrassed about the way that I look, I don't take care of myself and as a result, I have lots of medical problems, including mental illness.

I was born on a hot June afternoon. It was the 1960s; the world then was different than it is now. I was the eldest child with two brothers in tow, Jeff and Tom. We were your average family, living our ordinary lives. However, our lives weren't so average after all.

My mom and dad were opposites and grew up with vastly different lifestyles. My father, Mike, was born in Peace River, Alberta, on October 9, 1937. His mother was a Metis Cree Aboriginal and he had a Czechoslovakian father. His household was quite large, comprising ten children. He didn't have such an easy life growing up. They lived on a farm in a small shack with only two bedrooms without running water, electricity, or heat. It was my dad's job to chop the wood and stock the woodstove to stay warm during the harsh cold winter months.

My dad was particularly attached to his mother, which came

as no surprise since she was the homemaker. She was a very hard worker, having to hand wash all of their clothing, heat the water on the stove, kill chickens and milk cows for their evening meals. When she could afford fabric and hides, she would hand-sew moccasins and clothing for her large brood of children. She was an incredible cook, who made the meager food that she had taste delicious and go a long way.

My dad was never keen on talking about his childhood. We would often hear stories of how his mother would plant a huge garden when there was a full moon. Back then, the natives believed that the moon's gravitational pull brought forth the water from the plants and the earth. The bounties from the garden were always preserved to get the family through the winter months. My grandfather was also a hard worker, but he liked to indulge sometimes a little too much at the end of the day. The family was extremely poor, with barely enough money for supplies, and they produced most of their own food, milk, cream, butter, and meat. There was nothing left for any extras, which included winter boots and warm winter clothing.

My dad's school was almost three miles from his home, and he had to walk all the way there on a country dirt road. He lived in Northern Alberta, and, at times, it got extremely cold, sometimes even colder than -40 degrees Celsius. My grandmother fashioned a pair of makeshift winter boots out of a buffalo hide that she had skinned, and they used another buffalo hide to cover up whenever the kids could take the horse and wagon to school.

Whenever he would think back on it, Dad always said the same thing—that he was never too proud not to wear those ugly boots. He would always change his tone and in a very lecturing kind of way, would tell us, "I knew better than to disobey my parents, and they kept my feet warm. I never thought twice of it." He liked school, and he was smart, but he couldn't go to school for a long time. When he was just 11 years old, in grade 6, he had to quit and help out on the family farm. We had a standing joke in the family that he had finished half of twelve grades, and when asked why he didn't finish the other half, he used to say, "I didn't want to do another six years!"

When he was sixteen years old, Dad left home to try to make it on his own. He worked on the oil rigs in Northern Alberta for a while and decided that it was not for him, as you got incredibly dirty. Then he traveled the province, building grain elevators. All of my dad's siblings are pretty amazing and damn tough. Auntie Carol, who could still wrestle a cow at the age of 67, raised six children in a two-bedroom farmhouse in the 1970s with no electricity or running water. My Auntie Betty lived her dream in Vancouver as a movie extra still in her eighties. Auntie Margaret became a nurse and lived in the beautiful town of Jasper while raising six children. My Aunt Nancy was the operator of a large ski resort in British Columbia before becoming a fisherwoman out on the coast. Chickie, a nickname given to her as a child as it was her job to kill the chickens, worked hard as a school custodian and bus driver yet managed to open her home and be an incredible mother to five foster children—and is an absolute riot to spend time with. Then there is my Aunt Freida, whose husband had such severe arthritis that he was deemed disabled in his late thirties, so to take care of her family, she babysat during the day— people were lined up to get into her makeshift daycare as she loved kids and kids loved her. At one point, she had 28 children that she was caring for in her small home. My Uncle Bob was the entertainer; he was an incredible guitar player and singer, and teaming up with his dad to do a fantastic rendition of a chainsaw routine was his legacy. Unfortunately, he was electrocuted at work in his late thirties. The two youngest siblings were Phillip, who went on to become a top-notch lawyer, and Rosalie, who found the love of her life and travelled the world with him.

Each of my aunts is an incredible cook, using only the simplest ingredients and making the most delicious meals. I have numerous cousins on this side of the family, all of whom are quite successful. This family has lived one tough life, barely getting the essentials to live on, but it made them appreciate the gifts of nature, the gift of life, and each other.

Comparatively, my mother, Janet, lived a very easy life. She was born on March 11, 1939, in a small town in Central Alberta. Her dad John was a sheriff and an award-winning amateur photographer and movie-maker. Her mom Betty was a teacher.

For the longest time, the family comprised of just my mother and her younger sister Marilyn. Then thirteen years later, my mother's youngest sister, Dereka, was born. She was the apple of my mother's eye and my mother considered her to be her baby. Seventeen and eighteen years later, respectively, my two uncles were born, Brian and Barry. Yes, they are only two and three years older than me. They were more like my older brothers than my uncles growing up.

My mother had always dreamed of becoming a judge, however, her father didn't believe that a woman should be a lawyer or a judge but rather a teacher or nurse. My mother, disappointed as she was, opted to be a teacher and because she graduated high school so early, she finished the two-year teaching program at age 17. Her sister Marilyn went on to study to become a Psychiatric Nurse, eventually teaching the program. Her other sister Dereka went on to graduate at the top of her class as a Chartered Accountant and her two younger brothers became a doctor and a lawyer. My mom's dad passed away in his late fifties, which was a real blow to my mom as she was very close to her father. However, having five children all graduate with a university degree was a remarkable feat as my grandmother essentially was a single mother, yet managed to help guide her youngest children to all become very successful. My grandmother actually taught school until she was 83 years old. She liked to work, as did my mom, and anything they did, they gave it their all.

* * *

My mother started teaching at the age of 17 and her first class was grade 12. She had students older than her in her class and therefore, her first year of teaching was a challenge for her.

My parents met in the same place where they grew up—Peace

River. My mom was teaching in the local school and living in teacher's accommodations. My dad had seen her in town and asked around to find out where she lived. My dad thought it would be a good way to meet her if he approached her and pretended that he had to measure her floor for new flooring.

Of course, that was a complete lie. He was always the practical joker, and he could pull a prank on someone with the straightest face; this time was no different. What he didn't expect, though, was that it would eventually lead him to the woman with whom he would spend the rest of his life. He also didn't expect that my mother would get very excited about her new flooring, which was never going to materialize, but she was especially excited to meet this handsome young man.

They dated for a year and then, to my parents' dismay, they found out that my mom was pregnant with me. They knew they were right for each other, so they opted to elope and have a very small wedding. They rented a modest home in Nampa, a small town just outside of Peace River. Eighteen months after I was born, in 1962, my brother Jeff came along. Then in 1963, my brother Tom came along and my mother had her hands full.

That same year, when I was 3 years old, and Tom was still a baby, my mother fell while doing the laundry. Unfortunately, she was carrying a five-gallon washbasin of boiling water. She ended up getting third-degree burns all over her upper torso. She was burnt so badly that doctors had to operate just to remove her bra as it had melted to her body. She had to spend the next while in the hospital, healing and then enduring skin grafts. She had burns on over 80% of her body. Luckily, her face did not incur any damage from that horrible accident. It was amazing how family and friends stepped in to care for her small children that year as my dad was working out of town.

My dad was quite a figure in our family, though, mainly because of his tough childhood. He was used to living in harsh conditions, his parents were very strict, and he was an amazingly strong person, like a force of nature. Not to mention, he was quite proud; I don't think I ever saw my dad ask for help in his lifetime.

He was the kind of person who, when he talked, everybody would quiet down and listen. He had that sort of seriousness from an early age, however, he always loved to pull pranks on people.

There was a time when Dad had to get one of his wisdom teeth pulled. He was working in some isolated town in northern Alberta, where he found a dentist. The dentist's supplies were running short, and he didn't expect them to be replenished for another four days.

"Four days? I can't wait that long," Dad said. He then surprised the dentist by asking him to pull out the impacted tooth without any sort of freezing or anesthesia whatsoever. The dentist was shocked but couldn't refuse my father.

It just proved even more how much he was a man to be reckoned with. His childhood played a crucial role in turning him into the man he was, and it eventually made him kind of harsh. My dad was tough on my brothers, usually for things like taking the car or stealing his booze when they were underage. I screwed up as well, but he would never reprimand me the way he reprimanded my brothers.

My brothers hated how I would often get away with things, and it made me feel quite guilty. My Dad was very reserved in telling us that he loved us. The first time I heard those words from his mouth, I was 16 and going through a rough time. I was having suicidal thoughts, basically because I, like many others, thought teenage life was treating me unfairly. I will never forget my dad, not my mom, coming downstairs where I sat alone in my thoughts and holding me, telling me that he loved me. It was odd seeing such a tough man come down to my level and teach me, through his sincere compassion, how much I had to live for. It just made me realize how great he was.

The best part about Dad was his great sense of humor and how he loved to tease. While his tough spells were difficult to handle, there were also times when he would get crazy with us. I recall once, before I turned sixteen and was due to get my driver's license, he was teaching me how to drive. We somehow got onto the highway. I should have known that he would pull something, but I figured that it was such a big deal driving on the highway for the first time that he would let this opportunity for mischief slide. Oh, how little I knew him!

As I was driving down the highway, Dad thought the best way to teach me how to control a skidding car would be by pulling the hand brake. The car was at sixty MPH, and it spun like crazy. I screamed in surprise, and he burst out laughing, even though I found nothing funny about the incident. Somehow, I managed to stop the car and save it from any serious damage. I turned and asked him why he did that. He simply replied, "There! Now you know what to do if that ever happens to you."

All I remember thinking was how I would ever be in a situation like that again. Yes, it was terrifying at the time. While I sat there, gripping the steering wheel tightly, he couldn't stop laughing. In hindsight now, I see how funny it was and I ended up laughing as well.

It was around that same time that Dad taught me how to change the oil in my car. It was a warm day, and I was on my back under that car when he pointed out a bolt that was just above my face. He told me to undo that bolt, and I didn't really think about it. Now, I should probably mention that Dad had this thing where he would play pranks on us and keep a level and straight tone. That way, we'd never know when he was joking and when he wasn't. Since he did have a bit of a temper, we usually did what he told us to without question.

That day when I heard his smooth, even voice from above me tell me to look for a bolt, I didn't really think much of it and unscrewed it. Immediately, the oil splattered all over my face and in my mouth, sticking in my hair. I immediately spat it out and then gasped, and I could hear my Dad trying to control his laugh. I slid out from underneath the car and looked at him in disbelief. I asked why he didn't tell me about the oil before I unscrewed the bolt. He jokingly replied, "Well, you didn't ask now, did you?"

To be fair, he was right, I should have asked. My Dad was always on with his jokes, but he carefully placed them. However, his main achievement was parenting. My father always wanted to keep us out of trouble, and so his solution was to make sure that we spent a lot of time at the ski hill. He took us out there three nights a week after supper. On Saturdays, my mom packed our lunch, and Dad drove us out in the morning and picked us up at 10 p.m. when the ski hill closed. You would think that all that skiing made us expert skiers—my brothers, yes, me, no. I was too chicken of the black diamond hills and pretty much stuck to the green and blue ones.

One year, my brothers and two friends went to the mountains to ski and were in a horrific car accident coming home. Unfortunately, they had all fallen asleep. The steering wheel went through my brother Jeff's mouth, and he lost all of his teeth. We were at home, oblivious to what was happening. But a phone call from the Royal Canadian Mounted Police, or RCMP, brought with it a tragic sense of reality and we were soon on our way to Calgary, 90 miles away, to be with the boys.

We discovered that, as Jeff was being put in a helicopter to be flown to the hospital, he heard the paramedics say that the car would blow. Panic filled him, and he screamed that his younger brother was still in there. Luckily, they got Tom out just in time. He ended up having a cracked skull and a severe concussion, and the two had to stay in the hospital for a month. It was a difficult time for my parents, but they made sure that they were at the hospital as often as things allowed.

My Dad never let this incident faze him, though. Even as he grew older, he remained quite the hard ass. I learned this when we purchased a hot tub for our cabin at the lake, and we invited all our friends and family to help install it. It had to be carried down three stairs and through a bunch of rocks. The people we asked to help were all very well educated—we had a lawyer, a couple of doctors, an engineer, and a geologist, so we were confident that this job would be a piece of cake. Boy, was I wrong!

First, we broke the tub siding, taking it off the truck. Then, as we proceeded with it down the lane, my uncle, the doctor, felt something snap in his forearm. The pain shot up, making him cringe bloody murder. It turns out that he had torn a tendon and required surgery, which kept him off work for three months. The lesson was learned, and we never went back to the hot tub again. It remained on its side because I didn't want anything else to happen, so I said I would get professional movers to move it down by the lake next week.

My Dad was out of town at the time, and I called him and told him my plan. He replied, "What the hell do you need them for? I did it this morning. I just about lost it going down the stairs, but I managed to hang on. It's overlooking the lake, like you wanted."

I asked who he got to help him.

And he replied, "Why the hell would I need help? I did it by myself."

I have to say I was impressed. I then asked how on earth he did it, getting it over the rocks. His answer was, "How do you think the Egyptians built the pyramids? I rolled it on the pipe."

I felt the realization knock me with a laugh and I couldn't stop. I was dumbfounded, as were our friends and family that initially helped. My Dad was 71 years old! Yep, as I said, one tough son of a bitch.

* * *

My mother, on the other hand, was a very kind and caring woman. She worked with mentally disabled kids in a residential institution, which was an amazing and humbling experience for her. My mom already had the sweetest touch in her, but working with those children made her realize the fragility of life and how thankful she was to have us. She would do anything for anyone, and it was one reason people took a liking to her immediately.

Whereas my dad came from a household of twelve, my mother came from a family of seven. She had a great relationship with her siblings even though she was older than her youngest brother by almost eighteen years. All of her siblings went on to hold university degrees and were high achievers.

In 1965, my dad moved us to Red Deer, where my mom's

parents had moved, as he was going to live with them, get a stable job, and his family would eventually follow. When my Dad moved to Red Deer, my mom was solely responsible for the care of her three small children and holding down a full-time teaching job. I would have to say that she was a very brave woman, as one night when she was alone with us, watching television and there was a loud bang on the door. It was frightening and my Mom got up to check things. She opened the door and a man covered in blood practically fell into her arms. I was terrified, I thought he was dead. Honestly, after that, I don't remember what happened.

Then there was another incident; one night, we were in the small living room watching TV when my Mom screeched. There was a man peering in the window—he was a peeping tom. It terrified me but once again, my Mom put on a brave face and tried to calm us all and assure us that we were all fine. To this day, because of these incidents, I'm scared to be alone.

Mom loved cooking, and her baking was probably the reason I have such a sweet tooth. She loved to bake and was always baking something for when friends came for coffee, which was often. Her specialties were pies and chiffon cakes. I always yearned desperately for those days when I would come home to that wonderful aroma wafting through the house.

My mom never watched TV and always insisted that we do our chores right after returning home from school. We were always grumpy as most of our friends got to play after school, but we came home and took turns dusting and vacuuming; none of us liked cleaning the bathrooms, but Mom made sure she cleaned the bathroom daily.

When I was five years old, my parents packed up all their measly belongings and made their way to Red Deer, Alberta. She had lots of friends and friendship was very important to her. She valued every relationship she built, even with her students. She often brought the institutional residents who had no family home for the weekend. My Mom had the biggest heart and was never judgmental about anybody. And she certainly wasn't comfortable with gossip!

My mother taught for years. When the institution she was teaching at was phasing out its residential facilities, she quit teaching and went on to start a residential housing program for mentally disabled individuals. It was as though she had found her calling and made her way to doing what she was always destined to—taking care of her surroundings.

My parents lived from paycheck to paycheck, saving what they could. Regardless, my parents made sure my childhood was happy. All the money brought in by my parents was spent on necessities and a few extras. At one point, my parents bought a great big tent trailer so that they were able to take us on weekly camping trips. I could never really complain about my parents not working hard. Both Mom and Dad had hard and demanding jobs, and they did everything they could to make sure we were living as well as could be.

Despite not having little extra money after the monthly bills were paid, they wouldn't hesitate to help someone in need. My dad was always the first to offer what he could, whether it be a home-cooked meal, a place to stay, or a helping hand without any expectations in return. However, my dad did not like dishonest people and would try and make them pay for what they did. As I've mentioned, my dad was one tough son of a bitch. He was working about 60 miles from home, staying in a Motel, when one night, while trying to go to sleep, he went to the room below him and interrupted a party, asking them to quiet down. They invited him in and proceeded to beat the shit out of him, including carving symbols in his back with broken beer bottles. Not to be shown up, he drove all the way back home, bleeding profusely and surprised my mom with the announcement that he was there to get his goddamn gun. He was going to teach those assholes a lesson one way or another. It took everything my mom had to convince him to stay home and get some medical help; he still has those scars.

. . .

Unsurprisingly, with two such strong, determined parents, you would think that I would be tough. I am anything but—I am scared of everything, including walking on the grass, swimming in the lake or ocean, going to the dentist, worms, staying by myself, scary movies and I am deathly, phobia-style, afraid of snakes.

My mom and dad weren't perfect, far from it, actually. My mom yelled at us a lot, and I think it was because she was so unhappy with her body image (more on that soon), and my dad used a belt on my brothers when they misbehaved. Oh God, I hated that and I felt so bad for them. It pained me to hear them being spanked and I felt so helpless. Yet aside from that, my parents were pretty cool. When I couldn't decide who to invite to my Grade 1 birthday party, I asked my parents what I should do as I felt bad leaving anyone out. They suggested that I invite my whole class, that way no one would feel left out. I was elated— with my whole class and other friends, there were going to be many people coming to my party. My mom and dad managed to round up enough cars to transport everyone out to the lake for the day so we could all hang out at the beach. My Mom was famous for her chiffon cakes and she made four of them for the party. I really don't remember a lot about the party, but I do remember gathering in a large circle to open gifts. I came across a nicely wrapped gift and I opened the card. It was from my friend Steve Fredericks, who was a kind boy but very chubby and large for his age. As I was opening it, someone asked, "What did you get her, Steve?" He looked over and very loudly and proudly replied, "UNDERPANTS." Sure enough, two pairs of *underpants*. I was mortified and wanted to crawl into a hole, I couldn't believe someone would give me a gift of underpants!

My Mom and Dad volunteered for everything, from Canadian Girls in Training to Boy Scouts, from Girl Guides to swim club, the community association, not to mention countless other places, many involving the mentally disabled. On two separate occasions, my mother received prestigious honors. One was dinner with the Premier of Alberta to receive the Volunteer of the Year award from recognizing her work with the mentally disabled. She also was honored and was invited to dine at a banquet with Queen Elizabeth. My dad also got to attend dinner with the Queen, where they received formal instructions on greeting the queen which made my Dad uncomfortable since he wasn't used to being that formal or distinguished.

Whenever there were instances where people required help, my parents always stepped up. And there were many instances where they helped others voluntarily, but no one knew about them. There were also other places where my Dad volunteered, where he met a young Japanese man at the baseball field one day. This man and his family were told to leave British Columbia because of their heritage and he was trying to start over in Alberta. He wanted to start a new business, he had a building, but he didn't know how he was going to get it set up as he had very little money left and needed some construction work done. Without hesitation, my dad told him that he would give him a hand and not to worry, that he would help him, so he worked nights and weekends to help him get the store ready. They got the store open in a timely manner and my dad made a lifelong friend, an amazing man who hired my dad for many jobs after that.

When we were very little, we often made the trek to Northern Alberta, where my dad still had a family. We would pile in a red Volkswagen Beetle and off we would go for the seven-hour drive. My mom always packed a lunch for the road and they would make the three of us a nice little bed on the seat and a bed on the floor. I loved those trips and going to visit relatives, especially my aunts.

Every summer, we had two traditions. My mom drove the 11 miles to the lake and we would walk the ditch, picking up bottles to exchange for spending money. It was always fun, and in the end, we had a great picnic.

Picnics often happened in our house, and my mom always tried to find a reason to go on one. Our other annual summer tradition was to make a morning trip to the Hutterite Colony and buy 50 pounds of peas. The neighborhood kids would gather at our house and we all shelled peas for the afternoon, laughing and telling stories until the last pea was shelled, and the big finish came... Dairy Queen milk shakes for everyone. That was a treat!

Holidays were always special in our house. Regardless of which holiday we decorated, and my mom would paint our windows with snowmen, pumpkins, Easter bunnies, or hearts. Valentine's day was one of my favorites. The night before our big valentine's party at school, my mom would make each of us a double-layered heart cake. We could choose chocolate or vanilla and she baked them and then iced them and we got to help decorate them with cinnamon hearts, all the while signing our Valentine's cards for the next day. I always sent extra ones to the kids that I knew wouldn't get a lot, anonymously of course. My mom would drive us all to school the next day with our cakes on our laps, as proud as could be.

It's funny because I felt spoiled by my parents, yet I was not very confident growing up and I kept seeking attention. In my middle school years, I used to get migraine headaches, but I always made such a big production about it that it was ridiculous. One time, I hadn't studied for the morning social studies test and I faked a stomachache. My mom insisted on taking me to the hospital and, to this day, I am sure that she took the opportunity to teach me a lesson—as I ended up having appendicitis and getting my appendix out.

. . .

I was always jealous, sometimes, I still am and I wouldn't wish that emotion on anyone. At the age of 11, I got new downhill skis for Christmas. I pretended to be happy, but inside I was so upset because I wanted K2s so bad, but my Dad got me Yamahas. Nobody had Yamahas. Just like the time I wanted a Mustang bike but instead got a classic old lady–style bike. And then when I got a car, I didn't think of it as, *you lucky dog, you got a car.* Nope... my friend got a Mustang and I got an American Motors Matador four-door sedan. Not a cool car by any stretch of the imagination. My other friend had a Gremlin that was adorable and I was jealous of both of them. You would think that I would be thrilled to have a car, but no... it was a sedan, a family car, the only good thing about it was you could make it out in the back seat fairly easily!!

Some of my fondest memories growing up were going camping every weekend starting in May and finishing up in September. It didn't matter if it was raining, snowing, or in the middle of a blizzard, we still went camping—it was like a little adventure. We would pack up our tent trailer and because it was so big, we got to take along friends, or sometimes our uncles came with us, and the meals were always second to none, with my mom and dad trying out different fun camping meals. On every trip, my mom always did a scavenger or treasure hunt for us, usually with candies of some sort as the final prize. Everyone looked forward to those hunts and then sitting around the fire until the wee hours of the morning, playing games, talking and just being a family. I was always sad to be going home on Sunday when my dad would put the trailer back up so we could clean it, as my mom was meticulous about keeping things clean, especially the cooler. I hated that job, so my dad usually did it while we all pitched in with the other jobs that had to be done.

Besides all my other fears, I was also scared of heights, I didn't do roller coasters or ferris wheels. I would get nauseous on those little-kid roller coasters, it was bloody ridiculous. Then to top it all off and try and conquer my fear of heights, at the age of 18 I decided to go with a good friend of mine skydiving. A week before we went, a first-time jumper was killed when her chute didn't open properly at the facility we were to jump at. Because of that, we were forced to go to another facility four hours south of where we lived, and we had to drive back and forth four times until the weather conditions were perfect.

The day finally came, and we were packed into that little plane like sardines. I was first to go, and as I climbed out on the wing, I was terrified and started to cry. The jump master said, "I don't think you should go," and I passed out. Yup, high above the earth, I passed out cold. I came to and my parachute was open nice and even above me, and the ride down to earth was glorious. I had never felt so free as I felt then. My dad was the first one I called to tell him what I had done. I know that he had a hard time believing me, thank goodness I had some photos.

I had some really good friends growing up. My best friends were Trudy and Sandi, whom I am lucky enough to be friends with still today. We don't live in the same city, and we don't talk a lot, but when we do, it's like it was yesterday. We spent a lot of time together and had a lot of fun. We did some crazy things, including cruising up and down the streets of the city we lived in, after taking a phone from our house and pretending it was a car phone. Yeah, right, two chicks in a Matador sedan, with a car phone—like that's believable!

As children, we lived quite a simple life and looked forward to our mom's amazing cooking every day. She took the hour that she was allotted for lunch and came home to make lunch for us, always the same thing, soup and sandwiches. To top it off, every evening, she cooked us supper, which always consisted of meat and pota-toes, a vegetable, a salad, and usually fruit for dessert. It was very important that we always sat down at the table and ate dinner as a family.

We didn't mind, as it had become a routine, and we all looked forward to it. We had to be on our best behavior, however, as my father would smack us if we were sitting on our knees. There was always enough food for everyone, including our friends that were over, or if someone happened to drop by.

In 1974, my mother's weight ballooned to 350 pounds. She wasn't active, but my dad was the opposite; he was as fit as a fiddle. Us three kids, always had to help my mom roll down her panty girdle when she was going out. We would roll it down, and most of the time, it snapped back in our faces. We would laugh, and she would laugh, and we would try again, it was always a group effort, but it was hard on her, and it was hard on us.

I remember being at swim meets and hearing kids make fun of her. It was heartbreaking and embarrassing as a child. I could tell she felt bad about it. Eventually, she had tired of being the largest in the room all the time that she opted to have a gastric bypass operation, which removed her large intestine and decreased the size of her stomach. It was a relatively new procedure, and they only offered it in Vancouver and Toronto at the time.

My parents discussed it amongst themselves, and they decided on Vancouver. My aunt Marilyn and I were going to go with my mom. I was excited, but my excitement was cut short when three days before I was to go, I fell and broke my arm skiing. No, it wasn't because I was doing some crazy jump and I am a fabulous skier, it happened when I was taking off my skis and fell on my binding. It certainly wasn't a proud moment for me! I wasn't able to go, and it was hard without my mom home. However, we still managed, my parents had a lot of good friends who brought over meals and sent treats.

During the next 18 months, Mom lost over 250 pounds and looked incredible, except for her baggy arms. At her lowest weight, she was 105 pounds and very unhealthy. They had reduced her stomach size and she was eating very little. During the next few years, she was hospitalized numerous times because of the surgery. She was sent to Edmonton, which was 100 miles away, because they didn't have doctors specialized enough in Red Deer. A few times we were close to losing her. However, Mom was always a trooper and managed to bounce back every time. She did regain some of the weight but seemed still happy and she was healthy. She never slowed down either. The house was always clean, we were always well-fed, and she continued to work full-time and volunteer.

In 1978, my mother and her colleague started a non-profit organization that would house residents that were developmentally disabled and were being transitioned from an institution into the community even though there were few places for them to go. She was very excited about this and it gratified her that she would be really helping these people.

Even though my parents struggled financially, they tried to give us great memories. My parents managed to plan two extraordinary vacations for us, which I will never forget. When I was 12, we drove to California with our favorite neighbors, Ken and Marlene, over the Christmas break and had as much fun as we could fit in. It was truly a magical experience.

The second time we went away, I was 16 years old. That was when my parents took us to Hawaii for three weeks over the Christmas break. I remember it well, and I cherish the memories that we made there. Sometimes, I can almost feel the water. We splashed in the oceans and watched the sunrise over the Hawaiian skies. It was like something out of a movie.

That was the first time that I had been on a plane, and the excitement was overwhelming. I couldn't keep still, and neither could my brothers. In some ways, I was terrified to fly, but it was a good kind of fear, and in the end, it was a great experience. I was right. We had a wonderful trip, full of all sorts of adventures. One of the most memorable times was when my brother Jeff was surfing and lost his false teeth. He had to go for the rest of the vacation with no teeth. That certainly put a damper on his picking up girls!

Despite all the troubles they had to face, my parents managed to give us a good life. Our friends were always welcome in our home and often filled the sixth spot at the dinner table. We worked together as a family, my brothers and I were expected to do our chores to the best of our abilities. It taught us quite a lot about the responsibilities we had to face in the future. I would have to say that I enjoyed my childhood, it wasn't glamorous or filled with expensive gifts but it was well-rounded and what it taught me was to be kind, generous and independent. Finally, my parents taught us the value of family and how important that is.

Chapter Two

When I was 18, I moved to Edmonton as I was looking for a job, and wasn't having any luck finding one in my hometown. My aunt and uncle were kind enough to invite me to live with them and their two adorable little boys. I was lucky enough to meet a wonderful new friend, Marlene, who made me laugh so hard with her antics. Shortly, I snagged a job at a brand-new Racquet Club as the front desk receptionist. It was my job to make appointments to play, hand out towels, that kind of thing. It was a great job and I really liked it, but soon enough, my uncle offered me a job at his law firm as the receptionist. It was a common space that he shared with a few other firms and I would be the receptionist for all of them, including the Former Premier of Alberta. It was a great job; I worked with some magnificent people and it was all very exciting. It was then that I decided I would put in a year and then go back to school to become a lawyer.

Eventually, I found a great apartment that I shared with my two brothers at separate times. I had to get a second job delivering *The*

Globe and Mail, which started at four in the morning, but not only was it good for my budget, but there was a little extra to spend also.

Life moved on so quickly from when we were kids. As we grew older, we had to face more and more real-life and their challenges which every child does in that transition to adulthood.

Upon my return to Red Deer, I met someone. He was incredibly captivating, and I couldn't believe that he could be interested in me. His name was Gord, and he was one hell of a good-looking man.

Gord was tall, blond with blue eyes, and ruggedly handsome. He was kind, charming, and had a solid relationship with God. All of this combined made him the perfect guy for me, or so I thought. At the time, I was in the first year of my undergraduate degree and still aimed to go to Law School. I figured I was walking in my mother's footsteps and achieving what she wasn't allowed to.

It was a midsummer's eve of June when I first met Gord. One of the first things that I loved about him was that he never rushed me into anything. When I met him, I felt like I was walking on cloud nine. Gord was everything I needed in a man. However, there's always some catch. With Gord, it was that he did a little too many drugs for my liking, I was always scared to ask what kind, but he was often high when we saw each other. Apart from that, I thought he was special. He checked all the right boxes.

Gord managed to sweep me off my feet after just the third date. What could go wrong? Life was perfect; I had a man that I was falling in love with, I was on my way to building my career, I had good part-time jobs, and everything was going smoothly. Time passed by quite fast, and every day, I drew closer and closer to Gord. I found myself opening up to him and losing myself completely in his presence.

Even so, Gord respected my wishes and remained at a distance until October, when I realized I was ready for him. The chilly breeze chilled my skin, and I was prepared to feel his warmth surround me. Then, on that winter night, we had sex for the first time. Wouldn't you believe it, it turned out our condom was defective, and I became pregnant right after our first time. What are the odds?

I was young and didn't quite know how to feel. My emotions were all over the place; I was terrified of becoming a mother so soon, terrified of telling my parents, of letting them down, yet I was excited. Most of all, though, I was afraid of how Gord would react to the news. When I told him, I felt the excitement radiating off him. It would be a lie to say we weren't happy.

I was excited and nervous at the prospect of being a new mom, and we were doing everything we could to make ends meet. I was working as a photographer on the weekends and doing my dad's books, working part-time at my Mom's group homes and cleaning a couple of houses. Gord was a plumber. I felt blessed and happy, and I was in a place where everything seemed to be going right.

It did come with its downside, of course. I couldn't continue school while I was pregnant. So I had to quit studying, which was devastating to me. I was heartbroken about giving up my dream of becoming a lawyer. Nevertheless, I believed that maybe someday, I could just pick up where I left off and continue my education. It wasn't the end of the world; I was going to have a little bundle of joy in my life.

It wasn't long afterward that Gord came home on a winter's night. It was something out of a movie, so simple yet so amazing. He brushed off the snowflakes from his coat, and I watched as he made the fire. I sat unexpectedly on the sofa next to the fireplace, reveling in the newly-built fire and unconsciously rubbing my stomach. I turned my gaze and watched the fire crackle and the orange glow shadow Gord's smile. There, in front of the burning wood, he went down on one knee.

I didn't think much of it at first, especially since I wasn't expecting anything like that. However, when he cleared his throat again, I looked at him—really looked at him. With a smile on his face, he said the words that every girl wants to hear from the man she loves: "Will you marry me?"

I was dumbfounded at first, completely lost for words. I couldn't believe it for a few moments. I just blinked at him, my heart caught in my throat. Of course, I wanted to marry him! He was the father of my baby and the man I wanted to spend my entire life with at the time. There was no question about it, but, at the same time, my voice had left me. I simply nodded because I was so overcome with emotion I couldn't even speak.

I wiped away the tears that were running unchecked down my face and burst out laughing. It was perhaps the first time I was both laughing and crying at the same time. Gord lept to his feet, pulling me into an embrace. It was all like a dream for me. Life was good!

That wasn't it, though. We still had to do my favorite part, breaking the news to our families. I knew they would be happy, but I was a sucker for reactions and couldn't wait to see how they would react. It wasn't long afterward that Gord and I contacted our families and broke the news to them. My family was optimistic about my impending nuptials; however, I noticed that they seemed more worried than happy.

"Are you sure that he's the one?" they would often ask. It really wasn't the question I had expected they would ask every so often, but I knew it came from a good place. I told them I was, and I knew, in my heart of hearts, that Gord was the man for me. His side of the family was more accepting of our wedding. I adored them, they were all so kind, humble and gracious. He came from a very religious and close-knit Dutch household and was the black sheep in a family of six children. However, they were supportive, and his mother, especially, was an exceptional woman. I couldn't help but adore them all.

It all happened oh so fast and the next thing I knew, I was planning a wedding. We decided that the best time to get married was in February of the upcoming year. Neither he nor I wanted a small event. We wanted to celebrate the beginning of our lives together with style. We invited practically everyone we knew, which was more than 350 people. We whitewashed the entire venue, and the only dash of color was the red of the roses. I had six bridesmaids, and I remember him struggling to find six groomsmen.

Undoubtedly, it was a beautiful wedding, and it was everything I had planned since I was a little girl. I was so ecstatic to see how everything was unfolding just as I wanted it to. Well, everything except for the blizzard that occurred suddenly and resulted in a lot of guests being unable to attend. It could have ruined my big day, but I was okay with everything; I was with the man of my dreams. In the end, I guess that was all I could think about, even though I was still anxious about his drug and alcohol use.

I still remember how I felt as I was heading to the wedding with my mom and dad. I was nervous and scared, but again, the happy kind of scared. Of course, it didn't help that, until the last moment, my dad continued to say, "You don't have to go through with it, you know..."

I simply gave him a look and reassured him that I was going to be okay both at the time and in the future. He could see the same ferocity that he held in himself, and I could see the pride in his eyes. If only I had listened to them then.

* * *

We moved to Calgary right after we got married as Gord had a good job there. Gord was a good husband, or at least he was initially. Life was terrific after we got married. Unfortunately, it didn't stay that way for long. I didn't know what was going on, but it felt as though Gord had a switch, and the marriage had flipped it on. Maybe it was the prospect of us living together for the rest of our lives which made him believe that I had no other option. I would stay with him, regardless of what he did. Perhaps it was that sense of entitlement that rose in him from the fact that he married me. Until today, I can't really tell you what it was. I really didn't know what changed the man I thought I knew and loved.

Our honeymoon phase lasted about four weeks, and it was then that he started showing his true colors. It was like hell that had entered my world. I remember it clearly to this day. I was at home, reading a book when the door slammed open. I was in the bedroom, and I saw Gord stumble in. I expected the man I loved and the man I knew. I felt no fear. As I walked toward him, the stench of alcohol was so heavy on his breath that I wanted to throw up.

I was desperate to calm him; his entire demeanor terrified me, and I wanted him to rest. My husband, however, was more interested in picking a fight. One thing led to the other, I tried to help him, but he wouldn't accept it. That's when it happened—that's when my life came crashing down so fast, I couldn't believe it. What was a simple argument, a clash of words and desperate calmness of voices, suddenly ended up in a single slap, reverberating across my cheek.

The sound of the slap echoed in the living room and was abruptly replaced by intense silence. All I could feel then was a burning sensation spread through the right side of my face. Tears pooled in my eyes while my face and my heart went numb. I couldn't understand what was happening; how was this the same man I fell in love with?

I slowly turned my face back to my attacker, unable to comprehend what had just happened. What surprised me more was the look on his face. I don't know what I was expecting, but I knew it wasn't what I saw there. Gord had an evil smirk like he had been meaning to do this a long time ago. In his eyes, I could read the satisfaction of finally having done what he had wanted to do for a long time: to use his heavy, rough palm across my cheek so badly that it left a mark.

I felt the room turn in slow motion, and suddenly Gord wasn't ruggedly handsome anymore. In front of me stood a monster I didn't recognize. Before I could say anything, I was dragged across the room by my hair, and I could feel the rug burns on my bare skin. All I felt was pain. Sharp shooting pains erupted from places on my body that hit the furniture and where he kicked me. I tried to leave the apartment, but he slammed my fingers into the door as I tried to escape. A scream of anguish escaped my lips.

Then, it was as if someone had smacked Gord out of his reverie. Everything went still. I was no longer being dragged, no longer being violated. There was silence and stillness. I couldn't dare to look up, but I did. Gord simply turned around and went to bed without saying a word to me. All I could think of then was, "What just happened?"

I felt sharp pains, and I feared for my baby. Somehow, I dragged myself to the kitchen and got an ice pack. I sat on the floor all night, cradling the ice pack on my hands and face, trying to stop myself from crying. The baby inside me moved, and it was the only thing that gave me comfort, during that long, endless night.

It was that night that a part of me died, and I knew I couldn't remain quiet. As the day passed by and Gord had become more or less normal, I knew I had to talk to him. I brought up the topic of his violence, but he dismissed it as he would every time in the future. It was always the same; he told me I was overreacting and he never struck me as hard as I claimed he did. When he was sober, he could never remember what he had done to me, but he was very apologetic and usually brought home flowers. Either that or he would start crying and beg me to forgive him. He always promised that it was the alcohol and that he would never do that again. I chose to believe him; I couldn't see any other options.

The only thing that went through my head was, Is this still the man I loved? Is he the man who had given me a child and loved me, in those distant days past? The happier times of our lives seemed like eons ago, but it was the only thing I held on to. I kept those memories as a reminder of who Gord used to be. I always forgave him, believing that he was sincere and that he would never do that again, but he never stopped his behavior.

After living in Calgary for a few months, Gord lost his job, and we decided to move back to Red Deer, where our families were. With the help of my parents, we were able to get into some low-income housing, which was a godsend.

I thought with Gord's family close, he would stop the beatings, but I was wrong. They continued, mind you, only when he had been drinking. I would watch the clock like a hawk, praying that he would come home sober, as I was never sure of what I was in for.

The days would pass and to my relief, he would come home sober. But eventually, the inevitable would happen. He would come home drunk again and hit me—or his favorite was to throw me down the stairs and then kick my sore body. The vicious cycle would continue, and there was no way to stop it except to beg him to stop drinking, which he always promised he would do.

One time I was close to the basement stairs, and he pushed me down, but I didn't go all the way, I held my ground. But he came down the stairs and kicked me hard—thank god, it was in the arm and the chest and he missed my pregnant belly. The only thing I felt was the push and the pain with every hit my body took. It was excruciating, but it didn't compare to the pain that arose afterward. It seemed as though every bone in my body ached. I always thought that things couldn't get any worse, and I stuck it out, thinking they had to get better. I stayed with the man who hurt me, knowing that it really wasn't him, it was the booze. It was painful because, when he was sober, he actually made me believe that he loved me. He was the man that I loved, even though he was consistent with the booze and drug use, regardless of how much it bothered me.

Even though we were in low-income housing, we were still struggling financially. Gord had not been able to find a job, and I continued to work when I could. A month later, on June 29th, we were blessed with a healthy, beautiful baby girl. She was the light who brought happiness with her, and we called her Brooklyn. She was perfect, and she had my eyes. She was a beautiful baby, and I was so proud of her.

This baby girl stole my heart the moment she entered our lives, and I couldn't imagine loving anything more than I loved her. Brooklyn was the pride and joy of her maternal grandparents as well, and they were willing to help out with childcare every chance they got.

Financially, things weren't getting any better. Gord was having trouble finding a job, and so I had to take sole responsibility for the entire household. Honestly, it wasn't easy. I felt as though I was losing myself one day at a time, and only Brooklyn kept me intact. Apart from caring for Brooklyn, I was also working four part-time jobs; I was cleaning houses twice a week, taking wedding and portrait photos on the weekend, doing my Dad's bookkeeping, and still working nights in a group home for the mentally disabled. It was keeping me busy, but it was also bringing income in.

On the other hand, Gord continued his constant drinking and would abuse me when he got too drunk. I wouldn't say that Gord did practically nothing and never tried. He did land numerous jobs out of town, however, he had a tough time holding on to them. I guess his drinking would always get in the way and become his priority. So many times, I thought about leaving him, and protecting my child and myself, but I didn't have the strength in me. I was scared—I don't know what I was scared of—but I was scared, I was scared that he would come after us, I was scared of people saying, I told you so and I was scared of burdening my mom and dad with caring for us. And so I stayed to see what the next day would bring.

Life continued on the same path for the next couple of years. We were still struggling financially, but I was able to budget and stay within our means. We spent a lot of time with family and that was great. Gord was away a lot as he had gotten a job out of town, and for me, it was a sense of relief. He still abused me, sometimes severely, and I continued to ponder the idea of getting away. But when I would talk to him after a night of beating me and tell him that I was going to leave, he would beg me not to and promise me that he would stop. That he would change, that he loved his family and it would destroy him if I left.

Eventually, I found out that I was pregnant again and was

bringing another child into the world. I was ecstatic, but with every piece of good news came some darkness. In my case, it was something that I absolutely couldn't have imagined. I was attending one of my regular doctor's checkups, oblivious of the surprise in store for me. Then, out of the blue, the doctor informed me that I had a sexually transmitted disease, and if we didn't get it cleared up, I would not be able to deliver my baby normally. I would have to have a C-Section. I felt my world collapsing, and I could barely hear what she said after "sexually transmitted disease."

Regardless of how much he physically hurt me, I still always trusted Gord. Now, however, I was devastated. My life was shattered; he had been fooling around, and I didn't know what I was going to do. How would I handle this? How could he do this? I had entered that appointment looking forward to updates about my baby, but I left with my world shattered. I had the option to ignore the news that I had just received. I didn't know what I was going to do, I could confront him and we could have a terrible fight and who knows what he would do to me or I could look beyond it and just pray that it never happened again. That's what I did. I knew I couldn't handle the pressure, and it wouldn't be good for the baby. I was ashamed of myself for not being stronger and standing up to him.

I didn't know how I faced Gord, but I managed even as I chose not to confront him because I was scared of the outcome. Finally, after months of caring for the baby on my own, it was time for the delivery. That's when Gord reached a whole new low for me. When I was going into labor with my second daughter, Morgan, Gord decided to up and disappear. I was screaming out for him, I needed my husband's support, but he wasn't there.

Luckily, my best friend, Trudy, was the one who came into the delivery room with me and was my support. I had faced Gord's abuse, but never did I think he would leave me alone at a time like this. I couldn't help but wonder where he went when I needed him the most. He was a horrible person, but I always thought there was some good in him. I was wrong.

Morgan was only four pounds when she was born. She was so little, and I was scared even to hold her. However, she was a fighter, and she fought against the odds to make it into my arms, but she lost a pound while she was in there and it was a concern. My baby had to stay in the hospital for a month, and I would visit her every day. Morgan broke through all the odds, and, with every visit, I saw that she was getting healthier. She really was a fighter, and I couldn't be prouder. I was so lucky to have my and Gord's parents as they took turns caring for Brooklyn and I didn't have to worry about her.

A month later, we were finally able to bring Morgan home to her big sister, Brooklyn. Morgan was a tough baby as she had colic, would cry for hours on end, and it was trying. My dad would often come over and just walk with her in his arms to soothe her. Even three-year-old Brooklyn would take her turn in rocking her to try and make her stop crying. I remember Gord would pace the house with her face upside down while patting her back for hours on end. I thought that this time Gord would be okay, that he would change his habits at the sight of his little girl. He was so proud of them, yet, I couldn't have been more wrong.

I failed to realize that even the slightest bit of rationality in that man dissipated into thin air when he was drunk. Gord was an exceptional case, and not in a good way. My days would often end with my sitting, staring at the clock, praying to God that he would come home sober and everything would be okay. I prayed to God, so my girls wouldn't have to see their father that way, and I sheltered them most of the time. Regardless, it was a horrible way to live, as I was on eggshells all the time.

I remember one time when Gord came home drunk. It's a memory I desperately wish I didn't have, but I can't forget it. I was downstairs, fixing a meal for him to eat once he got home from wherever he had been. Morgan was in her bedroom upstairs, sleeping in her crib, and Brooklyn, who was three at the time, was sleeping in her own room.

Gord had come home and snuck upstairs without my knowing. Usually, I would be alert and prevent him from going anywhere upstairs. However, I was so consumed with my thoughts and the meal I was making him, that I was afraid he would throw against the wall. I didn't realize he was upstairs until I heard Morgan's cries. Immediately, my blood ran cold. I ran upstairs only to see that man standing over the edge of the upstairs wall, dangling my baby in her little blanket. Everything was moving so slowly, and I didn't know what to do. I screamed to make him stop, but he simply replied, "Fuck you, bitch . . . catch . . ." and pretended to drop her for me to catch. I screamed and I ran as fast as I could and then went upstairs to grab her and protect her from the asshole that he was when he was drunk.

She was safe in my arms while Gord had lost his temper and hit me again. I just tried to protect Morgan in my arms, but he was so powerful when he was drunk. I saw Brooklyn, looking from behind the parted door, scared and teary-eyed. I wish I could protect her from the horror she saw, and I did the best I could, but it broke my heart. I was terrified that he would do something like that again, or even worse, so that night, I brought her into Brooklyn's room and barricaded the door with a dresser while I slept on the floor to protect them.

Just as always, when he was sober the next day, he was very remorseful and apologetic and I once again tried to think of a way out.

"It will never happen again. I am so sorry." Flowers soon followed, along with more apologies and begging for forgiveness. I was so confused and eventually felt the strength that I thought I possessed disappear.

His words were becoming ingrained in my mind, and I would end up in tears, not knowing what to believe. It went around again, and soon he would show me that he wasn't to be trusted.

When I thought this was the worst he could do, he proved me wrong once again. He came home drunk one night and pulled out his hand revolver. He pointed it at me as I tried to avoid showing my fear.

"Let's play Russian Roulette," he said as he smirked.

What happened to the handsome, caring man that I had

married? I had no choice but to overlook the ugliness that disguised his face now. I had no choice but to sit there and show him I didn't care while my heart beat out of my chest. There were so many instances of him ruining moments—times when he would chase our neighbor down the street with a rake, hitting him repeatedly. Countless times, the neighbors called the police to our house because of his drunken behavior causing havoc.

I couldn't understand how Gord could have turned into the man that he did. It broke my heart to know that my girls had to witness all of this, and it would affect them forever. It broke me that they could never meet their real Dad, the man I had fallen in love with. Instead, they had to live with this monstrous version of him. I cringed when I thought of what people thought of me staying with him, yet I felt powerless to do anything about it.

I couldn't deny Gord's good side, though. When Gord was sober, he was a good dad. He cherished his girls; he loved taking them for bike rides and showing them off at church. It was like Dr. Jekyll and Mr. Hyde, and the evil would come out when he had been drinking. He would become a different person; he became a monster who seemed to have no idea when he hurt people.

One time when Morgan was just a baby, we had gone camping as a family. Brooklyn was so excited because we had hardly done anything like that. Money was too tight to spend on recreation. It was indeed a treat and something to be excited about!

We were all so thrilled and had been yapping about it for a while. However, nothing good would remain as long as there was alcohol. I didn't want to bring any booze, however, Gord did. "you can't go camping without booze, it's just a few beers." I got nervous when Gord opened the first bottle of beer and began to chug it down quite quickly. I tried to keep a watch on him, and every time he chugged down another beer, I felt something tighten up inside me. I was so scared something was going to happen to me, and then I fell asleep sometime during the night.

When I woke up the next morning, Gord was nowhere to be

found. I realized that the car was gone and was worried that he had driven drunk, I prayed that he hadn't gotten into an accident and hurt someone. I became very nervous as I didn't know what I was going to do. I decided that I would sit it out, take care of the kids and wait. Thankfully, we had food. We were out there for two days until he decided to come back for us.

I kept his behavior to myself because I was so embarrassed to say that I had failed in my marriage. I hated that I had failed in choosing a partner who would love and care for me. I often reached out to his parents, as I needed someone who I could count on when times got rough, but when I mentioned his bad behavior and what he did to me, I never expected their reaction. Whenever I tried contacting Gord's parents for help, all they would say was: "We are praying for you."

What I needed from them was actions, not prayers. They didn't understand that no amount of prayers could change the monster Gord became when he was drunk, as I knew because I prayed constantly. I just wanted to be able to have someone to talk to about it, to help me decide what to do, to give me the strength to leave. I thought about leaving more times than I could count. It was fear that always held me back, though. I didn't know how I would survive as a single parent, and I was scared of what he would do to me if he found out. Mostly, I was terrified of him taking my girls from me.

I thought that, eventually, things would get better. I had my father's pride, and it was that which made me not want to ask anyone for help. Gord struggled with getting a job as a plumber and had decided to go back to school. It was exciting for me because he selected instrumentation, and it seemed to be a career with a promising future. For once, I could say that things were, indeed, looking up for us, and it seemed as though we would finally find a way out of the dark spot.

At this time, being supportive of Gord meant we followed him wherever he went. This was the reason why, in 1988, we packed up our little house and moved back to Calgary. I was excited because I had seen how significantly he changed the last time we came here. My kids were very excited, as well. After all, the Olympics had just been there! It was a very happening city at the time. Once again, we were lucky enough to find low-income housing. Our rent was $450.00 a month now.

I needed to contribute to the finances because Gord would be a full-time student with no income coming in. I looked desperately for the right job; I needed to make sure my girls had the life I wanted them to have. Finally, after a lot of searching, I was able to find a position as an IT consultant at a bedding manufacturing company. My monthly pay was $1100.00. That, added with the $500 I got from my dad for doing his books, made sure we survived. At least we could handle the household expenses.

I still continued spending my weekends cleaning a couple of houses while also taking my two little girls with me. They would help me out as much as they could, though they were so young. It made me so proud of how good they were turning out to be, even after living through such trying situations.

Now that I think back on that time of my life, I have trouble figuring out how we could have ever survived on that little money. I remember thinking what we made put us about $9000.00 below the poverty line. Even so, I never reached the state where I would have to ask my parents for help.

Was it easy? God, no!

We were financially very constrained. I couldn't rely on Gord, no matter how much it pained me. He would often do drugs and beat me up in his intoxicated state. I would constantly reassure myself that things absolutely couldn't get any worse and that our situation would eventually get better. It had to, it was so bad now that it couldn't get worse. I constantly thought of ways that I could escape, but I was too scared to. If he found us, God only knows what he would do to us, as he kept telling me, if I ever tried to leave, he would kill me. I took that literally and as always, he was very apologetic the next day, yet he never seemed to stop his abuse. It was as though he couldn't control that side of him.

Brooklyn was only six at the time, but she understood her father's nature. That's why, whenever her dad came home drunk, she ran with Morgan and hid her under the bed or in a closet, making sure she was safe. Even though she was only six years old, she was so brave and always put her little sister first. I was so proud of her.

What I could never understand, though, was how he could hurt such innocent souls. There were a couple of times when Brooklyn didn't hide fast enough and, while she managed to hide Morgan, she got thrown against the wall by her violent father. I tried so hard to help and protect them, but I wasn't always home either. It was heartbreaking to see my beautiful little girl treated like that, and again I thought a lot about leaving. It was the abuse against my girls that I knew I couldn't forgive. I couldn't bear to witness the torture Gord inflicted on my kids. My fear would always get in the way, though. I would then beat myself up for being a lousy mother and not being able to protect my children and not having the strength to leave him.

Leaving a violent spouse is always easier said than done. The thought of just packing up our bags and leaving started with so many questions, the biggest of which was: where would I live with my daughters? I knew that my parents would take us in a heartbeat, but I was too ashamed to tell them what I was going through. Every now and then, I would think back about what they said to me on my wedding day, and I wished I could turn back time and walk away with them, but I didn't.

So I stuck it out. From the outside, we looked like a happy family, but we couldn't use that to escape reality. No matter what anybody saw, our life was not a walk in the park. I was scrambling for childcare for both girls. Brooklyn was in school but still needed after-school care, and I paid my neighbor to take care of her until I got home from work.

Finding someone for Morgan wasn't as difficult as I thought it would be, and I was able to get Morgan into the neighborhood daycare. However, it was expensive, and the money was very tight.

Christmas was tough, but it was around that time that I realized things could be much worse for me. I found out that my own neighbors were struggling, more so than me. It was quite an eye-opener. My neighbors were an immigrant family that had moved in next door with two small children. They were struggling so much, that they didn't even have money to buy blankets for their children. It broke my heart!

Looking at that family and then looking at my own, I was almost grateful for how lucky we were. I looked at my girls, and I couldn't imagine what that family might be going through. I thought about how I could help them. Initially, I had planned on giving the girls duvets for Christmas as the townhouse we had was quite cold and I had budgeted for the extra cost.

Later, I also realized that the neighbors didn't have anything for their children for Christmas. I talked to my girls, and they agreed that they would forego Christmas gifts from us, and we could spend the money on gifts for the neighbors. My heart swelled at how generous my kids were at such a tender age. I couldn't be prouder of how exceptional they were turning out to be.

I also talked to my mom that day and told her my neighbors' story. Between her and her friends, they were able to come up with gifts for my neighbors and a full Christmas dinner, along with a trunk load of more food. My mom and her friends drove up to Calgary with their cars packed, and we surprised my neighbors with a wonderful Christmas package. We had food, furniture, household items and wrapped gifts for everyone. The expressions on their faces made all our efforts worth it. That was all the happiness we needed that Christmas. They were so excited and so grateful that it made my heart full. It was an experience that wasn't just amazing for them, but it also taught my girls a great deal about spreading joy.

I knew my girls would have a good Christmas since we would be spending it with my parents, and they were always very generous when it came to my children. My family adored my girls and loved buying things for them. It was one of the best Christmas I ever had.

As for the financial situation, well, I had been in my IT position for a year, and the good thing was, I enjoyed my job. Enjoying it made me great at my job, and that's just what I needed at that time. However, my main focus was earning enough to give my kids a comfortable life, and this job simply didn't pay enough, and so I kept applying for new jobs. It didn't matter how much I enjoyed working; my kids were my priority.

After a few months of constantly searching, I finally secured an interview. However, it was a tough one. I had to write an algebra test and score 100 percent on it. Would luck be on my side? I really wished so, but only time could tell.

Chapter Three

It was October of 1990 when I got a call that would eventually change my life forever. It was the job I had applied for and, much to my surprise, I had actually passed the test! I almost teared up with joy! I desperately needed this opportunity, and just this one time, luck seemed to be on my side.

Soon enough, I started my new position as a chart interpreter and bookkeeper for an oil and gas service company. I have to admit, chart interpretation wasn't easy. I had to read a graphite chart through a scanner and record pressure and temperature readings for 360 hours. I also had to read accompanying gradients and determine if there was water, gas, or oil in the well according to the gradient reading. It was so tough; there were some days that I would stand after having my head down in a small microscope for eight hours and could hardly walk by the end of it.

However, regardless of how difficult things became for me at the job, I really enjoyed the work and the staff there was also fun to be around. Even though I was the only female employee, I managed to make good friends with a couple of the guys. We would go for lunch often and always had lots of laughs and they eventually became like family. The money wasn't great, but my bosses were great, and I knew there was the possibility of making more if I kept working hard.

Keeping my personal life aside, my work life was what often made me feel good about getting up in the morning. After I had been there for about a year, I discovered that two of the employees and another guy were slated to buy the existing owner out. I didn't know how to feel about it, but since I personally knew everyone, I knew the potential they had. I would be able to stay on at my job along with two other employees, and that made it all the more exciting for everyone.

My good friend, Jack, was one of the new owners, so that eased the process of getting over the "new employer jitters." Two of the owners were salesmen, Kerry and Bruce, and they spent most of their time downtown while Jack was handling the field operations and my job was to handle all of the office operations. Along with new responsibilities came a raise, so I was grateful for that. I was up to the challenge of my new position, even though it was going to be a lot of work, but I was looking forward to it.

I had worked with Bruce before and really liked him. Kerry, on the other hand, was new to the scene but seemed like a really nice man.

I never faced much appreciation throughout my life, which is why working at a job where I was constantly told what a great job I was doing was refreshing. It actually made me want to give my all to the job. The best part of my work was that none of my opinions went in vain. I was listened to, respected, and given a place where I had the authority to make the decision I thought was best for the company. It didn't take long for me to fall in love with my job, and it only got better with time.

However, regardless of how great my work was, I would still have to go back home and face the abuse at the hands of my husband. Just like I enjoyed my work, it felt like he enjoyed abusing us. One night, Gord failed to come home on time, and I started to get scared. I knew he would be late and drunk, and we all would have to face the consequences. I was not ready to do it all again. I looked at my daughters' innocent faces and realized they weren't ready either. They had faced so much because of their own father, and I knew I couldn't let them spend the rest of their lives huddled in fear over things that were completely out of their control. They were just little girls who didn't know what it was like to feel safe.

As I looked out the window, I saw the familiar silhouette of a man stumbling drunk towards the driveway. We had to get out. I quickly ran upstairs, grabbed the bag that I had filled earlier with clothes, picked up my girls, and got into the car. I had made up my mind that I didn't want to endure him slapping me around again, and possibly the girls too. I could handle it when he hit me, but it was devastating when he would push Brooklyn out of the way to get to me.

I had nowhere to go, and as I sat behind the wheel, looking at the empty street ahead of me, the girls crying in the backseat, there was only one place I knew I would be safe: my office. Thankfully, our office was set up in a way to help us lounge out whenever we wanted, and I used that to my advantage this time. We had a mezzanine with a couple of couches there that the girls could sleep on, and I planned to get up early and take them to school. I thought that I would then hurry back to work. No one would know or had to know.

I drove as fast as I could, afraid that Gord would somehow catch up with me. He was probably too drunk to understand what was happening, but I couldn't take the risk. I got to the office and got the girls settled in. I could see the fear in their big eyes that gleamed with fresh tears as they held onto each other. I hugged them and told them it was a little adventure, us sleeping at the office. I looked into their innocent eyes, my own filling with tears.

"Everything's going to be okay, you guys, we're going to be okay," I whispered to them as I tucked them into their makeshift beds, pushing their hair back and kissing their forehead. Brooklyn was old enough to know, and so she settled easily. Morgan was still young and fidgeted a little; Brooklyn hugged her to sleep. They were so frightened, but they had each other.

Once they had settled, I could finally breathe. I never thought I would love the silence so much, but I did. I looked at my girls sleeping peacefully behind me. Suddenly, the silence was disturbed by the sound of the overhead doors opening. Unable to understand, I ran to my girls, thinking it was Gord. Instead, Jack walked out. As soon as he saw us, a shocked and confused look appeared on his face. Who could blame him?

I never thought I'd be so happy to see Jack and yet, here I was. I told him what happened; it was the first time that I admitted to anyone the things Gord would do to my kids and me. I dove into the details of my abuse, asking him to let us stay here and not make us go back to that monster. Jack's expression changed as he held me and softly told me that I could stay at his house. I was reluctant, but it was better than living at the office, so we packed up, and the girls and I went to Jack's.

That night, once the girls had fallen asleep, I stayed awake all night with Jack, talking to him. For the first time in a long time, I realized just how amazing it feels to have someone to talk to and be honest with. He told me that he would protect the girls and me, and said that I deserved way better than the hand life had dealt me. I think that was all I had been waiting for because I got a boost of confidence listening to his reassuring words.

For the first time in a long time, I felt like I could actually ask Gord to leave. For the first time, it felt like I would be okay. I felt that I would finally have the courage to end things, and I felt safe with Jack by my side. I felt strong and no longer afraid and knew that I could do this. Jack was a much more muscular man than Gord, and I knew he would be able to protect me if things got ugly. There was really not much to worry about.

I went home the next day to see Gord, and once again, he was remorseful, promising that he wouldn't drink again. Seeing him in that state only made me angry. I couldn't even face him, he looked so disgusting to me. I told him outright that I was done, that he had to leave as soon as possible. Thankfully, he wasn't intoxicated at the time and didn't even argue. It was funny, it felt like he didn't even want to fight like he knew his faults and he needed to get out of this the first moment he got.

The truly troubling part, however, was telling the girls, but I knew in my heart that I had done the right thing. I knew that they would understand too. When I sat down with the two of them and explained that their dad wouldn't be living with us anymore, Brooklyn's response was, "Does that mean we don't have to hide under the bed anymore, Mommy?"

Before that moment, I never knew that a question so simple could hurt me so much. My little girls had faced so much at such a young age, but better days were coming. I knew it, and so did they. I held both of them tight and assured them that the dark days were over; we were safe now. They seemed relieved more than anything, and for the first time in years, I knew it was going to be okay.

* * *

After that fateful night, life became relatively smoother. It was the first time after many years that I could stay at home without fearing what would happen next. If I'm honest, it felt odd but in a good way. I felt free, and with this newfound freedom, I regained my confidence bit by bit. Living with a violent spouse and putting up with his abuse had done a number on my self-esteem, but my vision was slowly clearing up now. I knew who I was and what I was capable of achieving.

I also knew my priority was my children, and I had to be the best mom that I could be for them. They needed a chance to be children again. I guess they got it this time around because they also seemed different than the fearful girls they were around their father. They were calmer, relaxed, and carefree, although years later, Morgan confessed that wherever she went, she would scan the room and plan her escape if Gord came around to get her. This turnaround was a delightful sight to witness. After all, we all deserve a chance to live a happy life.

As for work, I couldn't complain. Work was going well; Jack

had been spending a lot of time with us and loved hanging with the girls. He was such a great guy that they, too, became close to him. He was a big tease and so playful, that my girls loved his attention. It felt as if my life was finally on the right track after so many years.

I was happy, and my daughters were happier. I was yet to find out that there would be an addition to my happiness. It was about two months after Gord had moved out, Jack had come over for dinner, and after we were done putting the girls to bed, I grabbed a glass of wine and sat outside with Jack underneath the night sky. It was perfect, we were laughing about something that happened at work, and then, out of the blue, he leaned over and kissed me.

The butterflies that I thought had died fluttered in my stomach. I was over the moon. Jack and I had been such good friends for such a long time that this just seemed right. I was comfortable, and now, I was also ecstatic.

Jack had something in his nature that brought so much ease to me. I felt like I could talk to him about anything. It seemed like the natural transition to take this to the next level. I kissed him back and let myself get lost in him. He was undoubtedly good-looking. He was a muscular, dark-haired man with a chiseled face and broad smile that could light up a million fires within me. He was what you would describe as a very ruggedly handsome male who seemed to care a lot about me, and I cared about him.

Jack seemed to be different from Gord in every way. He came from a small town in Southern Alberta and had small-town values. His parents were amazingly humble and kind. They lived a simple life but loved the outdoors and everything that came with it, including camping, hunting, and fishing. Jack had one younger brother, and both he and Jack loved the outdoors as much as their parents. It was a family thing that only ended up benefitting the girls and me. His parents were thrilled to be grandparents to my girls, and the girls took to them right away by calling them Grandma Barb and Grandpa Jerry.

Before I knew it, I was falling hard for Jack. It was scary yet thrilling, and he managed to give me goosebumps and butterflies in my stomach every time he kissed me. I must admit, I thought I would never feel like that again. It took me by surprise, but I knew that I was falling in love with him. Just like that, I had even begun looking forward to a new future. The dark days were over, so why not celebrate it by getting the well-deserved love?

* * *

The separation agreement went off without a hitch. That was a relief. Knowing Gord, I thought he would probably create more problems for me, but luckily, everything went rather smoothly. We agreed to a regular visitation schedule. No decision was made to get child support from him, and I got nothing from him to help raise my daughters.

The first time I took the girls to visit their dad, Brooklyn clawed at my arms, begging not to stay. She was terrified beyond belief, and it was absolutely heartbreaking seeing her like this. We were both in tears and, when I sat privately and asked her how she would like to visit her dad in the future, she stated that she would like Oma, her paternal grandmother, to be there. It was then decided that Gord would visit his children at his parents' home.

Other than that, everything went quite well. A year after I had asked Gord to leave, Jack and I bought a house together. Never in a million years would I have dreamed that it would be possible to ever own a home, and here I was! I was so excited about moving, I literally even dreamed about it. We had it built, so it was brand new, and the girls were excited about having a beautiful house to move into. They kept telling everyone that it had three bathrooms. Living their entire lives in such a small townhouse with only one bathroom, definitely made it so much more worth it seeing their excited faces light up every time the house was mentioned.

My love for interior design came in handy when I had to pick out the paint colors, carpets, and wall coverings. It was right up my alley! Finally, when the day came for us to move in, I saw the beautifully decorated house and was filled with a sense of pride.

The thing is, it wasn't just the house that excited me, it was what the house represented for my girls and me. We were happy as a family, and the girls felt so comfortable with Jack that they started to call him Dad. We were moving forward, and we were all on board with where the ship was heading.

As for the divorce, nothing was settled as of then, and Gord had yet to give me a dime for the girls. Thankfully, Jack never complained about that, and he put me in charge of our finances. It really helped build trust amongst us, which was a great way to start our lives together. Things were going really well, but of course, Gord always had a way of making my life worse. This time, however, a dreaded phone call stole away my sleep once again.

When my lawyer called, asking if I would be able to come in, I knew something was wrong. My blood ran cold when I heard his next words: he informed me that Gord had applied for full custody of the girls. How anyone thought that was a good idea was beyond me. My girls were terrified of him, of the monster he was, and now he wanted them to himself. I knew he was only doing it out of spite.

I was blown away by the lawyer's words. Here's a man who does countless drugs, has a drinking problem, whose children only want to see him in a supervised manner, who can't hold down a job, and he's willing to fight for full custody of the girls. His argument was that I was heavily into drugs, while I had smoked pot twice in my life. I didn't think that constituted a drug problem. My lawyer told me that there would be a court-ordered psychological assessment, and all four of us would have to attend separately.

I was okay with that, I had nothing to hide, and I knew that my girls were stable and happy. I knew the hell he had raised for us and how my girls were terrified of him. The girls and I attended our assessments and finally, the day came when Gord had to get his assessment done. He was the last one. The day after his assessment was complete, I got a phone call from my lawyer. I almost stopped breathing as I picked up the call and heard his voice. I could feel the world around me get dimmer when he asked me if I was sitting down, and I replied that I was. He then proceeded to tell me that if I gave Gord the set of red pots that I was saving, the $1000 RRSP and the $800 in the girls' bank account, he would never see his girls again. He would never pay child support; it was all up to me.

It seemed impossible to me, maybe this was all part of Gord's scheme to get the girls, but I knew in my heart of hearts that he never cared for them. If he did, he wouldn't treat us the way he did. Regardless, the blow of the lawyer's words hit so hard, that I was beyond shocked, and I started to cry, wondering what kind of man would trade his kids for a couple of thousand dollars and some red pots. Gord was willing to sign an affidavit stating as much, and I accepted it for what it was. No matter what happened, it was so much better than losing the girls.

I took a deep breath and agreed. I would do anything to keep my girls with me. When I broke the news to the girls, they danced and never questioned the reasons why. Thank God because I didn't know what I would tell them if they did ask. Saying that their own father traded them for money would have been heartbreaking beyond belief, and I couldn't do that. They actually seemed content with the news. Jack was the father figure in their world, and he was doing an incredible job of being a father to them. He adored them, and they loved him to pieces.

I was so happy; my life and the girls' lives were finally going right. Jack and I rarely fought—he didn't know how to raise his voice, he was such a kind and gentle human being that I almost couldn't believe he was in my life.

Chapter Four

E very Thursday, the four of us would make a list of cleaning chores and tackle the house, so it was spic and span. It became a sort of family ritual, and we made it fun. Neither Jack nor the girls ever complained about this, and we were all very happy. My girls began to thrive after they lost all contact with their god-awful father, and they actually began to excel academically as well as personally. Jack was their dad now, and they loved him just as much as he loved them.

We bought a camper for our truck, and our summers were filled with coastal vacations, including taking our boat and going salmon fishing. On our way home, we would always stop at a pristine lake where Jack and the kids could go waterskiing and wakeboarding. We had never been on vacations before, so this was a real treat. I couldn't ask for a better life for myself or my kids. I was over the moon, and I was glad I had Jack beside me. Do you know how there's always a rainbow after a storm? Well, we were living in that rainbow, blissfully making sure we enjoyed every day to the fullest.

After a long time of dealing with all of the hardships, our lives were finally full—we were all so happy. The girls were thriving, and they both had a very special relationship with Jack. I could tell that they felt free in his presence and were able to talk to him about anything that was bothering them. In return, he would always have sound advice to give them.

I was happy because not only was my personal life thriving, but work was also going well, I couldn't have asked for a better job or better bosses.

Jack and I had yet to get married. While we did talk about it and our imminent future together, that was as far as it went. I didn't think much of it, neither did I want to make a big deal out of it. I loved things as they were at the moment, and why wouldn't I? Our life was amazing. Little did I know, it was about to get so much better.

One day, I wasn't feeling well. My stomach was all over the place, and it was churning. A part of me suspected I might be pregnant, but I had to be sure. I went to the store and bought a pregnancy test that very day. Lo and behold, I was pregnant!

When I saw it, I didn't really know what to make of it. I was excited and not so much at the same time. I had very mixed feelings about it; my life was complete, as far as I was concerned, and the girls were getting older. Brooklyn was 14 and Morgan was 11. Was I ready to start it all again? Was I ready to raise another little one? I thought about it, long and hard and realized that this would be Jack's first child, and I knew that he would be thrilled with the prospect of a new baby in our home. I figured it was time to let my secret out and tell him.

I was right! He was so excited when I told him that I was expecting. What I was worried about, however, was work. While I didn't want anyone else to raise my child, I also didn't want to quit my job. I had decided to approach my bosses and ask them if they would consider letting me work from home. I must admit, I wasn't expecting a positive response. However, they were happy that I wasn't leaving and allowed me to set up an office in my home. My plan was to take care of my child during the day and work at night.

Now that I had taken care of work, my next move was to tell

the girls. I knew this wasn't going to be easy. We had never talked about having a baby in the house. I braced myself and talked to Jack—he agreed we would tell them together and relief washed over me. It was nice to know I wasn't alone—not anymore.

When we told the girls, we had a mixed reaction. Brooklyn was thrilled, while Morgan, not so much. She ended up in tears, crying that she was the baby of the family, and she didn't want another baby to take her place. As much as I hate to admit it, I could've laughed at how adorable she sounded. However, I knew that she would eventually come around to loving the baby with all her heart. Life was taking a turn and we were all on board with a change.

That's when Jack and I finally decided that it was time we got married. We planned a very small wedding within two weeks, and it was for immediate family only. We got married in our family room and had a small reception at a local hotel. It was perfect; I had never been so happy and thought that life couldn't get any better. Finally, everything was falling into place and I couldn't be happier.

Our routine visits to the doctor always reassured us that everything was fine with our baby. Then, on December 3rd, we were blessed with a bouncing ten-pound baby boy. The delivery was tough and I ended up cracking my pelvis. It was quite painful and made it difficult to walk. However, when I saw that little bundle of joy, I couldn't help but smile.

Jack picked out our boy's name: Zach. He couldn't get enough of his little son. Even the girls were thrilled, and Morgan had completely let go of the grudge she harbored against Zach for taking her place. What was even more special is that Zach was born on Jack's Grandma's 82nd birthday.

All of my doubts about having a baby in the house were unfounded as I cherished every second of being with little Zach. I knew that he was going to achieve great things in life and that he was special. All this time, I had experienced what it was like raising two beautiful girls; I was excited to find out what it would be like to raise a boy.

The girls loved him unconditionally and, at times, fought over him as well. Brooklyn, being the eldest, was always happy to babysit and we knew that he was in good hands. In Morgan's case, however, we had to take some care. She was a child herself and had never before had to take care of another kid, which is why it was so difficult for her.

I recall the first time Morgan babysat. We received six phone calls asking about changing his diaper, feeding him, and putting him to bed! She had absolutely no idea and was freaking out. Morgan wasn't a fan of babysitting and we tried to work it out so that she didn't have to, though we had a good laugh at her concerns.

My arrangement at work was going well, although there were times that I would work until three or four in the morning, depending on the workload. However, I was usually able to have a quick nap when Zach was napping and I loved spending my days with him. He was thriving and was a happy child, and he absolutely loved cars. He would often sit in a car and pretend that he was driving. Zach could spot a car from a mile away and tell you what kind it was. His favorite hobby was lying on the floor, lining up all of his cars, and naming them. He was obsessed with them.

I had a girlfriend who drove a very popular mini-van. When two-year-old Zach noticed it while we were out driving, he immediately pointed to it and exclaimed, "There's Layna's van!"

It was quite surprising and I replied that I didn't think it was since it was a block away. However, sure enough, when we got close, it turned out to be true. He had a remarkable memory for cars.

Our family of five was now complete. We were so happy and felt very blessed. Jack and I rarely fought and when we did, it was about work. I never dreamt I could be so lucky. Gord had managed to make my life a living hell, but it was through my courage that I had finally found the love that would turn my life into everything it was now.

We had absolutely no contact with Gord; he made his choice and was out of our lives as far as we were concerned. I never even thought about him as time went by; he simply became a figment of a nightmare we once lived in. He had no idea where we lived nor our phone number, and I was so happy with my new life that I rarely thought about him.

Every now and then, though, the creeping question would enter my mind. The question of my decision to stay with him for as long as I did. The truth was I never thought I was strong enough to leave. Now, I was strong and confident enough that if he ever decided to try and come back into our lives, I would know how to handle it. I never told the girls that he had traded them for some red pots, I still couldn't believe it myself. They didn't deserve a father like him, and I was glad that he wasn't around.

One night, at around 2 a.m., the phone rang, and Jack answered it. I was asleep, but the call had woken me up and I watched Jack's expression. Jack had turned red. It was Gord on the other line, drunker than a skunk. As soon as Jack hung up, it rang again and we chose to take the phone off the hook rather than be disturbed anymore. Every resolve I had made with myself went swimming away. I suddenly didn't feel quite so strong, knowing that he had our phone number.

Gord had a darkness in him, a darkness that could drain my energy and throw me into a deep abyss of self-doubt. The next morning, when we replaced the receiver on its cradle, the phone rang right away. Again, it was Gord, still drunk. This time, Jack refused to hang up.

"What is it like to fuck that sixteen-year-old daughter of mine? You must love doing that rather than fucking that fat bitch you are married to," Gord said to him.

Jack turned red with anger. I don't think I had ever seen him so upset. Jack gripped the phone so tight that his knuckles turned white and he replied, "You asshole, you have no idea what you have missed out on, they are both amazing girls and if you ever come near them and hurt them again, you will be sorry."

Without even waiting to hear what Gord said, he hung up. Jack was visibly shaken and his voice wavered as he repeated the conversation to me. I couldn't believe what had just happened and how Gord could say such a horrible thing about his own daughter. He was their father, did he have no sense left in him?

Even though they hated him, Gord was still the girls' father and it would break them apart knowing he had said something like this about them. That's why Jack and I made a conscious decision not to tell the girls what had happened. It was a terrible thing, but we were both very careful not to speak badly about Gord in front of them. If they ever decided to have a relationship with him, we wouldn't want them to know of the horrible things he had said or done.

It was anything but easy to move past that, and I kept thinking, what kind of father would talk like that about his own daughter? But was it really so hard to believe? This was Gord we're talking about and anything he did shouldn't really be surprising. Eventually, I realized that dwelling on him wasn't doing me any favors. I had to move past it and be grateful for so many things— most of all for the fact that I was not with him anymore.

Part Two

Chapter Five

Life was good, and I didn't think things could get any better. I was happy, the girls were happy, and Gord was finally out of our lives for good. Our business was thriving, but there was one little hitch. Jack came home one day and shared his concerns about one of his partners. He looked quite flustered, and it worried me because I had never seen him like this. I asked him what had happened, but he didn't tell me much. At least at first, he avoided it the best he could.

I sat him down, made some tea, and when he was calmer, he said that Bruce didn't seem to be doing his job. He was fixated on starting another branch of the business. Jack felt as if, instead of being out there selling during work hours, Bruce was looking for investors for a new company. It hadn't been long since we had expanded our company. We had added another service, which, according to Bruce, was going to make us millions. Instead, it was just losing money. So, at this point, another expansion was out of the question.

As expected, Jack seemed stressed out by the events. He was also clueless about handling the situation. He had already approached Bruce and asked him out-and-out if he was trying to sell for this other company, and Bruce had denied it.

It was then that Jack and his partner, Kerry planned to hire a private investigator to see if they could come up with proof that Bruce was, indeed, trying to start up another company. It took a lot of planning, and while Jack wasn't all too happy about spying on Bruce, he knew it was something he had to do. They went ahead with the plan. Later, when Jack brought home the video-tape of Bruce's daily activities, it was unnerving to watch, to say the least. We felt like we were doing something wrong and invading someone's privacy and the tape proved our suspicions were right.

With substantial evidence, Jack and Kerry could now openly question Bruce. They approached him with the evidence and made it clear that they wanted him out. Since the business was doing so well, it was not going to be cheap. I suggested that they give Bruce all the assets of the second business we had started. After all, it was his baby. Bruce seemed happy with that and parted ways with the company.

I was now down to two bosses. Our business was doing better than ever. Financially, we were finally stable and had enough to build a new home. We had spent eleven years in our home and figured that it was time for a change, and we wanted something bigger.

We began to look at homes out in the country. Initially, I didn't really know how the girls would take the news; I was a bit nervous about having Morgan change schools in Grade 11. However, she seemed on board and was excited about the move. Morgan was a very outgoing young lady with a bubbly, vibrant personality. It wouldn't be too difficult for her to make friends. Zach wouldn't be much of a problem either since he would start kindergarten in the new school. As for Brooklyn, well, she would have graduated Grade 12 by then, so she was all right with the decision as well.

After a lot of discussions and an extensive search, we eventu-ally settled on a location that had a mountain view and a natural pond in our backyard. The view was absolutely stunning. It seemed perfect, so we found on a builder that we were both happy with. We sat down with the architect, and I told him exactly what we were looking for. We laid out the entire structure for him and told him all the details that I didn't want them to miss out on.

I told them that I wanted a round shower where you didn't have to squeegee it down every time. I also wanted a covered deck, a loft above the garage that served as an office, and a murphy bed so that it could double as a guest room when needed. I asked to include a movie theatre, a wine room, a secret playroom and built-ins in all the bedrooms. The entire time I was laying out what I wanted, I could hardly believe it. I was actually building my dream home! It was a home that I would have never imagined myself getting, not even in my wildest dreams. I was beyond excited!

Every day, we drove out to the lot and saw the progress of the house. It took forty minutes to get there and another forty to come back, which means that we spent a lot of time just going back and forth, but I was okay with that. I was so excited every time, and each trip was worth it. I could hardly contain myself! My girls were excited, too. They had spent a large portion of their lives in low-income housing, and moving into a million-dollar estate home was unbelievable. I would ask myself several times a day how I got so blessed.

However, things were going to take a turn for the worse. When Brooklyn was getting ready to graduate Grade 12, the final semester brought us some unsettling news. I received a call from her Biology 30 teacher, who broke the news to me that he feared Brooklyn had a severe learning disability. He thought that it was for this reason that Brooklyn struggled with reading. It wasn't too surprising to me when I thought about it; we had always wondered about it.

What was surprising, though, was that she got 75% on her Biology 20 exam, and when the teacher gave the same one to her as a review, all she got was 20%. Then he gave her the same exam on audio, and she achieved a whopping 79%! It was then that we decided to get her tested, and it confirmed our suspicions. Brooklyn was diagnosed with dyslexia and another learning disability that escapes me. However, if she were to join a university, she would get coded. This would allow her to write exams on audio.

Brooklyn didn't take the news too well. It was a real blow to her to find out she had a learning disability. I thought back to the times when she was growing up and still in the junior classes. I would talk to her teachers and voice my concerns about Brooklyn's learning difficulties, but none of them were worried about it. They just dismissed me. Brooklyn was very good at making concessions to get by, so we never bothered to get her tested, either. I so regretted that decision now and blamed myself.

Regardless, I knew my daughter. Even though she had been given this spirit-breaking news, she still decided to go to the local college and get a degree. Brooklyn didn't really have a direction, though; she was still uncertain about what she wanted to do. Eventually, she settled for general studies.

Everything seemed to fall into place then. After a couple of months of studying, Brooklyn came home and announced that she wanted to take a year off. She wanted to travel to Australia. I was surprised; I knew she loved to travel, but I didn't know she would want to be so far away from her family. Australia was on the other side of the world, after all!

Brooklyn told us that she planned on going by herself. The only thing I could think of was how brave she was to venture out all alone. It blew my mind, and I was proud of her at the same time. Brooklyn deserved happiness, and I knew that she was going to get it this way. I hoped that she would make some lifelong friends on this adventure and grow as a person. Travel transforms people in countless positive ways, and I hoped that would happen for my daughter as well.

After a lot of planning, we agreed that she could go if she earned enough money. I still remember the happiness on her face. It was December when she finished her classes, and that was when she began working full-time to reach her goal. She planned to leave in the middle of October.

In the next few months, we continued to drive out to our new home every day. My excitement for my home made me fall in love with the long drive and watching the progress made it all the more worthwhile. The house was coming along really well, plus the experience of watching something of my own built up from scratch and taking solid shape was more profound than I had ever imagined it could be. There were times when I reflected on my own progress in life—thinking of where I came from and wondering how I'd found my way where I was.

There were times when just the girls and I would drive out to see the progress on the house. One beautiful summer evening, we sat on the edge of the uncompleted deck. We were talking about how lucky we were and how happy our life had become. I mentioned that I felt like Cinderella living with her prince in a dream castle. It felt like home, sitting underneath the night sky and feeling the cold air caress our faces. I looked up at the stars— those silent witnesses to our conversations. All of a sudden, the conversation turned to questions about Gord's behavior and the things that he had done.

The girls wanted to know if what they remembered was true, and they wanted validation. I knew we were treading dangerous waters, but they needed to know the truth about the man who was, unfortunately, their father. We had never talked about Gord or his actions before. After I answered some of their questions, I found it rather cathartic, and I think that, for the girls, it gave them the green light to feel the way they felt about their birth father. They deserved to know who he was, but I wasn't prepared to tell them all the details. I didn't elaborate on some of the incidents, but all I said was that it was time to move on and that it was okay to do it. I believed that they had moved on, but they undoubtedly had some questions and maybe some lingering feelings of abandonment as well.

Now the kids were all doing well, and when they could, they came with us to see the new house. Work continued to thrive, and

I still held an immense love for my job, even though I would find myself rather tired during the day.

Zach had begun to grow, and he no longer needed a nap during the afternoon, which meant that I was unable to sneak one in as well. The lack of sleep didn't seem to be affecting me, and I was still able to keep up with my daily chores and work.

One Friday night, Brooklyn announced that she was going out with some friends to a party. I was happy for her as she didn't go out a lot. We were just happy that she was socializing. I will never forget that day, especially since it was Mother's Day weekend in May. The memory is engraved in my mind. I remember how she didn't come home that night. It may not be a big deal for many people, but in Brooklyn's case, it truly was. She had never come home before. She always let us know where she was, so we were worried.

We woke up on Saturday, and the dread only grew as the hours passed. I was freaking out, and Jack was too. I didn't know what to do when suddenly, the phone rang. My blood ran cold as I slowly walked towards it and picked up the receiver. I didn't want to hear any bad news; I was not prepared for it. I heard my dad's voice on the other end. I took a deep breath, a little reassured.

My dad was in Red Deer, which was about 100 miles away, and he told us that Brooklyn was with them. He also mentioned that she would be home on Sunday and had something to tell us. Once again, my blood ran cold. I didn't know what was happening or what the news was, but I just wanted her home.

Sunday morning. I went to church and prayed. Once I arrived home, Brooklyn was there, waiting to talk to us. Her beautiful, soft features were marked with disappointment and despair. She kept repeating that she was sorry for worrying us so much. I tried to calm her down, but it didn't work. She told us that she had gotten very drunk at the party and that there were some drugs involved. She said that her memory was very foggy about the incident, and all she knew was that she had woken up in a bed completely naked. She thought she had been sexually assaulted.

I never doubted her for a minute, and I hugged her as she cried helplessly, hearing the anger and pain in her words. About six months ago, I had to convince her to go to the doctor and get a prescription for birth control pills. Brooklyn argued with me, saying that she wasn't sexually active. The only thing I could do was tell her that she was in college and that you never knew what could happen.

Reluctantly, and after a lot of convincing, she came with me to the doctor and got the prescription. She had also never had a problem with getting drunk or doing drugs. Every time she went out, she came home sober. We felt very lucky that both girls weren't too much into partying and I always conceded that they didn't like to drink too much as they saw what it did to their birth father.

What I was worried about, however, were the consequences of the sexual assault and so we arranged counseling sessions, thinking that was the best way to go about it. Brooklyn didn't seem to want to report the incident, however, so we let it go. I still don't know whether or not it was a good decision, but it was a choice that we both made. She seemed to want to get over it and put it behind her.

In the beginning, it was very difficult to see Brooklyn change. It was like a piece of her had died. However, as some time passed, she seemed to be getting her old self back. We talked often, but never about that night. We were close, and I knew she was getting excited about her upcoming trip. We had another short, tough phase at the end of July. Brooklyn had to have tonsils removed, but she was a trooper and never dwelled on that. I was glad to see my daughter knew how to handle unexpected bumps that life threw at her.

The date to move was getting closer: September 30th. Zach was already enjoying his new school, Morgan had settled in nicely, too, and had made some very good new friends, both boys and girls, and Brooklyn was working. She had gone into Zach's school a couple of times to volunteer and had shared her upcoming adventure with her class. I drove Zach to his new school every day, and I met some wonderful women as well. It wasn't always easy, though; there were times when it was a bit of a struggle since we lived in a very prominent neighborhood. I would look around, and the women were all maintained, slim and beautiful. I felt like a turnip around some of them. I had severe body-image issues as I was so overweight. There were very few people that had a weight problem, such as I did. It was a large community, and there were only four women who were overweight like me.

It was tough not being self-conscious there. I would feel like an alien because I didn't fill my day with yoga and going to the gym or running on a daily basis. It still wasn't all bad; I made some amazing new friends there. However, there were a lot of pretentious and wealthy people. I wasn't quite sure how I was going to fit in, but I tried my best.

Brooklyn was busy working and had taken on the task of cleaning our old home to make some more money for her trip. She had decided to go for a whole year, and she was scheduled to leave on October 15th. Initially, I was happy for her. However, as the date for her departure came closer, I became more and more anxious. I didn't know how she would fare in a foreign country all by herself, and I didn't know how I was going to survive without her. I knew that the last thing she needed was my nervousness, and I wanted her to be able to go and fulfill a lifelong dream. So I let her go.

Eventually, the day arrived when we moved into our new house. I could hardly sleep the night before. Zach was in Lethbridge with my aunt, and my parents had come down to help us unpack and get set up. As exciting as it was, I still had to pinch myself and realize that this was my home. I would have never imagined that I would have a home like this. How did I get so lucky? I had a wonderful husband and three great kids and I had never been happier. Life was good, really good! I only hoped it would remain that way.

Chapter Six

W e were quickly settling into our new home and I was totally in awe of it. We had some wonderful neighbors, and it was fun to get to know everyone. Everything was going perfectly according to plan and right on schedule. However, my anxiety was creeping up on me, knowing that Brooklyn was just two weeks away from leaving. We spent half of our time getting her ready for her big adventure. I was a bit concerned because I thought that she would be more excited than she was. Yet, something was gnawing at me, and I couldn't put my finger on it.

We had planned a big family party the night before. It was the first of many parties that I would hold in my new home. While I was excited to show it off, I also knew that my emotions might get the best of me when I thought about my eldest going so far away for so long.

Regardless, the party was fun. We had more than twenty-five guests that showed up, and Brooklyn tearfully gave a little speech during the cake cutting. I tried hard to hold my tears back, but the moment she began to talk, I teared up. I did not know how I was going to survive without her. She was such a help to us with Zach, and I didn't know how her little brother and sister would cope without her here; after all, they were very close. That night, some of our relatives stayed over so that we could all go to the airport to say goodbye.

When the much-awaited, yet much dreaded, morning of October 15th arrived, I was anxious about what would happen and how I would keep my emotions in control. We took some pictures before Brooklyn began sobbing. She started sobbing as soon as she came up the stairs with her backpack, and I gave her a big hug. As soon as I did, it was like the barrier holding my tears back broke, and then the waterworks started and didn't stop.

We promised to stay in touch, and I kept telling her to be careful. I was counting every second the closer we moved to the airport, not wanting time to pass. Alas, it did, and once we got to the airport and said goodbye to her at security, we could hear her sobs through the doors. It was heartbreaking. I wanted nothing more than to run to her and bring her back home. However, I knew she was old enough and had to leave the nest. I took a deep breath and walked away, trying to block out the sound of her sobs.

Once we got home, I immediately noticed the silence in the house. Her absence weighed heavy on all of us, and I realized that I had never felt so lost in my life. It was overwhelming, and I honestly didn't know if I was going to make it through the day. I yearned for my daily conversations with her, our daily hug, our "I love you's" just because.

In no way was it easy and everyone felt it. Our only way to survive was to look forward to the phone calls and emails.

During the next couple of months, I began to feel better. Brooklyn and I emailed regularly and talked on the phone a couple of times a week. She was doing well but was very homesick. At the end of November, while we were having a conversation, she told me about two young men that she had met, Pierce and Ollie, from the UK. They had decided to share an apartment on the Gold Coast of Australia.

I wasn't too happy about it; I was afraid of any kind of trouble she could get in. However, she assured me that the boys were waiting for their girlfriends to join them in March. The arrangement was that Brooklyn would cook and clean since she was a great cook, and the boys would cover her part of her rent.

While she was managing her money okay, she still didn't have the budget for such an apartment in such a popular spot, which is why this was a good arrangement for her. Often, when we talked on the phone, she would end up in tears. It made me worried; I knew she would be homesick initially, but I didn't expect her to be so broken.

It was during one conversation closer to Christmas when I absolutely could not handle being away from her. Her voice broke my heart, and I told her that she should come home. But she just continued to sob and said, "No, Mom, I have to prove something to myself and have to stay."

It broke my heart to hear her cry like that, and I assumed that it was because we were getting close to Christmas, and it would have been the first Christmas that she would be alone. Being the eldest, she was always pampered with the best holidays, and spending it away from us wouldn't be easy. I, too, didn't know how I was going to handle the holidays without her. We were such a close family, her absence was certainly going to be felt by all of us.

Finally, an idea popped into my head: My brother, Tom, and his wife Sandra lived in Indonesia. I emailed him, asking him what his Christmas plans were. I then proceeded to tell him about Brooklyn and how distraught she was every time she spoke to me. He mentioned that they were going to New Zealand for Christmas and that maybe Brooklyn could join them.

It seemed like the perfect plan; at least she wouldn't be alone during this time. I was delighted and very grateful for his suggestion. He said that he would call Brooklyn and ask her if she would like to be a part of their vacation. I didn't know how she would respond to it and only hoped that she would take it positively and accept the offer. It was a relief when Brooklyn called and told me that she was going to be with her Aunt and Uncle over Christmas.

I could finally relax. However, I didn't know that there was a secret that was yet to be revealed.

Christmas came and went. There was definitely a void in our celebration without Brooklyn. I was happy knowing that she was with family and was very grateful to my brother and sister-in-law for including her. I still missed her so much.

Everything was going great. I had figured we would focus on our own celebrations and leave Brooklyn with her uncle. When New Year's Eve came, we were celebrating it with friends when suddenly the phone rang. The blessed ring made my heart jump because I knew it was Brooklyn. I picked it up and went into the bedroom. I found that it was my sister-in-law, Sandra.

I was surprised to hear her voice and even more surprised when she asked me if I was sitting down. A tingling feeling spread through my body, and I knew something was wrong. I replied that I was. All of a sudden, I got a sick feeling in my stomach.

There was a silence on the call, the struggle evident in the ominous quiet. I held my breath as Sandra broke the news to me: Brooklyn was pregnant. I couldn't speak. It felt like the air from my lungs had been knocked out. I had just assumed that it happened recently when I suggested that she come home right away. I knew that we would be able to handle everything here. However, Sandra went on to tell me that she couldn't make such a long flight as she was eight months pregnant.

This newfound information made the blood drain from my body, and I couldn't believe the words. Brooklyn had not seen a doctor and was still wearing the same clothes that she left home with. She had planned to have the child and give it up for adoption in Australia. Sandra said that Brooklyn was very ashamed and didn't tell us because she didn't want to disappoint us.

I couldn't make Brooklyn understand that she didn't disappoint us; I wanted her to know that we knew and that we didn't want her to be by herself.

Sandra also said that she would take her home, but the jungles of Indonesia, where she lived, were no place to have a baby. On top of everything else, Tom and Sandra had small children and jobs of their own. I knew they would do anything to help, but it was too much to ask. They couldn't help by staying with Brooklyn. Brooklyn's plan was to have the baby in Australia and give it up for adoption so no one would have been the wiser. I then understood why she wanted to move into the apartment with Pierce and Ollie, as they were going to take care of her.

At that moment, I felt forever indebted to Tom and Sandra. Who knows what would have happened if they hadn't come along and been there for Brooklyn? I didn't know how I was ever going to repay them for their kindness. I just wished I could be with her during this time. I talked to Brooklyn and told her that everything was going to be alright, that she shouldn't worry that we would figure this out. She begged me not to tell anyone, to keep her secret. I had no idea what I was going to do, I couldn't go and be with her as I had a small child and a job that I couldn't leave for that long.

I was devastated to think that my child was on the other side of the world, handling a teenage pregnancy all alone. My world was crashing down on me, and I could do absolutely nothing about it. After the phone call, I tried to pull myself together and pretend that everything was okay. Everything was—it had to be, at least until Jack and I were alone. That night, I told him what was going on. None of it made sense to him either. He was as upset as I was and we came to a decision to tell my parents to see if they could go over and stay with her.

I slept very little that night, and I was sick to my stomach. When I awoke, I felt like I had been living a nightmare. It was rather an out-of-body experience, and all I could think of was *this wasn't happening*. I had such hopes for my kids, so many visions of how their lives were going to be, that I didn't know how I could handle this. I don't recall having feelings like that before. It was very unpleasant and terrifying.

All I wanted to do was hold my daughter and tell her that everything would be alright. All I could think of was the pain and anguish that she was going through, and she was doing it alone. I couldn't be there for her, even though she was always there for me. My memories kept coming alive in those days, and I recalled the Mother's Day weekend. I was sure that that was when she got pregnant. I could understand why she didn't want to keep the baby and why she was adamant about giving it up. However, I couldn't help but feel a slight ache towards never having to experience my first grandchild's life.

The next day, I called my parents and got them both on the phone at the same time. They were both very close to Brooklyn, and I knew that they would do anything for her. They listened to me carefully, giving me just the right input I needed. There was absolutely no hesitation when we asked them if they would help. They were as distraught as I was but not judgmental in any way.

Within a week, we had my mom on a flight to Australia to be with Brooklyn. She was more than happy to go and help out. My father was still working and would have to finish a few jobs that he was currently doing. He planned to go after the baby was born and be there for Brooklyn postpartum.

My mom arrived there and found a small motel at the base of a hill, where a hospital was situated at the top of the hill. She contacted social services, and they put together a team of nurses, a doctor, and social workers to work with Brooklyn in arranging the adoption of the child once it was born. Australia's adoption service works in a way that the mother would be with the child until she gets released from the hospital, and then the child is placed with foster parents for one month until going to a permanent home. That way, the mother has one month to change her mind.

My mom met everyone on the team and scrutinized each member. She needed to know that her granddaughter was in good hands. She said that everyone on the team was amazing and all very good with Brooklyn. She also mentioned that this, indeed, was what Brooklyn wanted. Every time I spoke to Brooklyn, she also reassured me that it was important for this child to have a father and that she was not ready to become a mother.

It gave me some relief that she seemed so sure of herself, but I also knew that this would be the hardest thing she would ever have to do. Just thinking about what would come ahead made me want to reach through the phone and hold her tight. I just wanted to be with her, to take care of her, but I knew my Mother was offering the comfort that she needed.

It was tough when friends and family would say, "I'll bet Brooklyn is having the time of her life."

Their words came from a good place, but they didn't know half of what my daughter was going through. We would just have to respond with a brave face and tell them that yes, she is. After all, we promised that we wouldn't tell anybody. Life had to be normal, regardless of how difficult it was. We tried to continue our daily activities with a very heavy heart and prayed that this was the right thing.

Life was as normal as we could make it until February 6th arrived. It was an ordinary day until we got a phone call from my mom stating that Brooklyn had an emergency C-Section, and she'd had a beautiful baby boy. It was actually February 5th in Canada, as we were a day behind Australia. I was so worried. I needed to see her, but my mom said that Brooklyn was doing well, that the two young men she lived with had gone into the operating room with her. She also mentioned that she thought that if it were a girl, Brooklyn would have a more difficult time giving it up.

Jack and I were having a hard time relating. We had not seen Brooklyn pregnant and we had not held this precious little gem in our arms. We wanted to and we missed the experience of it. Though Jack was very supportive, I could tell that he hated missing it too. We were struggling with how hard this was going to be, yet we were trying to be very sensitive to Brooklyn's needs. She was told that she had to give him a name, and she wanted to name him after her grandpa, Mike, and her dad. However, Michael Jack was too close to Michael Jackson, so she opted for the opposite, Jack Michael, with his last name being McNair since Brooklyn had taken on her stepdad's last name when she was 18.

Brooklyn spent a week in the hospital with her baby. He would be sent to the foster home two days after she was released.

As expected, she grew rather attached to him. We thought that a part of her would think again about her decision. We were concerned, but she was still adamant that she wanted what was best for him, and that was a father.

The day that Brooklyn had to say goodbye was an extremely hard day. After she was released, my mom called me and said that she didn't know if Brooklyn could do it. She said, "Leianne, you didn't hold that beautiful baby in your arms and knew that you would never see him again." My mom, normally a very strong woman, was in tears.

I felt incredibly distraught, but I understood what she was saying. I agreed with her, and yet, I didn't know what to do. I could hear Brooklyn sobbing in the background. I asked my mom to have Brooklyn call me when she calmed down, but, unfortunately, I had plans that evening to go to a woman's show with some friends. I couldn't get to talk to my daughter and tell her it was all going to be okay. I was so glad my mother was there.

I was finding it really hard to hold it together. When we got to the show, there was a woman reading cards and telling fortunes. I was reluctant to sit down, but my friends all convinced me to do it. All I wanted was to go to Brooklyn. Regardless, I sat down, and she proceeded to tell me that she saw a house, and that it was a dream house. I told her that we had just recently moved into our new home. She then went on to tell me that my love life looked good and stable and that my financial situation was good.

It was all true, which is why I wasn't too impressed. I thought that anybody could say that, but then she showed me three cards and said, "You have three children, and I struggle to see what this means, but I see a small male far away, and I have to bring him and put him with your three children."

I stared at her, gaping. I got chills up my spine and struggled with finding words. Tears welled up in my eyes, and I started crying. She said to me, "I see that might make some sense to you, and all I can say is that it's going to be okay, it's going to be wonderful."

She covered my shaking hand, looked deep into my eyes, and said, "It's going to be okay."

I returned the look and arose from the table. I could see everyone's eyes on me; all my friends were wondering what the matter with me was, and I just said that I had to go home. When I finally got home, Jack was pacing. He was normally in the lazy boy with the remote in his hand. However, this time, he looked worried. It worried me to look at him being like this. He was often the one controlling my anxiety. He said that he didn't think Brooklyn could leave the baby behind. He was adamant that she couldn't do it. He then said to me, "Tell her we will adopt him."

I looked at Jack and said, "Hey, we need to talk about this" "We will be 60 years old when he's 18, I don't know if I can do this." At that moment, everything began to fall into place. It seemed possible. Why wouldn't it? When I finally talked to her, I asked her if what she really wanted was to give him up for adoption, and she said to me, "Mom, if I could just bring him home to Alberta and then we could adopt him out just so you could see him."

I began to cry and said, "Brooklyn, you need to do whatever is best for you, and if that is what you want, then that's what we will do, honey. You need to take these next few days and pray about it. Whatever you decide, we will support you in every way that we can."

Jack's words stuck with me, I never told her what he had said; I thought that we needed to talk about it. When I got off the phone, I was shaking. I couldn't imagine her bringing him home and then adopting him out after spending that much time with him. But I also knew that she wasn't ready to be a mom, she had mentioned that several times. I considered what Jack had said and talked to him about adopting the baby.

He said, "We have Zach, who is five, and he needs a little brother. We know that we can handle a child, we don't know if we can handle a child coming home without her child."

I reminded him again that we would be sixty years old when this little one was graduating and that we should really think about it. Some part of me was still wondering just how this would work. I knew that I would do just about anything for my daughter, and if this was what she wanted, then we would become the new parents of that baby. I didn't have to think twice about it. I also knew that I couldn't imagine a mother giving up her child, and if we adopted him, then essentially, Brooklyn would always know about him as her little brother.

I called Brooklyn and got her on the phone; she was extremely distraught. I had never heard her voice like this, and it broke my heart. I couldn't help but sob, and I could barely get the words out. I said, "Brooklyn, if you don't think that you are ready to be a parent, then your Dad and I have talked, and we will adopt him. There is absolutely no rush in you making that decision, we just want whatever is best for you and that baby. You can take all the time you need, and we are here for you when you decide."

There was silence on the other end, just the sound of her breaking voice. Finally, she uttered the words, "Mom, I don't know what to say, but I do know I can't leave him behind. Maybe February 6th will have a different meaning for you, it will be his birthday, and it won't bring back bad memories of your first wedding anniversary."

The day Jack Michael was born was the twentieth anniversary of my first wedding, and every time that day came around, it was a reminder of the hurt. I would end up reliving it all over again.

I remember my mom telling me about a young man, Brad, whom Brooklyn had met and who had been a good friend to her. Brad had flown in from wherever he was to meet the baby and made sure that Brooklyn was okay. My mom thought Brad liked Brooklyn, but Brooklyn assured her they were just friends.

For the next two days, we sat in limbo, unsure of the decision that Brooklyn was going to make. The day kept stretching on. Then we got a phone call. She had gone to the hospital and picked the baby up to bring home. It was amazing that their team at the hospital had gathered baby clothes, diapers, a stroller, and a car seat for them. They were all standing at the doorway to say goodbye when they left with the baby. There wasn't a dry eye in the hospital. When we got the news, I told Brooklyn that we were thrilled. We reassured her that she could take all the time she needed to decide whether her dad and I would be parents or grandparents to this child.

My dad was on a flight to Australia when they brought the baby home. I knew he would be a lifesaver to Brooklyn and this baby; he absolutely adored babies, and I knew that he would be excited about helping care for this child. I was right, my dad was very helpful and made sure all the needs were taken care of.

For the next two months, Brooklyn, my parents and Jack Michael made their way across Australia, seeing the sights. They were staying in small local hotels, and my dad would make a little crib out of a dresser drawer or put two club chairs together for Jack Michael to sleep in. There was a plan in place for my cousin, Erin, to join Brooklyn to travel further through the country for a couple of months, and my parents were going to bring the baby home to us to care for him. Erin was only six years older than Brooklyn and had just finished her psychology degree; she and Brooklyn were close, so it was a good fit.

Meanwhile, we were working with a lawyer here and a lawyer in Australia to make sure we had everything in place for this child to come home to us. My parents had been there for over three months, and they were ready to come home. They had all up and left and none of their friends knew why they were staying in Australia for so long.

We knew we were making the right decision and we felt confident that we had everything in place. Children that young did not need a passport at the time, so we had not bothered to get one. The day came when it was time for my mom and dad to come home. Jack and I were bursting with joy, and we fought hard to contain our excitement. Brooklyn and Erin had left the day before on a trek to the Outback. We had told Brooklyn that we wanted her to travel and have fun; she deserved to enjoy the country without the worry of being pregnant and alone and to take that time to decide what role she wanted us to play in the upbringing of this child. This was her time to enjoy her life, and she was already so excited about the trip. Now, she could finally see the true joy she had planned.

The trouble occurred when my parents arrived at the airport and were told that they couldn't go anywhere without the baby having a passport. The state laws had changed that week due to 9/11. They were told that they could get on the flight but that they would have to leave the baby behind. Terrified, my mother started to cry and said, "We just about left this baby behind once, and we are not going to do it again."

They had given away the stroller, the car seat, and the phone that they had, so they were scrambling. They were clueless, alone, and had no idea what they were in for. They called me, frantic and upset, not knowing what to do. To get a passport, we needed Brooklyn's signature, and she was somewhere in the Outback, and we had no way of getting a hold of her. I told my mom that I would try and reach a friend of Brooklyn's, Belinda, who was from Sydney. I desperately hoped that she could help us.

I called Belinda, and her response was, "I will see what I can do, but it's the Outback, there is nothing there."

Desperately, I told her that if she found Brooklyn, we needed her signature along with a Justice of the Peace's signature on the passport application, so we would have to get her to fly into Sydney right away. My parents were exhausted, and they just wanted to get home.

What was supposed to be an easy process stretched on for two days while we sat in limbo? We waited to see if we could find Brooklyn, and then on Friday morning, I got a call.

It was Brooklyn. Her voice sounded like the most beautiful music then, and I started to cry, I was so relieved. She told me that Belinda found her at a sheep ranch where they had a working fax machine and if you can believe it, the owner of the sheep ranch was a Justice of the Peace. The universe was setting everything up in place. If that wasn't a sign, I don't know what was. It was like a miracle. My parents were relieved, and once they received Jack Michael's passport, they finally began their journey home.

Now that Jack and I were able to enjoy the excitement of

things moving forward, we went out and bought a crib, car seat and some other essentials for the baby. We didn't have an extra bedroom, so we set everything up in Zach's room. We didn't have to worry about Zach being jealous, he just seemed excited about getting a little roommate. After thirty-six hours, my mom called and said they were in Vancouver and would be arriving home in a couple of hours.

I couldn't contain myself, my heart beat fast throughout, and I couldn't wait to see the baby. Jack, Zach, and I all went to the airport to greet them. I was so excited to meet this new little man, as we all were. He was now 2 ½ months old, not a newborn anymore.

At the airport, we stood with anticipation, awaiting their arrival. Finally, we saw two familiar, elderly, exhausted people coming through the doors. They still kept a smile on their faces, and my dad was holding the baby. This little man was extremely handsome and bright-eyed, taking in everything around him. He had his mother's eyes and the same curiosity she held at his age. He had dark hair and a fair complexion with blue eyes. As soon as I saw him, tears welled up in my eyes, and I was overcome. I can't explain how I felt, except that I couldn't believe this little man was ours.

I knew right then how my mom and Brooklyn felt at the thought of giving him away. I didn't even have to hold him to feel the ache of him being taken away from my arms. I had only met him, yet I loved him with all my heart.

By the time we got home, we saw how apparent it was that this baby was extra special to my father. He insisted on showing us how he liked his baths, how a little bit of red wine on his soother soothed him, and how he liked his back rubbed. I made sure I took all the tips from dad and loved the little guy like he did. We took pictures, and Zach was thrilled with this new addition to our family. When Morgan came home, she, too, greeted him with tears in her eyes and couldn't wait to show him off to all her friends.

She acted so maturely through this, loving her sister's son and caring for him like an adult would. She was no longer the child we thought she was.

The next day, my mom and dad were leaving, and at the doorway, my dad had tears in his eyes. I had never seen my dad cry, so it was tough to see that. He kept his eyes on the baby, holding him close. Dad remarked, "If it doesn't work out, I would be happy to take him."

It broke my heart to hear my dad say that because I knew that he was having a tough time leaving him behind. My dad had gotten more attached to Jack Michael than any of us.

At this point, we didn't know what we were going to tell people because we didn't know if we were going to be parents or grandparents. We had to hurry, though, because people would begin to wonder where a baby suddenly came from. We had already told all of our family that we might adopt him, and only one family member thought that would be a bad idea. However, we were still determined to do what was right for Brooklyn.

Zach had asked if he could take the baby to show and tell. He was in kindergarten, and I had gotten to know the mothers that dropped off their kids quite well, which is why I agreed. I didn't know what I was going to say to them and was rather nervous about it. Jack and I discussed it a lot and none of us came up with an appropriate answer. When I arrived at the end of his class with the baby, he went up to the front to tell his story. Some of the mothers were there and the corner where Brooklyn's postcards and pictures were still intact. Brooklyn had volunteered in Zach's classroom a couple of times before she left and the children had even written to her in Australia.

Zach stood there proudly and said, "This is Jack Michael, he is my baby brother, and he is adopted. And if none of you know what adoption is, it's when your sister, Appie, goes to Australia and has a baby and sends it home with your Grandma and Grandpa for you to love."

I was shocked, watching my little boy take control better than I ever could. I felt so proud of him at that time, and I smiled, trying to hold back the tears.

Some of the mothers looked at me and couldn't believe it. Some of them had tears in their eyes, giving me questioning glances. I just smiled and said, "Yes, that is what happened." I explained to them that we did not know if we were going to adopt him or not yet, that decision was up to Brooklyn. It came out so easily from then on, I just decided to tell the truth.

I didn't care if people would judge me, all I cared about was Brooklyn and this baby. I knew that I would do anything to ensure that they were both going to be okay. It was going to be different, having a little baby around, and I didn't know how I would be able to handle it and still work full time. However, I knew that, as a family, we would figure it out. I was excited about the whole idea and wouldn't have had it any other way.

Chapter Seven

Brooklyn was enjoying her time in Australia with her cousin Erin. We continued to talk on the phone a couple of times a week. I knew in my heart that she was probably going to ask us to adopt Jack Michael. Though she was his mother, I still felt as though she, too, felt like she was too young to have a child. Every time she called, she didn't come across as a new mother missing her new baby. She was just a young woman who was enjoying her time but missing her family. We would talk about Jack Michael, but I knew the bond that a mother has with a new baby just wasn't there.

I was getting used to having a little man around the house and enjoying my time with him. I found that I was still able to work at night while taking care of him during the day. More than me, little Jack had become Morgan's baby, and she mothered him like he was her own. She was so helpful with both Zach and Jack Michael that I really became dependent on her. I felt blessed to have him in our life, and we showered him with love. It was impossible not to! His older brother, Zach, couldn't get enough of him and wanted to carry him everywhere he went.

Initially, I was afraid of how Zach would react to Jack Michael having all the attention, but I was calmer when I saw the two of them together. I guess Zach was just happy to have another boy in the house! With the five of us at home, there was no shortage of people wanting to spend time with this new addition to our family.

In July, we were all out, and when we arrived home, we found the biggest gift waiting on our doorstep. Brooklyn had arrived home to surprise us all! She had given us no prior notice of her return, and it was such a joyous sight! I was overwhelmed by emotion that I began to cry. It was fun to see Zach run into his Appie's arms and not want to let her go. He looked at her and said, "Thank you for the baby, Appie, I really love him." It made my heart melt. When Morgan came home, she just about fainted when she saw her sister and after she realized what was going on, she hugged her and they both ended up sobbing in each other's arms. It went on for at least two minutes, maybe longer. They obviously were close, and Morgan said, "Thank you for Jack Michael."

After all the hugs, Brooklyn looked at her dad and me. With tears in her eyes, she said, "Mom and Dad, if you would still be willing to, I would love it if you adopted Jack Michael."

It wasn't shocking. We knew it was coming. There was no hesitation, and we both had the biggest smiles on our faces and said, "Absolutely!"

I felt a twinge of excitement, becoming a mom again to this little man, and I knew that we could offer him a great life. This way, he could even be part of our family rather than going into a completely new home. However, I was worried about how Brooklyn would handle the transition. Jack and I talked and decided that if it were too difficult for her to continue to live with us, we would get her an apartment so that she could live on her own.

At that time, Brooklyn also informed us that she wanted to be an airline pilot and would like to start instruction right away. We were thrilled that she had found something she could be passionate about. She was equally excited to get started on her next adventure.

The first few months of Brooklyn living with us went well; she pitched in whenever she could and attended school the rest of the time. The pilot school was going well for her, and she loved it. I was very worried about her mental health, though, now and then, I could see that she seemed to be depressed.

Brooklyn had always been a bubbly, happy person, and I didn't see that in her anymore. It was very unlike her, especially since she didn't talk much about it. As her mother, I felt as though it was something I could not take care of on my own. One day I took her to the doctor, and between the three of us, we decided that she would try some anti-depressants. She was reluctant and felt as though they wouldn't really help, but she was willing to give them a try.

I don't know if it was getting better because I couldn't see a difference, and she wouldn't talk about it. Time continued to pass when, one day, something happened that I still remember as clearly as day.

Brooklyn had gone out one evening with some friends and came home looking really upset. Though she didn't cry, she was visibly drowning in that bout of depression again. I called her to the dining room, and the two of us talked about it. She couldn't pinpoint what was wrong, so we both went to bed, hoping a good night's rest would help her. However, it only got worse.

Jack and I were woken in the middle of the night by the sounds of someone screaming bloody murder and crying. I felt the dread creep up on me, and both Jack and I ran downstairs to see what was wrong. It's no exaggeration when I say Brooklyn had literally gone berserk. She was throwing things, screaming out of control, and shaking as I had never seen before. Her hair was in disarray, tears streamed down her cheeks, and her clothes were disheveled. Morgan was standing there and Brooklyn jumped on Morgan, clawing at her face and punching her. I was horrified and Jack tried his damndest to pull her off. When he finally freed Morgan, she was bloodied and her eye was swollen. It was as though Brooklyn had no control over her actions.

Brooklyn went running to the bathroom and we could hear her rustling around in the drawers. When Jack finally got into the bathroom, she was cutting her wrists with a razor blade. She had torn the toilet right out of the floor and so Jack called 911 while I went upstairs to check on the kids. It was horrific.

The little ones were both crying, so I carried Jack to Zach's bed and held them both until they calmed down while the screaming continued. The paramedics arrived and went down-stairs where Brooklyn was, with a gurney. They were down there for over an hour, and when they came back upstairs, Brooklyn was strapped in the gurney but still shaking uncontrollably. It was one of the most awful sights I've ever seen, and I wished so desper-ately that I could help her. While I was stroking her forehead, sobbing, she looked at me and whispered, "Mom, please just let me die."

My heart broke at the desperation in her voice, and I promised I wouldn't. I told her she wasn't speaking sense, and she was going to be just fine. However, she had a look in her eyes, the distant look that pulled her away from me, and desperation clawed at my heart. The paramedic said, "We have given her enough shots to knock out an elephant, so she should be calmed down soon."

I opted to stay with the little ones while Jack went to the hospital. The kids were so scared. They had never seen Brooklyn this way, and they wouldn't stop crying. I tried to calm them down and put them back to sleep. Then I had to tend to Morgan, whose face was a bloody mess, she was in tears. Nothing like this had ever happened before and I said, "Morgan, if you never forgive your sister for what she did to you tonight, I will under-stand, but I need you to understand that she is ill and she did not do this on purpose."

Jack returned home a few hours later. "Brooklyn has been admitted to the psych ward," he said. I rushed to get my coat and keys, but he stopped me.

"She's heavily sedated, and there is no point in going into the hospital until tomorrow night to see her," he told me, taking me in his arms. I hated the thought of leaving Brooklyn there alone, but I had no choice, and Jack assured me that she would be fine.

I didn't sleep at all that night, wondering what I had done wrong. How could I have prevented this from happening? I was exceptionally careful that I did not make her feel guilty about giving up Jack Michael. I made sure that she knew she had given us a gift that we would cherish forever.

I had never dealt with someone who had a mental illness before, and I did not know what to expect. I did not know how this was going to affect Brooklyn's life. I didn't know if what she was suffering from was curable or if she would eventually be okay. These might seem like stupid questions, but they were my questions, and I knew that they would also be Brooklyn's questions. Throughout the night, I pictured Brooklyn how she used to be— my happy little girl. It broke my heart. It absolutely broke my heart.

The next night, Jack and I made our way to the hospital and to the psych ward. The smell lingered in my nostrils and haunts me even today. The doors were locked, and you had to buzz to get in. I had never been in a psych ward before, and I was terrified. My stomach fell down to my knees, and I thought I might faint. We went to Brooklyn's room only to find her lying on her bed very quietly. I had never seen her so still, so lost. She didn't even turn towards me when my footsteps echoed in the quiet, empty room.

When I touched her, she grabbed me and just held on. She didn't look at me, but I could see the fear in her eyes. I just sat there and held her, and we both sobbed quietly. She didn't seem herself at all. She didn't seem to want to talk. She actually seemed a bit groggy, like in a fog.

"I'll let you sleep, sweetie. We'll be back tomorrow night," I said after a while and kissed her forehead. She didn't say anything, but a tear dropped from her eye. Visiting hours didn't start on the psych ward until 5 p.m., and they were very strict about that.

When we arrived home, Morgan greeted us and was anxious to hear how Brooklyn was doing. Brooklyn and Morgan were like two peas in a pod and were very close as sisters. Aside from the cuts, Morgan's face was black and blue; she looked like a truck had hit her. Morgan loved her big sister like no other and often looked up to her for advice. They spent a lot of time together, and I knew that this latest turn of events was going to impact Morgan immensely. I made sure I was there for her the best I could be, calming her down whenever I felt like Morgan was getting too anxious.

Two days after Brooklyn's admission to the hospital, I got a call from her psychiatrist stating that they had diagnosed Brooklyn with bipolar disorder. He stated that, usually, patients don't get diagnosed with bipolar until their late twenties, but he was sure that was the problem. He said it was probably brought on by a traumatic event. I tried to think back and figured that it was Brooklyn being in Australia alone and wanting to give up her baby for adoption or even the sexual assault.

I was devastated when I heard this, but I knew that, with her family's support, Brooklyn would be able to deal with it and lead a normal life. I didn't know a lot about bipolar disorder, so I got on the computer to learn as much as I could. I read up on it until I felt that I had a good handle just to prepare me for it.

The psychiatrist said that he was going to put her on some strong medication, and with that information in hand, I learned the side effects of her medications. There were some ugly side effects, one of which was weight gain. That night on my daily visit to the hospital, Brooklyn and I talked about her diagnosis, and she seemed to be handling it pretty well, I was very proud of her. The doctor was relieved as well; he had mentioned that most patients often remain in denial and refuse medications, making it worse. I took Brooklyn's hand and promised to be by her side.

The next month I spent going to the hospital daily and spending the evening with Brooklyn. She was very bored there, so I would bring her crafts. She seemed to enjoy that, and it helped pass the time. Soon enough, it was time for Brooklyn to return home.

Upon Brooklyn's release from the hospital, she continued to

stay with us. However, eventually, I knew it was too hard for her to see Jack Michael every day, so we decided that we would get her her own place to live. She seemed very relieved and happy with that decision. She was getting better, so we had no second thoughts of leaving her alone. Besides, I was there whenever she needed me. She was excited to start her flying lessons once again, but a week before she was scheduled to go back, we got a letter from the Aviation Board stating that, because of the diagnosis that she was given, she would have to withdraw from the program and would never be allowed to be a pilot.

It was like Brooklyn's world came crashing down. This was a devastating blow to her, not only because she was so excited about piloting as a career but because she didn't know what else she could do. Once again, she was falling into her pit, but this time, we knew how to handle it together.

She decided that even if she couldn't be a pilot, she would still like to work for an airline. She had hope, and it encouraged her more. Finally, she received great news one day. It was a happy day when she got a call announcing that she had gotten a job with Canjet, a national airline. She was so excited about working there mainly because she had heard what a wonderful employer Canjet was. Starting her new job seemed to take the bitterness away about not becoming a pilot. We were all so excited for her, and we knew it would help make her better.

* * *

Brooklyn was thriving in her new job, had a new boyfriend, and seemed happy in her little apartment. We weren't all that thrilled with the new man in her life as he seemed controlling and conniving. We were still wishing that she would give Brad a chance, the young man she'd met in Australia. Brad was planning to come out and see her with a friend from Vancouver, and we were hoping that she would dump her current boyfriend before Brad arrived.

However, contrary to our expectations, when Brad arrived, it turned out to be somewhat awkward. I could tell that he really liked Brooklyn, but with her having a boyfriend, it was difficult for him to find a place in her life. We hosted Brad and his friend while he was visiting. They were both very nice young men, and I was secretly hoping that Brad and Brooklyn would become an item.

During the next few months, Brooklyn had two other episodes and ended up back in the hospital. The third time she went back, a different psychiatrist diagnosed her with borderline personality disorder, along with the bipolar disorder. A borderline personality disorder is a mental illness that makes it difficult for a person to feel comfortable with themselves. They end up having difficulty controlling emotions and have a difficult time relating to other people.

We were devastated by this latest diagnosis. I didn't know what to think. I was scared for her, and I didn't want her to go on more medications. However, we had to do what the doctors thought was best for her.

Brooklyn was also devastated by her latest diagnosis, and one day, when Brooklyn was 21, she came to me.

"Mom, I don't want to be on the drugs anymore," she said. Her voice cracked as she said it, and I didn't know what to say.

"I've heard about a fairly new therapy called cognitive behavior therapy that I want to try. I'm willing to pay for it myself, and it would take a year for me to complete it," she said before I could answer. She was on disability from work, so it wouldn't be difficult to carry that over. She also mentioned that if she chose to go this route with taking no medication, she would not have the support of a psychiatrist anymore.

I thought about it. It all seemed too much, but she had thought it all out. Brooklyn's psychiatrist told her that she would not be his patient anymore, and it really bothered me because it was essential to have consistency in her treatment should she have to return to the hospital.

However, Brooklyn seemed determined, and so I gave her my blessing. I told her that her dad and I would do whatever we could to help. We would support her in any way. I was so thankful for

Jack at this time because I really needed someone to be able to lean on, and he was my rock. I felt like I was breaking apart, and I might have if it weren't for Jack. We had such a great relationship and were able to talk about anything and get through it together. We rarely fought, and it was a great feeling to have a partner like him.

One good thing that came out of this was that Brad and Brooklyn started dating. He was a great guy, and he was so supportive of her. They were a great couple, and we were thrilled about the relationship. They even had plans to buy a small home together, so they were thinking of their future. We adored Brad and were so thankful for him. He somehow did make her better, and he knew how to handle her disorder.

Life seemed to be getting back on track. The kids were all well, life with Jack Michael was going smoothly, and I couldn't have imagined a life without him now. We were all so happy, and I felt so blessed and grateful to have everything I had with my family.

Chapter Eight

I was so happy that Brooklyn was doing well. She had faced her mental health challenges head-on and decided that she would do whatever she could to conquer them. It was a big blow to her, having been diagnosed with borderline personality disorder and bipolar disorder, but she was making great strides with her psychologist and the Cognitive Behavioral Disorder course.

Brooklyn had dealt with the worst that she could, and now she was determined to turn her life around. Her strength gave us all strength, and I never once felt as though she was giving up. She pushed herself to be the best. I was very proud of her and knew that she was going to be successful. It also helped that she had a great job with a promising future, a supportive and loving boyfriend, and her dad and I was there for her whenever we could be.

I felt so happy and blessed. However, my latest challenge was childcare for Jack Michael. Zach took the bus to school every day, and Morgan was always home for him when he got off the bus. I don't know what I would do if I didn't have her. She was amazing with her little brothers and never balked at helping out with them. She even made sure that she took them to the playground or swimming or did some other activity in her downtime. They loved spending time with her just as she loved spending time with them.

I had recently given up trying to work at home and take care of Jack Michael. I found that I just couldn't work into the wee hours of the morning anymore. It often left me exhausted, and so I searched around for daycare for him. I spent my time searching for a good one, and, finally, I found one; it was not ideal, but it seemed okay.

Jack Michael was still quite young, and it was tough to get him up and out the door in the early hours of the morning, and he did not want to go. He would cry every time I left him, and it broke my heart, but I had to do it. After three months of this, I decided this simply wasn't working out, and I talked to Jack about us getting a live-in nanny. We were both reluctant to have a stranger come and live with us, but decided that we would try it out.

At that point, I didn't see any other solution that seemed to be feasible for us. I called and made an appointment with an agency that specialized in live-in nannies. Jack and I both attended the appointment, found out the logistics of having a nanny, and then interviewed two girls who had recently arrived here from the Philippines and were looking for work. We decided on a pretty young girl named Kathleen. She seemed experienced enough and seemed to handle kids well in the brief meeting we had with her. She seemed eager to work for us, but it was still uncertain how Jack Michael would react. After all, not all kids take to their nannies.

However, Jack and I both liked her and were sure that Jack Michael would like her as well. He had just turned three and was quite stubborn. The day we brought her home, Jack Michael took to her right away, much to our relief. Kathleen settled into our home and seemed very comfortable that night at dinner.

We guided her on everything regarding Jack Michael and what we expected from her. We told her about his likes and dislikes and that we expected her to discipline him when he misbehaved. We told her that her job was not to clean the house or do the laundry, but if she had free time, she could do it. I still had a house cleaner who I brought in once a week.

I noticed the next morning after her arrival when I went off to work that he was quite happy to stay at home with Kathleen. After about a week, I realized how much happier Jack Michael was. Kathleen was always playing with him, reading him stories, or listening to music with him, and I was thrilled at their relationship.

Kathleen also offered to cook meals, and she was an excellent cook. She had given Jack Michael the attention he was lacking, and in turn, she helped all of us become more relaxed. I felt like my life had gone from chaotic to calm, and I couldn't believe that I had it so good. Honestly, I felt as though we were all finally able to take a breath and move on with our lives without any stress coming our way.

Kathleen was like a gift from God, and gradually, we all came to love her, and she became part of our family. We treated her with the respect that she deserved and showed her just how grateful we were for having her in our lives. Kathleen had mentioned that she didn't know how to drive, so in the next year, we taught her and bought her a second-hand car so she would have more freedom to come and go. I remember how ecstatic she was when she got the car and kept on thanking us. It made my heart swell with happiness. It certainly wasn't a fancy car, but it was nothing less than she deserved.

Kathleen quickly made friends with other nannies that lived in our neighborhood, and there were a lot of them! It was great because they would schedule playdates together, big picnics in the park, little field trips, and the like. Jack Michael made so many new friends. It was amazing.

Life at work was good as well. We were extremely busy, expanding at a steady rate, and the company profits were excellent. In fact, we were doing so well that Jack and I decided to look for a lakefront cabin where we could spend our summers. We made a trip out to British Columbia and looked at a variety of properties.

But we had no luck in finding something suitable. We were hoping to find something in the interior of BC, where the weather is beautiful and the lakes are big.

Someone suggested that we look around Sylvan Lake, which was only 12 miles from where I grew up. I really wasn't interested in Sylvan, but Jack and I thought we would give it a shot anyway. So, one day, we headed out there to visit my parents and to look at a few properties that were for sale. The whole time I was somewhat in denial. It was funny how my mind simply couldn't accept that we were in this position now. I couldn't believe that we were actually going to buy a cabin! It was like a dream come true.

We immediately fell in love with a small partial log cabin with a beautiful interior. The exterior needed work, but we could get it done. It was the most beautiful cabin I had ever seen, and I couldn't wait to purchase it.

After taking a second look at it, Jack and I decided to put in an offer. That's when we found out that there were two other offers on the place. We chose to bid slightly above the asking price so the scales would tip a little towards us. Over the next few hours, we sat on pins and needles, waiting to hear if our offer had been accepted. The phone rang, and Jack quickly answered it, and the smile on his face told me everything. Our offer had been accepted! We jumped for joy! Man, were we excited.

All we had was a picture of the real estate listing, but it didn't take long for us to tell the kids and grandparents. Everyone was very excited. I already knew how I was going to decorate it. I quickly got on the computer and researched log furniture because I wanted beds, tables, bookcases, and bunk beds for the place.

There was a cute little log shack in the back of the property called The Sugar Shack, where I was going to put log bunk beds. The actual cabin itself had only two bedrooms, but with queen-sized bunk beds in one room and a pullout sectional in the living area, we would have lots of room for guests. I had it all planned out.

The cabin was lakefront, situated on a hill from the lake, so my dad built a nice lower deck overlooking the lake. We brought in a hot tub, and placed it on the deck and cleaned up some hedges. We landscaped the front with brick and put tiers down the hill, which we planted with shrubs and bushes. It took some work, but it turned out to be amazing, just how I pictured it in my mind!

It was beautiful when it was complete. We made sure that we invited all of our friends on the weekends so they could enjoy it with us. It was our happy place. During the summer, the boys stayed out there during the week, and my mom and dad stayed with them while Jack and I came back to town to work. We would go back on the weekends, and my parents would go home.

Kathleen, our nanny, was also out there helping with the boys all week, and she would go back to Calgary during the weekend. The boys were happy there, and it got them more in touch with the outdoors and closer to their Grandparents. Eventually, they were busy during the week with swimming and sailing lessons, which they weren't too keen about because the swimming lessons were sometimes held at the lake, and it could be cold. Bu the cabin was terrific and we made some very happy memories there.

One good thing about having a cabin was that the family time spent together is second to none. We were a pretty close family, but we all became closer and loved spending time on the water and with each other. Besides that, we had an awful lot of fun and laughs. The cabin was like a haven that brought us all even closer, and that, in itself, was a blessing.

We couldn't help but be in a good mood when we were there. We would have the cool breeze of the water, the exciting thunderstorms, and the laughter of everyone sitting around. It definitely provided a kind of family time, which was difficult to forget. As soon as you walked into the cabin, the stress and anxiety just seemed to fade away; it was a wonderful sigh of relief. The kids were so happy, so relaxed, and we spent so much time outdoors.

There was a lot of work that went into maintaining the cabin, though, since the grounds constantly needed weeding, and there were so many trees to take care of and clean up after. However, my father was more than happy to do this for us. He loved the cabin and spending time there, so did my mom. They made it their home during the week, inviting their friends out for dinner, and even though neither of them felt comfortable using the boat, they still really enjoyed being there.

I was like Jack, and I could hardly wait for Friday to roll around so we could take off for the lake. Often, we would have the company out for the weekend. Even though it was small, we always managed to make the sleeping arrangements work, and we always had a good time with our friends and family. I can easily say that the cabin helped make us all very close-knit.

When summer was over, we would take out the dock and put the boats away. It was always a sad moment, but if time allowed, we could go out and spend the weekend at the cabin during the rest of the year. It was a cozy place to be in the winter with lots of ice skating, driving on the lake, having a roaring fire, and playing in the snow. Unfortunately, the boys both played ice hockey, and it was hard to find a weekend when they weren't doing that. Still, every so often, we would get the chance to escape the hustle and bustle of the big city and the challenges at work and go to the cabin for a quiet weekend with our kids. It was such a beautiful, peaceful family time.

We were very blessed, and after everything we all faced together, it was something that we all very much needed.

Chapter Nine

Life in the McNair household couldn't be better. The kids were all thriving, and Brooklyn was doing well with her program and was very much in love with Brad. Her health had improved significantly, and everything was finally falling right into place. I was so incredibly proud of her. With all the research I had done on borderline personality disorder and bipolar disorder, I had found it was a very difficult illness to overcome without drugs.

Brooklyn and Brad moved forward with buying a small house together. They chose a newer neighborhood on the west side, and we helped Brooklyn out with the down payment. She assured us that she could cover the mortgage, so I took a step back. I wanted her to feel as though she could turn to me when she wanted without my smothering her. They were very excited, and we were excited for them.

Kathleen fit into our family like she had been a part of it all along. She was very close to my mom and dad, with whom she spent the summers. They adjusted well to her as well, and they were all very happy together.

We spent the summers at the cabin, and, every winter, we

would try and take a vacation to a tropical place, including a Caribbean Cruise with my brother Jeff and his family. We were making family memories, and we all felt incredibly blessed that we were able to do such things. I couldn't help but take a step back and admire how far we all had come. It was hard to believe that there was once a time my girls and I had to face abuse at the hands of someone who should have loved us. Now, here we all were, happy, healthy and safe.

At times, I would reflect on my life and couldn't believe how lucky I was. My life now was one that I could only have dreamed of in my former life. I rarely thought about my life then, except when I had to take the stairs, or someone wanted to throw a set of keys at me, I was terrified. The remnants of abuse still lingered strongly within me. The girls had nothing to do with their birth father, and we'd completely forgotten about him and the things that he did to us.

I was at the point of my life where I rarely thought of him. Even when Jack Michael's birthday came around, I enjoyed the celebration without a single thought of my ex. I was happy, but I still worried about Brooklyn. Yet she was stable and seemed to be doing really well. Morgan and Zach were both well-adjusted and good kids. Zach was so good with his little brother and made sure he played with him whenever he got the chance. They built a bond together that no one could break.

Morgan was in her first year of university, having the time of her life away from home for the first time. I missed having her around so badly, and the boys missed her terribly. We were lucky she was close enough to come home on weekends. I was happy to see how she had grown and become a responsible young woman, so full of life.

One beautiful October evening, we had made plans with friends to go out for dinner. Morgan was home and offered to babysit, and we agreed. We had a wonderful time. Our friends stopped in for a drink on their way home, and Morgan said that she was going to meet some friends at a downtown pub. It was about 11 p.m., and I remember thanking her for babysitting, hugging her and telling her to be safe and not to drink and drive. This was something we always instilled in our kids. She assured me she wouldn't and went on her way.

It was about 4:30 in the morning when the phone rang. We were all asleep, and when the ringing rang out in the empty room, my eyes opened to a sinking feeling in my gut. Something was terribly wrong.

My husband answered it, and all I heard was, "How many are dead?" I hadn't realized I had gotten to my feet, and suddenly, I sank to my knees and felt a knot in my stomach that I had never felt before. It was the longest minute of my life until Jack got off the phone. Tears had already started running down my face. I just looked at him and asked, "What happened?"

He was struggling too, but he still kept his calm. He proceeded to tell me that Morgan had seven kids in her car, a Volkswagen Beetle, and had been driving on a country road where the turn was a very sharp 90 degrees. She had taken it too fast and rolled her car. One young man, Josh, 21, died in the accident. All the other six were okay and at the hospital. Jack had to go to the hospital to be with Morgan.

I said I would be there in the morning when I could get a friend to take care of the boys. I wished Jack could stay back with me so we could support each other. This was one of those times when being a parent was the priority. I couldn't stand the thought of it, but I had to.

I knew Morgan, and I knew that this would destroy her. I couldn't imagine what she was going through right now, but I knew that Morgan wouldn't be the same for a very long time. It broke my heart, and I wanted to hug all her pain away, but that wasn't possible either. I had to gather my strength and be there for her.

I lay in bed for the next few hours, just wishing I could be with my daughter. Kathleen was on her days off, so as soon as I thought it was okay to do so, I called my friends Tracy and Sue and asked if they would come and take care of Jack and Zach. Tracy lived down the street and had a daughter the same age as

Jack, and Sue lived quite a way away, but her son, Adam, was Zach's best friend. They were both happy to come, and I knew I had nothing to worry about on this end, leaving them for the hospital.

All I knew in my heart of hearts was that I needed to be there for Morgan. I rushed to the hospital and walked into Morgan's room. As soon as she saw me, she started sobbing, as did I. I rushed to her side and held her, then rocked her back and forth for at least five minutes until her sobs subsided. My heart was broken; I did not know what to say to her. I had no idea how she felt, except that I knew she was devastated.

Jack wasn't very good with this kind of thing, and I needed Brooklyn to be with me, but she was out on the coast, visiting Brad's parents at the time. The doctor came in and said that we could take Morgan home. He also told us that the other five were being released, too, as there were no other major injuries. Relief washed over me, but Morgan was different. I could see the despair in her eyes and could only try and imagine what she was going through.

Morgan rode home with me, and when we got in the car, I asked her to tell me what had happened. She took a deep breath, gathered her strength, and then began. She explained that she got to the bar, had a beer with the girlfriends that she was meeting up, and they had met three guys. One of the guys was asked to leave the bar as he had gotten sick. They all left together and told Morgan that she had only had one beer, so she could drive them all; it would be fun.

They all piled into her little car, two buckled in the passenger's seat, the three guys in the back with one girl sprawled over their legs. The intention was to go to a party not very far away. However, they missed the turnoff and ended up out in the country, where Morgan showed them where she went to school.

They were heading back on the main highway, turning off on a secondary road, which has a very bad reputation for being dangerous because of its hairpin turns and narrow road. They had to stop a couple of times so that Josh could get sick and vomit.

But other than that, the car was filled with singing and music. They were just having a good time.

Morgan came across this 90-degree turn, took it too fast, and rolled the car in the field. One of the boys started calling out everyone's name, and when he came to Josh, he didn't answer. Morgan yelled out at him, "Over here," and he found Morgan crying and trying to give Josh mouth-to-mouth and administer CPR.

He had vomit all over him, and subsequently, Morgan got it all over her. Morgan never shared this information with me; we found this out two years later at her hearing. Morgan was shaking, and the horror of the night was still evident on her pale face. For the first time, I didn't know what I could do to make her okay.

We went home, and I knew I had to be there for Morgan; she was devastated and could barely function. I knew she was riddled with guilt, and I also knew that the upcoming days would be challenging for her, having to face Josh's family and friends.

I was trying to help her prepare for that in the best way that I knew how. I told her to be honest, be sincere, and that it was important for her to show her grief. However, regardless of what I said, it didn't translate properly for her. She nodded, but I knew she was spaced out.

Once again, sleep was hard to come by, and I couldn't stop thinking about the tragedy and the family who lost their son. When I did sleep, I awoke with a sick feeling that was similar to when I found out that Brooklyn was pregnant. It wouldn't go away, and it was hard to function during the day. I had to be there for the boys, but Morgan really needed me now. More than anything, I had to dig deep inside to find the strength to be a mother right now. I was desperate for things to say to Morgan without breaking down myself. Often, I would hide in my closet, trying to get my sobs under control.

Morgan and I decided to attend the prayer service on Friday night that Josh's family set up. It was just going to be the two of us, and then our whole family would attend the funeral service for Josh. We were both very nervous walking into the funeral home for the prayer service; however, I wasn't going to leave my girl to deal with it alone. I held her hand tightly, and we both took a deep breath upon entering the service. I could feel Morgan shaking.

There were quite a few people there, and we noticed an open casket up front with a man and woman standing beside it. I assumed they were Josh's parents, and I led Morgan up to them. I stood back, and she looked down and said to them, "I'm so incredibly sorry. I am Morgan, the driver of the car, and I just want you to know..."—and then the sobbing started. It was heart-breaking, and I couldn't hold it together either.

By this time, she was sobbing but had managed to utter the words, "Please forgive me." Everyone was staring at her and you could see people whispering.

Even though I stood at a distance, I heard it all, and I was sobbing too. It was so hard to see her in so much pain. It was hard to see the body of a promising young man and accept it for what it was. He was an incredibly handsome young man, one whose time had come way too soon. My heart was breaking for Morgan, standing there sobbing uncontrollably. I hadn't expected anything good, but I watched as something magical happened: Both of his parents took her in their arms. With tears in their eyes, they said, "We forgive you, Morgan. We know this wasn't intentional. God forgives you."

I was so grateful to these incredible people, and I felt that a 1000-pound weight lifted off my shoulders. They extended their arms to me, so I joined in the hug, and they introduced them-selves. I asked them if, when this was all over, they would be inter-ested in our families going out for dinner so they could share stories of Josh with us.

I felt it was important for them to see that my family was grieving Josh's death also. Although we hadn't lost a son, we were the cause of that loss, and that was something that we would have to deal with for the rest of our lives.

I couldn't begin to imagine how Morgan felt; all I knew was how I felt as her mother. How could I have prevented this? Could

I have said something to her so that she wouldn't have put those seven kids in the car? Oddly enough, I came up with nothing. Instead, I dealt with helping her heal if that was at all possible. I knew the emotions and grief were bigger than I was capable of understanding. Yet I had to help her try and get through this.

The next day, we all attended Josh's funeral. It was a beautiful service with lots of friends and family in attendance and, though we didn't know him, it was hard not to cry through it. Morgan wasn't capable of holding back her emotions. On the inside, I was glad that she was so distraught as I felt everyone's eyes on us.

We did get a chance to see Josh's parents, and they gave all of us a big hug. They were very devoted Christians, and I knew that their faith in the Lord would help them through this incredibly difficult time.

I also knew that I had to get Morgan to see someone as soon as possible. I saw how much she changed; we all did. Morgan was not the same kid who used to be vibrant, funny and happy. She was always a glass-half-full kind of girl. I couldn't remember the last time I had seen her upset; she was usually so upbeat and positive about everything.

Now, however, she seemed broken. Her spirit was broken and I wanted to do everything in my power to try and help her heal. We decided that she would withdraw from school and come home. She would continue her studies when she was stronger. It seemed the most suitable thing to do in the situation.

We had been in touch with a lawyer who offered some distressing news. Morgan could very well go to jail since she was charged with, "dangerous driving causing death," and the penalty for that was five years in prison. I was sick when I heard that and struggled to believe that my beautiful young daughter could go to jail. I couldn't even picture her there, and she was in no way capable of handling the horrors that lingered in such a place.

My nighttime prayers became desperate, and I didn't know what to do. On top of that, Morgan was terrified of what might happen to her, and I had to try and keep her calm. No matter what happened, I knew that I wouldn't be able to handle it if she had to go to jail.

We were able to find an excellent psychologist who worked with her on a regular basis and, with her help, Morgan was able to function through daily life. I had never been so scared and worried, but I had to put my fears in God's hands, knowing that He would help me get through this and accept whatever the outcome would be.

There was no way that I knew if I would ever have the daughter that I once knew back, but I was determined to do everything I could to help her become her normal self again. It was painful watching her day in and out, and I knew it was going to be a painful two years before we went to court to find out what her destiny would be.

It was if the days were stretching interminably. The dread of what was in the future weighed heavily on our backs. I felt sick to my stomach at the mere thought of my girl in jail. What was worse was that I could see the sadness in Morgan's eyes and wished that there was something I could do to take that away. But I had nothing except the words that continued reminding her of the love I held for her and the support I was willing to give. I didn't know what that support could be, all I knew was I was there for her, to hold her when she needed to be held, to listen when she needed to talk and to love her and let her know that it was unconditional.

Chapter Ten

As life went on, we mentally prepared ourselves for the dreaded court trial. It seemed to consume all our waking moments. Stress increased for each one of us, eventually taking its toll. It was two years later that we entered the courtroom.

The moment we had all feared so much was finally here. Even my parents came down so they could attend. It was comforting to have them there, and I know Morgan appreciated it. She needed all the support that she could get. I could tell that they, too, had lost sleep. They seemed just as scared as the rest of us. However, my main focus was on my terrified daughter.

We got to the courthouse early in the morning, and the first people we recognized were Josh's parents. They hugged us and assured us that they were there for support. It was hard seeing them, but I was grateful for their thoughtfulness. It was more than what any of us could have asked for and showed just how amazing they were.

We had driven past the crash site only once and seen Josh's photo, flowers, and a cross that had been planted there. It was too painful to drive past it, especially for Morgan, which is why we avoided it whenever we could.

We had hired a top-notch lawyer but, as it happened, he got appointed to the bench just before Morgan's trial, which meant that our case went to one of his associates. His associate was a local celebrity boxer who lost his mother and brother in a car accident caused by drunk driving. I was upset when I found out that the lawyer we had initially hired wouldn't be able to represent Morgan, as he had developed quite a rapport with her while the associate barely knew her.

The tension was in the air. Our hearts seemed to beat out of our chests with every minute that passed. After what seemed like forever, the trial began. Josh's mother was sitting next to me, and she held my hand tightly as we heard the testimony together.

The young people present in the car that night testified. Many tears were shed, including my own. Often, I would look at Morgan, who had her back to me. However, I could read every movement and twitch of her face from the side. It was evident that she was sobbing because her back constantly moved up and down. It broke my heart, and I just wanted to get up and hug her.

Living through this difficult time was one of the toughest things that I'd ever had to endure. I couldn't sleep, couldn't eat, and could barely take care of my younger children. It was like living the nightmare all over again, and I was trying so hard to be strong for Morgan.

Often at times, we would just be talking and she would break down. She would tell me just how the incident haunted her. It had consumed her dreams and every waking hour. I couldn't get it out of my head that she could go to jail for five years. I honestly didn't know what I would do if that happened. I felt so powerless at that time and so vulnerable. I was constantly sick to my stomach with grief.

Morgan had always been so full of life and now it was hard to get her to smile. She had been through so much; she didn't deserve this. There was no doubt that she was a great kid with a great future. She'd made one stupid mistake. I only hoped that the judge could see that. I knew in my heart that she would never forgive herself for that night, and I kept thinking maybe that was enough.

However, as I sat there and listened to all the recollections of what happened that night, it was nearly unbearable. None of the kids blamed Morgan. It was a dangerous corner of the road, and it was noted that, since her accident, they'd lowered the speed limit at that particular corner since Josh's wasn't the only fatality that occurred there. The other thing that came out of the trial was Josh's best friend testified that he found Morgan trying to administer CPR and mouth-to-mouth to Josh, even though he was covered in vomit.

After a few more agonizing days, the moment finally arrived for her sentencing. The anxiety had stolen my sleep, and I couldn't stop thinking about it. That morning, I got out of bed, made coffee, and just felt sick to my stomach. The air that day seemed different as well. It was gloomy and oppressive, but it might only have been my anxiety.

I put the mug to my mouth and held my hand in front of me: it was shaking. The only comfort I had at the time was my parents. It was nice to have them and know that Jack and I weren't alone in any of this. Jack was just as nervous as I was, but he was able to hide it better—or perhaps deal with it better than I could.

When we all got dressed and sat in the car. Thick silence filled it. Our car rides used to be happy and chirpy, but that day, all of us were quiet and solemn. Upon arriving at the courthouse, Josh's parents greeted us again, grabbing Morgan and hugging her.

"Morgan, the one good thing to come out of this is we got meet a wonderful family," they said to her.

I couldn't believe it when they said that, there were tears in my eyes. I was so incredibly grateful. I knew that if it were anyone else, they probably wouldn't share the same sentiments. They were very kind people, and even in this tragedy, they were able to see some good come out of it.

I admired them so much, and I wanted them to know that, even though we didn't know Josh, we grieved his death. I felt that this family would always be a part of us, and we would never forget them.

We entered the room and took our places while Morgan stayed outside until called upon. I gave her one last hug and assured her everything would be alright. I didn't know if it would, and I hated that she could see it in my eyes. The judge walked in and sat down. All of a sudden, I couldn't breathe. It felt like all the air in my lungs was suddenly forced out of me.

"Now is not the time to have a panic attack! Breathe deep," I thought to myself and kept on repeating it. I knew that I had to keep it together, to remain strong. I couldn't imagine what Morgan was going through or what her thoughts were. I just knew that I had to hold her and tell her how much I loved her before she went and sat down.

Once again, I sat beside Josh's mom, with my mom on the other side. I held both their hands when the judge arrived in the courtroom. I felt like I was in a movie and wanted to fast forward through it all. Alas, this was actually happening, and we all had to face the agony of waiting.

As soon as the judge sat down, he proceeded to read the charges. He then asked for a victim's statement, and Josh's dad got up to read his. It was lengthy and heartbreaking, but it was kind. After that, the judge looked at Morgan and said a few words. Morgan's back was to us and I could tell that she was crying but trying to keep it together, as was I.

Finally, the judge cleared his throat and laid down the sentence. As soon as I heard it, I felt all the tears release from me. They were tears of relief. I had never been so relieved in my entire life.

The judge gave Morgan six months of house arrest and five years of loss of license. Finally, I could breathe again, and before I could even react, Josh's mom leaned in and hugged me. I knew they weren't disappointed in the sentence. She had the same look of relief that I did and as we hugged, we both sobbed. I wanted to get up and run to my daughter, but we had to wait until the judge dismissed us.

When the proceedings were over, I made my way to Morgan so that I could hold her tight. She was crying, and her face was red and covered with tears. "We'll get through this together," I held her face in my hand and whispered.

She nodded and took me into her arms, and her head slumped onto my shoulders as she cried. Everyone came around to meet with her, and luckily, she had the strength to get through it. We had a long road ahead, but I knew we would be able to make it through. I thanked God for watching over us and I was extremely grateful for the light sentence that Morgan got. I could once again sleep at night.

* * *

On the first day of house arrest, I took Morgan to a parole officer, where we found out how this was all going to work. He informed Morgan that she was allowed to attend school, work, and be home, and that was it, which is why he needed her schedule. She could be contacted at any time during the day or night to see if she was home. Then he told her to be prepared to be contacted at least once a day.

Since we lived out in the country, Morgan would be relying on me for transportation. She worked downtown at a club, so it was going to be a bit of a challenge, but I was up for it. I was so relieved that she was spared imprisonment that I was ready to do anything to get her through this.

As for Morgan, she seemed to be doing well. She was happy to be able to continue her education and keep her job. Her friends had stopped coming by a long time ago, and I only imagined that she would have very little interaction with them now that she was stuck at home for the next six months.

Once summer made its way to us, we got permission from her parole officer to move her permanent home to our cabin. There, she was able to get a job at the local golf course. She still had to abide by the rules, though. There was also no boating involved because when she wasn't working, she had to be in the cabin in case they checked up on her.

I knew that spending time at the cabin would be good for her. It was such a family place, and that is what she needed. She needed to be surrounded by people who loved her, who cared for her and who did not judge her.

The summer went by fast, and every day, Morgan coped even better. We were abiding by the rules, and the phone calls to check that she was home came at all hours of the night, even in the middle of the night. It was annoying, but nothing we couldn't handle.

The six months seemed to go by fast. During this period, Morgan and I spent a lot of time in the car together, and we grew closer than ever. It seemed like life had drifted us apart, and we had become too busy to be in touch. Now, however, we had the opportunity to talk about our day, her future, and her dreams. I guess that was the silver lining to the dark cloud.

Morgan was fortunate enough to spend some time sailing on a 130-foot wooden schooner out on the coast during the past few summers. There was a trip coming up for young people that sounded amazing. The ship was making its way around the world, and you had the choice of different legs to sail.

Morgan showed interest and asked if she could take the leg from Papau, New Guinea, to Japan. I was skeptical and afraid, of course. It was a three-month trip with about six different countries on the docket. There would be thirty-eight people aboard the ship.

The ship itself would be at sea for a year, and the captain had brought along his entire family. There was no running water or electricity aboard, so it wasn't like any cruise ship; it was more like survival at sea.

Eventually, however, I did agree to it. When Morgan boarded the ship in New Guinea, it was 58 degrees Celsius/138 degrees Fahrenheit. She lost her visa and her debit card when they arrived in Guam. She was without money for the rest of the trip, as I couldn't get a new visa for her. The good thing was that she was making some lifelong friends, although I knew that she was at times homesick. She mentioned in one of her letters that at one point when they were at sea for twelve days straight, she was so homesick that she was physically ill.

We missed her too. Morgan was very close to her little brothers, and they missed having her around. She had a way around the family and had left her mark on each of us.

I missed her so much and was anxiously awaiting when she would come home. We were in Edmonton at a hockey tournament one weekend, and I was sitting in the rafters. Suddenly, I felt a hand go over my eyes, and I couldn't figure out who it was. I turned around, and there were Brooklyn and Morgan, surprising me with Morgan's homecoming. It was quite a surprise, and I had tears in my eyes when I held her tight. After so long, she was finally home safe and sound.

Morgan had the trip of a lifetime, one that she would never forget.

She talked about her trip, sailing in the intense heat and the vegetables down below becoming mush, eating homemade yogurt and oatmeal, trying to bathe in the ocean and have others on shark watch, and then arriving in Japan, where it was 12 degrees Celsius/53 degrees Fahrenheit and very cold.

Morgan often reminisced about the good times, which I loved to hear. She talked about the one day that they spiffed the ship up for arrival in Shanghai and, just before they were to be accompanied down the Yangtze River, a cable broke and oil spilled everywhere.

Well, they managed to clean it up, and then it took eight hours to go down the Yangtze River to their destination. Apparently, the river was quite filthy, and the air polluted and even though she thoroughly enjoyed seeing those different countries, Morgan was glad to set foot on Canadian soil again.

Once she started school again, it was different for her. This time, she didn't have the weight of the world on her shoulders, and she seemed to be able to concentrate better. I was enjoying our time together in the vehicle when I would take her to school and work. We talked about everything, and she shared a lot with me. We had some great mother-daughter bonding time. It was much needed, and we both knew it.

I was also grateful to Kathleen, our nanny. She was taking such good care of Jack, Michael and Zach. Zach was in school, but Kathleen was there for him when he got home. She truly was a gift from God, that's for sure, and we were fortunate to have her.

Because Morgan was home during the weekend, she spent a lot of time with her little brothers. She adored them, and they loved her back. I could tell they were making up for a lost time; they had been so sad ever since she left the house. Now, however, they made sure they were constantly by her side.

One night, close to Christmas, Morgan asked if we would drop her off at a party. We decided that she would call us if she needed a ride home. I was happy that her life was getting back on track, and Jack and I both agreed that this would help her.

Little did we know Morgan would meet the love of her life there! She told me about it the very next day and said that she wasn't quite sure how she was feeling about this guy. I told her to give it time, and eventually, she would figure it out.

Morgan continued to date Bryan, a tall, thin, handsome young man five years older than she was, and they eventually fell deeply in love. Things were finally coming together for her and our family. Despite everything we had been through, we came out on the other side, together and stronger than before. We could still call ourselves happy and blessed.

Chapter Eleven

L ife was back to somewhat normal. Chauffeuring Morgan
back and forth wasn't as challenging as I thought it would
be. All I knew was that, although I was putting a lot of miles on
my truck, I was still happy for the opportunity to become closer
to her and try and help her through a very tough time. I was sure
she was never going to get over the guilt that she felt.

Through all this turmoil, we did get some fantastic news one
day and that was when Brad and Brooklyn came over to share that
they were going to be parents. We were over the moon, thinking
that we were now going to be grandparents, even though our
youngest was only three years old.

The boys were busy with hockey and loved playing it. It had
become a big part of our routine, as well as our social life. It was
great for everyone because we had made most of our good friends
through the sport.

All in all, hockey wasn't just great for kids, but parents too!
We attended every game, and Jack was quite often an assistant
coach. Now and then, we would do our part and loved hosting
the parent party in our home. Hockey was constant and the great
thing about it was that Jack was becoming very close to his boys,

coaching them and spending hours in the vehicle with them, shuffling them back and forth.

At least four nights a week were spent at the arena. I was at Jack Michael's game one night when a mom sat down beside me. We started talking, and I felt an immediate connection with her. Tammy was tall, with raven-colored long hair. She dressed like a man, and she liked logos, which was evident because her coat was covered in them. She was one of those people who you meet and know that you can share anything with them. I adored her. She was a mother of two boys, and her eldest, Bodie, was my son Jack Michael's best friend.

Jack Michael and Bodie were inseparable, and it allowed Tammy and me to spend a lot of time together. Tammy was a chiropractor and quite intelligent. It was interesting, though, the second time I met her, she complained about her husband and, at that time, I really didn't think we were close enough to share that kind of information. However, the more I got to know her, the more she complained about him.

Before we knew it, six weeks had passed into our friendship, and we ended up in Hawaii at the same time. I got to know her husband, who I quite liked. The family dynamics between Tammy and her husband were rather evident: Her husband was clearly disciplinarian while she was quite a pushover. You could also tell that there was no love lost between the two of them.

The more I got to know Tammy, the more I chose to ignore some of her inclinations. One of my quirks is that I like a clean, tidy house. I make sure that everything gets put away when you come home and pick up accordingly, and I'm quite anal about it. Tammy was not like that at all—when you visited her place, you actually had to remove the skates off the sofa in order to sit down. It was easy to see why she didn't want people there. Despite that, I tried my best not to judge her, as she was becoming one of my very best friends.

Jack Michael and Bodie were joined at the hip. They had to do everything together, and I mean everything! When they made different hockey teams, Tammy would email the head evaluator and see if they could get put on the same team. I was not impressed when she did that, but for some reason, it was important to her that they were on the same team.

In all the time that I knew Tammy, she kept on berating her husband, Jason. I honestly did feel sorry for her, as it seemed like she was in such an unhappy marriage. It's no wonder the news of her third pregnancy came as a big shock. It was difficult to believe that one person who was so unhappy could still be expecting another child.

Tammy's husband was one of the top chiropractors in the city, and he held the honor of being the chiropractor for the Canadian Olympic Team. Thus, his career allowed him to attend many Olympic Games as an official chiropractor and being friends with him certainly had its benefits—and it wasn't just the fascinating stories he had to tell.

When the Olympics came to Vancouver, he told us that he could get us accommodations where the athletes' parents were staying. I was ecstatic and jumped at the chance, knowing that it would be the opportunity of a lifetime for us.

When the tickets came out, I was lucky enough to get Ski Jumping, medal ceremonies, a hockey game and closing ceremonies for the entire family. It was a hectic travel year since it was also my parents' fiftieth wedding anniversary, and we were all going to Mexico to celebrate. It was nice to spend time with family in Mexico, and the experiences we had in Vancouver for the 2010 Games were remarkable. Both trips included memories of our lives together that I will always cherish.

During the Vancouver games, we made sure we didn't miss a single thing. It was a once-in-a-lifetime opportunity for us to be there, and we experienced everything there was to see in Vancouver. The closing ceremonies were unforgettable. The best part was that it didn't end when we got home. Jason was kind enough to include our boys to meet some of the gold medalists.

We started spending a lot of time with Jason and Tammy, and eventually, we were just as close as Jack, Michael and Bodie were. She was a very good friend to me, and I felt like I could tell her almost anything. What I liked about Tammy was that when you told her something, you knew it stayed with her. Not only was she incredibly bright, but she was also humble, helpful, honest, and brave. It was even more exciting that, on my fiftieth birthday, she gave birth to a baby girl.

She was honest with me and said that she wasn't sure how on earth she was going to be the mother of a little girl. Tammy was a tomboy, and she was hoping that her girl would be the same rather than a girlie girl.

Tammy loved sports, loved watching them, and could really connect with men on that level. She loved crime shows and gory programs, so in that regard, we had nothing in common. However, she was the sweetest friend and always agreed to go to my kind of movies rather than the ones that she enjoyed. It's one of the things I liked so much about her; her ability to compromise for my benefit felt selfless. When we were together, we always managed to find something to talk about.

One day in July, I got a phone call from her, and she was crying. Tammy was tough, and I had never seen her in a vulnerable position like that, so I was taken aback. When I asked what was wrong, she told me that their doctor had run some tests and confirmed that their baby girl had cystic fibrosis.

It was so shocking and heartbreaking. However, I knew that I had to be strong for Tammy and let her know that I was there for her. I knew that it was one of the worst pieces of news that a parent could receive. My heart went out to both of them, and I vowed to be there for them whenever I could.

I guess things were getting to her husband, however, because a few years later, he requested a divorce after thirteen years of marriage.

I felt sorry for Tammy. She didn't know how she was going to survive financially. She would have to go back to work, and I knew she was worried about her daughter and what she would do for childcare.

The one thing I had to say about Tammy and Jason was they had great kids, they really did, so they were doing something right.

While Tammy was finding comfort within our family, we tried to do everything we could to help her out. Our life was going rather smoothly, but our business was starting to see some effects of the recession. We had to lay off staff, which was heartbreaking, as we had good staff members.

Eventually, we felt our business slow down dramatically. Jack and his partner, Kerry, took a huge pay cut, hoping to help the bottom line. For the first time in a long time, we actually had to watch our finances.

Jack and I had done everything in our power to give our kids the best life, and it meant that they didn't want for anything. That's why it was tough to see the monthly financials. It was hard to see the monthly losses when we hadn't had a profit loss in years.

The oil business was getting tougher to be in because of all the safety requirements. Safety protocol expenses were about 25 percent of our total expenses. It was costly to keep on top of things.

Our other concern was that our equipment was getting old and was breaking down more frequently. That meant more expensive repairs were required, which was challenging to manage, considering our situation. We started sourcing out repairs that we had never done before.

It did weigh heavily on Jack's and my shoulders, but we worked together, and we were all working very hard to keep the company up and running. It was then that we learned just how stressful it could be to own your own business. In its own way, it was also very rewarding, and we never regretted it. The stress was overwhelming at times, and it was difficult to keep a positive outlook and try not to worry our employees. There were not a lot of options for us, so we just had to wait it out and see how things would unfold.

In 2007, Brooklyn and Brad got married. It was a beautiful wedding, and everything was perfect that day, the one special moment that stood out for me was when Jack got up to give his speech. We had worked on it quite a bit as Jack struggled with reading things, so he was trying to memorize it, which he was having difficulty doing. In the end, he decided to wing it and when he was finished, there were a lot of people with tears in their eyes and he received a standing ovation. I was so proud of him, as was Brooklyn. I knew what he had done was totally out of his comfort zone, yet he did it for love. I didn't think it was possible, but he made me love him more that day. My kids were very lucky to have a dad who loved them as much as he did. He is a good man, and I am so lucky to have him.

Chapter Twelve

My mother was one of the most influential and important people in my life. She taught me everything I've always needed to know. She taught me strength, independence, and other essential things in life. Because of her, I know how to prioritize, work full time, and still be a hands-on mother. Because of her, I know how to love unconditionally.

My mother taught me how to accept things for what they are and not be judgemental. I would definitely say that those are some of the most important tools to have, and I think they are necessary to guide you through life. She taught me to be kind to others and sympathetic and to try and help those who are less fortunate. Because of her, I know I must never turn my back on people who need me. She was also my best friend, whom I could talk to about pretty much anything, and she never judged me.

My mother always loved to have fun and laugh. She was an incredible cook and loved to bake. Our family reunions often took place at the cabin, and a couple of times, I held a car rally for everyone to participate in and have a great time.

When we were together, we always experienced moments that I would never let go of. Our reunions were so much fun, and I made some great memories. My mom would often go down to the dock and take the sea-doo for a spin, and nothing would ever hold her back.

My mother had a lot of good friends, and she was close to all of her siblings. Her sisters-in-law always liked her and were some of the first to sing her praises. That's why it was exceptionally hard to see her suffer and be in a lot of pain in her late sixties. It was determined that the arthritis that she had suffered from all her life had taken its toll on her hip. She now needed a hip replacement.

The strong, amazing woman I had grown up with and had put on a pedestal was now beginning to show the weakness of age. It was difficult to witness. Regardless, mom was strong and never let anything stand in her way. She had begun to walk with a walker, and her surgery was finally scheduled for November 2010. She wasn't scared or nervous. Instead, she was looking forward to walking properly again.

I had suggested that she and my dad move in with us while she recovered. I was even willing to give them our bedroom, which had a walk-in shower and would make it easier for her to shower. They thought that was a good idea, and I think my mom was quite looking forward to spending some time with her grand-children.

We prepared for my parents to move in, and everything was going great. Finally, after a long wait, the day of the surgery arrived.

She had it in Red Deer, and so I drove down after work to see her. She looked great, her spirits were high, and she was just looking forward to getting out of there. While I was there, her surgeon came to see her, and he mentioned that they had to discharge her ASAP because there was a superbug in the hospital. They didn't want any complications and so were trying to get people out of there sooner rather than later.

They kept her in for another day and then released her. My dad picked her up, and they drove up to my place, where I tried to make them as comfortable as possible. They had everything they needed; now, we just had her to help her get better.

We kept note of everything the doctor had said, and she followed everything she was supposed to do for a quick recovery to a tee. A week passed, but there didn't seem to be a lot of improvement in her recovery. I could tell she was trying everything to recover from her end, but this wasn't in her hands.

As for me, I enjoyed having my parents there, and my dad was amazing with her. He catered to her every need, and it was sweet to see. He took such good care of her and never left her side. It was the kind of love you watch in movies and read about in books. Seeing it there in front of me brought comfort to my heart.

Mom still wasn't recovering, though, no matter how much attention she was getting. Every day, a physiotherapist would come by and do the exercises with her, and it caused her a lot of pain. She was in so much pain that we decided to take her to Emergency as this wasn't normal. They sent her home from Emergency, but we were still very concerned about her health. The next day, we took her back to the hospital emergency with the same results. There was nothing they could do for her because she seemed okay. Since we lived with her, we knew differently. Finally, on our fourth trip to the emergency room, they decided to operate again and check out her hip.

Mom was in the hospital for three days before the operation took place. It was all very frustrating as she wasn't able to eat that whole time and they didn't know when exactly they would have an available room to operate. They finally took her in, and when the operation was over, I got a phone call from the surgeon. Immediately, I thought of the worst.

A sinking feeling automatically made its way to me when I saw the call. I picked it up and heard the surgeon's voice. She stated that she had never seen such an infected area before and that she took out over four liters of infection of the MRSA super bug. I was stunned and at a loss of words, but at least now we had figured out what was causing Mom so much distress.

The surgeon said that she wanted to put Mom on the most powerful antibiotic, Vancomycin. This antibiotic killed not only

the bad bacteria but the good bacteria also. She would be suscep-
tible to other bugs.

I had a decision to make. I thought of my mother, thought of
how much pain she was in. After a lot of consideration, I prayed I
was making the right decision and then agreed.

She spent another three weeks in the hospital, but she didn't
seem to be improving that much. It was suggested that she be
moved to an extended care facility. I was desperate for her to get
better, and if I had thought it through, I wouldn't have agreed to
that. I can't stop thinking about how I should have told her to
come home to recover. Instead, I thought the doctors knew best
and never thought to question them and that it would be easier
for her with medical care at her disposal.

What was supposed to be weeks ended up being months. And
my mother spent it all in an extended care facility. At one point,
they put up notices that the C-Diff infection was going around
their facility. My mother eventually caught it, and we were devastated. She had barely recovered from having the first superbug
that she caught and now this.

I remembered who my mom used to be, and I saw her
becoming . . . numb. She wasn't interested in eating and seemed
to be fading away daily. My father spent the days with her. After
dinner and getting the kids settled, I spent the evenings with her. I
tried to keep her calm and positive, but it was so difficult to do,
especially when I felt the opposite inside.

Worst of all, though, was having to watch the cleaners. It was
downright distressing. They would basically wipe down the bathroom that four people were using and then run a mop quickly
through the room. They were done cleaning in less than five
minutes. I expected a lot more care to be taken for this kind of
things.

I had read that the only way to kill off C-Diff germs was to use
bleach, and there was no bleach being used to clean these rooms.
When Mom got C-Diff the second time, my dad had had enough.
He decided to get her discharged from the hospital and take her
home to take care of her. After seeing their cleaning conditions, I

wasn't too opposed to the idea either. He took a lesson on how to inject her medication into her and it was heartwarming to see him become so proficient at it.

We expected Mom to recover quickly, however, after two months, Dad decided that Mom needed to be back in the hospital. He was too scared to leave her alone, and her health seemed to be slowly declining. We were watching her die, and my dad was hoping that being hospitalized would save her life. My uncle was a doctor in the Red Deer Regional Hospital, and he told my dad of a special rehab ward for patients like my mom and he was able to get her a room. We were very grateful to him.

As if dealing with Mom's condition wasn't difficult enough, life decided that our stream of bad luck would begin once more. One night, when I returned from the hospital and was sitting with Jack, the phone rang. We immediately braced ourselves because there had hardly been any good news of late, and it was the middle of the night. It was Jack who picked it up, and I could never forget the look on his face.

It was Jack's dad who had called to inform him that his mother, Barb, was diagnosed with stage 4 lung cancer. I couldn't believe it. I was as devastated to hear that news as was Jack. His parents were both heavy smokers for a long time, which was even harder to take.

The next morning, Jack and I packed up our things and went down to see his mom, who had also been hospitalized. When we spoke with the doctor, it turned out that she didn't have much time to live. Barb was such a lively woman, so it was heartbreaking to see her looking so very frail. She spoke with a raspy voice, and to know that she had such little time left, was tough to take.

Barb was a good woman, and this was going to be very hard on her husband; they were soul mates and had been together for fifty-one years. Jack's dad was heartbroken, and I didn't know what was going to happen to him when she was gone.

It was going to be tough on Jack and me since we both had our mothers in the hospital dying on opposite ends of the province. Jack would have to spend the time with his mother, and I would have to spend the time with my mother.

I felt like I was letting Jack down, and I wanted to assure him that I wanted to be there for him, but I just couldn't. I had to be there for my mom, and he had to be there for his mom. This time was a very tough period for us. Besides juggling this, work, and our kids, it was a lot.

The kids were very understanding, and it was a great help that Morgan was still at home. She was enrolled at a university, but she was still a big help with the kids. I tried to get up to see my mom at least two times during the week, and we would all go up on the weekend.

Life had taken a turn for the worse, and all the good times we had throughout our lives suddenly stopped making sense. Now, we lived in constant stress of having our parents in the hospital at the same time, both so close to death.

However, it wasn't just that; Jack and I were also stressed out about our company as the recession was hitting it hard. A recent large investment had gone belly up, and we lost a helluva lot of money. I didn't know how we were going to make up those losses. With the company doing so poorly, both Jack and I had to take another pay cut, so we now really had to watch our budget. On top of everything else going on, this simply made matters so much worse.

I kept visiting my mom in the hospital; she was wasting away. She never ate anything during the day, and it was a chore to get her to drink a Boost or eat some yogurt. We had read that probiotics were the key to recovery from a C-diff bug, so I searched the internet to see if I could get some probiotics in capsule form. It didn't matter what we tried, she was fading away to nothing, and it was very difficult to watch.

On May 18th, Jack said his final goodbye to his dear mother. Barb was literally worn out completely, and there was nothing left of her. At least she wasn't in pain anymore. It was difficult to see her suffer like that, so it was a blessing in disguise that she no longer suffered. Heaven had received another angel, and though she was at peace, it was still hard to say goodbye.

I remember trying to be so strong. I was sitting in my closet when, all of a sudden, everything that had happened overwhelmed me, and I just burst into tears. It was like a collision that burst it all out. All the stress that had built up inside of me was finally out. It was funny, my husband was not particularly sensitive, and when he saw me bawling had to ask what was wrong!

Normally, I like to take care of things, to try and fix things. Lately, however, things have been beyond my control. My mother-in-law had to be buried; I had to put together a slide show for her that was fitting and portrayed what a beautiful soul she was. I had to go to work and try to put together revised budgets as things were slow. I also had to go down and make sure that I spent some quality time with my mom, as I had no idea how much longer she would have. It was all piling up, one on top of the other, until I felt it take a toll on me.

We got through my mother-in-law's service, and I knew that she would have been proud. My father-in-law was very strong, although I didn't know how he would survive without her. The two of them had always been a team, never once leaving each other's side. It was odd seeing him by himself; it was really heartbreaking. It was going to be tough, that was for sure, but he was determined to stay in his own home.

My mom's condition continued to deteriorate. We spent a lot of the summer at the cabin, so it was easy to go and visit her. Things started to pile up, and the only ray of sunshine then was Brad and Brooklyn and their little bundle of joy. When they came for a visit, we were lucky that their family now included another little boy and a baby girl.

However, when life went south, it left no stone unturned. It was during their visit that Brooklyn gave us some bad news. Kaitlin, their baby girl, had been diagnosed with infant epilepsy. Brooklyn was in the final testing stages of having an MS diagnosis. I was devastated to hear the news and at a loss for words.

Brooklyn was a very strong player, but a diagnosis of MS was just too much.

To top it all off, my father-in-law had diabetes, but he didn't take it seriously. As a result, he was hospitalized and due to get his toes amputated. Once again, we were left with two people in the hospital. I was desperate for something to go right—anything—but there was nothing.

Our business continued to be a challenge and go downhill, constantly requiring that I adjust budgets and continually watch expenditures. On top of that, the major loss of our investment was a huge blow to our savings. Now, we were at an all-time low, but it didn't end there.

I guess it was all the stress, but I had begun to experience a lot of pain in my hip, and it got to the point that I couldn't bend over anymore. I was starting to walk with a limp. When I visited the doctor, it turned out that I needed a hip replacement and possibly two knee replacements. Even though the pain was unbearable at times, I decided to hold off until things calmed down a bit and to see how my mother fared after her hip replacement.

I tried to visit her as often as I could, Jack was in Calgary with his dad, and things were getting tough. I was really feeling stressed out. We couldn't catch a break, and that was the worst thing. One beautiful morning, as I lay in my bed trying to get my mind to be calm, I received a call from my niece.

She told me that my brother had been in a horrific motorcycle accident in Montana. He was lucky to be alive but suffered broken bones, a broken jaw, collapsed lungs, broken ribs, and the list went on. He was in the intensive care unit at the hospital in Montana, and it did not look good.

Oh my god, what else could go wrong?! My mind scrambled to find hope, any glimpse of light there was, but it couldn't. I was starting to feel overwhelmed, at times, I had a tough time breath-ing, and I was beginning to feel weird. This was not the time to be feeling unwell; I said to myself, "Get it together!"

It was hard to be present and in the moment, but I was trying my damndest. About ten days later, my brother was flown to

Cranbrook, which was about 4 ½ hours from where we were. He was admitted to the hospital there.

Jack and I decided to go and visit him and see for ourselves how he was doing. I hadn't slept for two days, and I was exhausted. My mind was doing funny things. It was like I was talking to myself, yet I wasn't speaking. I had spoken with Morgan that day and told her as much, and I told her I was worried about my brain. I was very open with her about everything and told her that I felt like I wasn't in control of my mind. It felt so weird; I really couldn't explain it.

We made the trip to Cranbrook and saw my brother. His spirits were good, but he seemed like he was in a lot of pain. It was hard to see him like that, but we spent as much time with him as possible. We then went to a hotel and stayed the night before making the trip home the next day.

I didn't tell anybody because I had too much on my plate already, but I heard my niece and my daughter screaming at each other in the hallway. I didn't want to know what it was about, so I just ignored it. What scared me the most was that I wasn't sure if it was real or if I heard things.

Something was wrong with me, and I didn't know what it was. I knew I had to get this sorted out, but I couldn't do it just yet—not with so much already happening.

We stopped at a 7-11 on the way home, and I went in and got water. I remember the look the clerk kept giving me. He kept on looking at me really funny, but again, I just ignored it. I kept hearing things in my head, and I wasn't sure if I was talking out loud or if I was just hearing things.

My mind was constantly circling with thoughts of my mom, my brother, Brooklyn and her MS, Kaitlin and her epilepsy, the money we lost, our company and trying to make sure it survived. My father in law was in the hospital, my hip replacement and the pain that I was in, and then my kids, who I had to help get through all this.

I had to be strong, and I had to sleep. I hadn't slept in three nights, and my thoughts were so strange and erratic that I couldn't explain what was going on. All I knew now was that I had to see a professional because something was very, very wrong.

I talked to Morgan again, and we googled psychologists. Once we found someone suitable, we called and made an appointment for the next day. I kept to myself the rest of the night until it was bedtime. I constantly had this dreaded feeling in me; I was terrified that something was not right, and yet I couldn't explain it. I was so glad that I was going to see someone.

Again, I didn't sleep, I tossed and turned, and I couldn't turn my mind off. My mind screamed at bizarre things, and I would blink my eyes because I thought I was seeing things. I would blink to see if what I saw was gone and, sure enough, it was gone, and then it wasn't. It was back.

I got out of bed to get some water. I thought I saw something in the backyard. I looked in on my son's room and...OH MY GOD, OH MY GOD, OH MY GOD, I saw him, lying lifeless and covered in blood. I didn't do anything; I didn't scream because I couldn't, I had no voice. I tried again and nothing. I went to the back window and saw my ex-husband with a bloodied knife in his hand.

I went to my other son's room, and he, too, was lifeless and covered in blood. I felt my entire life circle me, everything was loud, and it kept on whirling around. Was this in my head? Was I screaming? I didn't know. Please make it stop, please... I started to sob, and Jack came to see what was wrong. I was shaking so bad, that I could hardly stand.

"The boys are dead!" I whispered under my breath, and then the shock that came next shattered me, I killed my kids.

Once again, my mind screamed. OH MY GOD, OH MY GOD, how could I have done such a horrific thing? I love those boys more than anything. There's no way I could have done this. Oh my god, what have I done?

Suddenly, I couldn't breathe. There was no air, and I couldn't speak, in my head, it was screaming that I killed my kids. I wanted it to stop, please no.... I would never do that... I adore my kids... please stop... stop the screaming... Everything had to stop; my mind was doing strange things to me, and then I realized I deserved to die. I knew that I must die. However, I needed to apologize to my girls and my family first before I die. All I kept thinking about was I did something horrific, and I deserved to die, and I needed to be with my boys now.

I asked Jack for some pills for my headache, and he brought me back two pills. I knew that if I took them, I would die. Jack was trying to kill me. Those two little pills were arsenic, and they would kill me. I knew that he wanted me to die because of what I did and I didn't blame him, but I needed to tell my girls that this wasn't my fault, that I didn't even remember doing it, that something was terribly wrong with me, that my eyes couldn't focus, and my head was spinning, and it wouldn't stop. They wouldn't understand, how could they, I did something horrific that no mother should do, I don't know how I did it, I loved my boys more than anything, I didn't mean to, honestly, I didn't. But one day soon, I would be with them again. Oh my god, why? Why?

I had to set things right, so when Jack left the room, I called 911, and quietly whispered, "I need help," then, under my breath, I whispered, "I killed my kids."

Part Three

Chapter Thirteen

There was confusion and chaos and fear. I felt it all. I was aware of everything around me and that we had reached the hospital. However, the screaming wouldn't stop. When we arrived at the hospital, I threw those deadly pills that Jack had given me in the little bush. When they wheeled me down to get a CT scan, my ears were pierced by every sound in my surroundings. Once again, I heard my niece and Morgan screaming in the hospital waiting room. At first, I didn't understand what they were screaming about and then I realized it was about my brother.

"OH MY GOD, I killed my brother too!" I adored my brother and I would never hurt him. What have I done? My God...

It dawned on me then. The tension was made worse by the incessant screams coming from the waiting room, which simply would not stop!

"Please stop! I'm sorry, I'm so sorry, I didn't mean to do it," I kept saying, vaguely aware that I was holding my hands over my ears and trying my best to cover it up. I was wondering how I would die in the hospital. I saw people pointing and staring at me, people whom I recognized from when we went to visit my brother Jeff in the hospital. I was hoping I would die soon, as the pain of what I had done was unbearable. I just stared straight ahead, like a zombie, just praying over and over to die, while tears continuously streamed down my face.

Every minute of it was agony. I needed them to end my life—not only did I deserve to die, but I also wanted to die so badly. I wanted so desperately to get the images of what I had done out of my head, but that wasn't something that could happen so easily. Things were happening in my head that I still couldn't explain. I would see and hear things all around me. I wanted to scream for them to stop, for the screams and the noises to stop.

I wanted so badly to see my boys, and I was sobbing and couldn't get my emotions under control, I was shaking, and I was so scared. Not only was everything so dark and gloomy, but nothing made sense. All I could do was try to be as still as I could and close my eyes to the horrors my mind was screaming.

When I opened my eyes again, I was in a cold room with just a bed. I could smell the horrid smell of antiseptic that I hated so much, and there was white all around me. I looked around in confusion, not knowing what was real and what was not.

There were four of those rooms and one washroom where the floor was covered in pee and the toilet seat was gross. For some reason, when I went to use it, it didn't bother me, I never even thought of it. My eyes then wandered to the security guard standing there the entire time. He was still as he looked outside; it was just like prison, and for a moment, that's where I thought I was.

Regardless of my state of mind, the events of that night are engraved in my mind, clear as day. I still remember every detail. And then, all of a sudden, the memories stopped, I have no recollection of anything past that night for the next two and a half weeks. All I remember was darkness, as if somebody had taken away that piece of my memory.

My Psychiatrist explained my situation in these words: "The

mind is so powerful and you had so much stress in your life that it just wanted to shut down. It needed time to heal and time for you to forget the pain."

After two and a half weeks, I was able to take in the details of what the psych unit was like. The unit itself had a lot of beds in it. In each room were two or three patients, and each patient had a small night table and a bed. It was pretty sparse. If a patient got flowers, the flowers had to be put in a plastic container. There were no glass containers, no razors, no dental floss as one could use it to hang themselves, and absolutely nothing sharp.

I missed my home, and I missed the comforts of it, but I had to manage my life here now. It was even more difficult because I had nothing that I could call my own. Every patient's belongings were taken when they arrived at the hospital, and so were mine. The doors to the unit were locked, and if you were allowed access, you had to be buzzed out. Visitors were permitted from 5 p.m. to 9 p.m., and they had to be screened and buzzed in through the locked doors.

There were four rooms right in front of the nursing station, which were all glass, and behind that glass, I could see that the beds were on the floor. These were the rooms dedicated to really sick patients, and they were known as the "high observations" rooms. They had put blinds on the outside of the glass so that the nurses could control what the patient saw outside. Often, you would hear the patients inside those rooms screaming or banging on the windows to get out.

During the two and a half weeks that I was there, when I can recall nothing, I asked my children what they remembered about that time when coming to visit me. None of them would talk about it and all they would tell me was that every time I saw them, I would scream as if I had seen a ghost. They said that the memories of that time for them were too painful and they didn't want to relive them.

On the other hand, I don't remember any of that, and I can't imagine how they must have felt. I would give anything to feel the relief of knowing that the murders my mind told me I committed hadn't happened, to take back all the things my children faced because of my condition.

My time in the hospital was a blank, but there was one thing I had in there—my journal. I wrote in a journal while I was there, and I wrote a lot. While writing this book, I found journals in my closet for all the times I was admitted to the hospital and I remember the first one was a red journal. I don't have it anymore. I think I didn't want to revisit that time, and at one point, I must have destroyed it.

Going through those journals, I truly understood just how powerful and unexplained mental illness really is. There are so many spectrums of it, yet they all fall under the same umbrella. It's scary because the illness itself is so debilitating and sometimes even deadly—it changes people. In my case, my Doctor told me that I was neither homicidal nor suicidal, even though I had spent the previous weeks thinking that I had killed my kids.

The mere thought of it would send me reeling into another fit of sickness and insomnia. It tortured my very existence until the moment I realized that it was all in my head. Yet, even that understanding didn't stop me from feeling as terrible as I did. How was I going to live with that for the rest of my life? How would I ever forgive myself? How would I ever live with myself for having such thoughts?

My biggest worry in the hospital was my mind and the lasting effects of my condition—that fear inhabited the loneliness surrounding me in the room. I honestly didn't know how psychosis was going to affect me or my future, but I did know that it was not just going to go away.

Is it permanent? Would I ever be able to have a normal life? The questions kept circling my mind, driving me even more over the edge. No one could explain my condition like my doctor. It was he who said that what I experienced was like having numerous severe concussions to my brain. There were physiological reasons that I shut down and lost my mind that I failed to remember.

Even though I didn't want to, I still had to learn how to accept that. I had to recover from this and countless medications. Moving on from something so major didn't just happen overnight; that was the worst thing. The mind holds power over you that even you don't know and realize. That was what had happened to me when I thought I was a murderer. I was living with the memories of something that wasn't even true.

The scene in my mind was just so very real, though, etched like a vivid painting. It haunted me repeatedly, and I wondered to myself, *What makes me different from the man who killed all those people, from the man who decapitated an innocent victim on the bus, from the young girl who killed her family?* I began to question myself over and over and no one else.

I would keep these thoughts to myself because I was too ashamed to talk about them. I would cry a lot in silence, and it was hard, so hard to hold my head up. I didn't know why, I couldn't understand it; I didn't know why I couldn't accept it and move on. It was like I was stuck in quicksand and trying to get out. My head had never felt so full, but at that time, it was so full it hurt. It hurt really bad and I begged God to help me forgive myself. But sadly, forgiveness never came.

The hospital was a safe place to be. Things became routine. Very slowly, I started returning to my old self again. I got to know some of the patients and even befriended them. I still felt like I was in prison because everything was so calculated and strict. You weren't allowed any kind of electronics—your phone was locked away, there was only one television for the entire ward of thirty-two patients, it didn't turn on until 3 p.m., and then it was too hard to focus. My mind was constantly running.

One Saturday afternoon, a lot of the patients went home for the weekend. Since I was still recovering, I was not allowed to take a step outside of the ward. Much to my luck, the nurse decided that I could pick a movie to watch. I chose the MASH movie since I thought it would be funny, but oh my! What a mistake that was!

I started watching the movie, and soon there was blood, death and gore everywhere. It triggered so many of my senses, tapping into each one that I was trying to recover from. I kept closing my eyes because to top everything off, there were snakes all over the movie—they were wrapped around people, crawling through the tents and, oh, it gave me chills as I was terrified of snakes, I had a phobia ever since I was a little girl. I couldn't stand to look at the movie, it scared me so badly. I was shaking, and I started to cry. I didn't want to open my eyes, I couldn't get to the TV to turn it off. A gentle nudge on my shoulder forced me to open my eyes to the nurse's kind face looking at me with concern.

I took the courage to glimpse over at the TV and noticed that somebody had changed the tape.

"I can't watch it," I managed to get the words out, and she nodded in understanding. She was so sweet; I think we talked for a while, and then I just went back to my room and lay on my bed. I did that a lot; I wasn't very social, and only saw people at meal-time. Some of the people in there were scary, and I sometimes struggled to figure out if a person was a staff member or a patient. Everybody dressed the same. Some of the patients were kind of funny. One in particular, Annabelle, was always so proud of the way she looked and strutted around with her head held high. Nobody ever had the guts to tell her that she was wearing her bra on the outside of her shirt!

I wasn't a fan of the food either. The loss of appetite made me lose a lot of weight, and that was something that didn't go unde-tected by my friend, Tammy, whenever she came to visit. I had tried every other trick in the book to lose weight—who would've thought that going crazy was the way to do it? Maybe I should market that idea?

* * *

As far as I know, I had a lot of visitors. My Aunt Dereka came often, and she kept updating me on how my Mom was doing; it was never good news. It was devastating to hear, but I knew it would drive me even more insane if I didn't know. Mom had shut down at that point. It was a battle to try and even get her to eat a yogurt or drink a small protein drink.

Tammy and her daughter came to visit, Morgan was there as often as she could come, and Zach came but only when I could visit outside. Jack Michael didn't like to visit because it was uncomfortable for him and I think he was scared of some of the patients. I understood, of course. As for Jack, he was my constant. He visited every night. He was such a rock, and it was so comforting to know that he was there for me. I could tell this latest turn of events really shook him up, but he was a quiet man and didn't talk about it. Then there was my cousin Shirl; she came at least twice a week, and when she did, it was comforting. We would go to the chapel and pray together.

Whenever I think about it, I find it rather funny how I've always had a relationship with God. However, I find I only pray when I need Him to come through for me. It's not like I don't thank Him. When I pray, I always thank Him for my blessings, of which I have an abundance and I also ask Him to show me the way.

I was different than a lot of the patients because I had a family that was there for me, a family that really cared about what happened to me and I had some wonderful friends. I also knew that God had a plan for me; I wasn't sure what it was, but I knew I was going to get well. I felt so lucky.

I find that I'm never really calm. There is a kind of desperation in my requests to God, yet I have such high hopes that He will come through for me. When I was in the hospital, I knew I needed all the help that I could get. That's why I was always looking forward to Shirl's visits.

The hospital routine eventually became comfortable. Then my doctor told me I could go home. It was just for the weekend to see how I would make out, but I was over the moon with excitement. Oddly enough, the one thing I was most excited about was sleeping in my own bed, and that excitement actually kept me up at night.

I was also very nervous about walking into the house again

and seeing everything. It had been a while since the incident, but I was afraid that it would trigger another episode. I didn't want to remember any of it, so I focused on sleeping in my bed and braced myself to see the house again.

When the weekend finally came, Jack picked me up. He really was my soul mate, and I was very impressed with how he held it all together. It felt so good to be out of the hospital and to smell the fresh air. I felt like I had earned my freedom, and in this short time span, I wanted to do everything.

I looked out of the window at the trees and the people and the buildings as though it was my first time. I smiled at the feel of the sun against my skin and the AC blasting on my face. I loved the feel of everything around me.

Finally, I saw the familiar house come into view, giving me a tinge of bittersweet emotions. I didn't know if I was ready, but I had to be. When we got home, I stepped inside. The first thing I noticed was how nice and clean it was. As I walked through, I tried hard not to think about that night. I forced my mind to think about the good times, and there were many good times in that house.

I smiled at the thought of how many parties I used to throw, at the fun and laughter that had echoed in these walls. We played a lot of games, and, on special occasions, I even hired impersonators to come and entertain our guests. There was one time I had a fabulous quartet perform and another time when 140 choir members came for dinner and we all ended up singing in the back-yard. Back then, I would always pull out my collection of various hats, and everyone was happy to participate and wear one, which was always good for a laugh.

As I looked at the hallways, I realized how much I loved hosting parties. However, right now, all of that love was gone. I felt numb, and even the memory of the fun I used to have, didn't make me feel light. My spirit was broken, my sense of joy was gone, and I didn't know how to get that back. It wasn't that I was terribly sad or depressed, it's just that I felt . . . numb, like a different person. I was a different person.

The moment I stepped into my house, I realized how much I didn't want to be there, and the thought was terribly sad. I didn't even enjoy sleeping in my bed, the thing I was looking forward to the most.

The weekend came and went, and I realized that I was actually looking forward to going back to the hospital. I wanted to be home with my family, and they needed me home. I knew that the boys and Morgan needed me; they needed to know that I was going to recover. I wanted to make Morgan feel alright. I hated how worried she was.

Tammy had told me that when Morgan told her what had occurred the night I was hospitalized, she burst into tears and sobbed. It hurt me how broken Morgan was to see me this way. Mental illness is hard on the individual it affects, but it is extra hard on the family. It can destroy people, relationships, and families. It's something that changes people, sometimes forever.

I returned to the hospital sooner than I was supposed to. I couldn't stay home anymore. I had another week to spend in the hospital before being released to go home with a mitt full of meds, a date to visit my psychiatrist every week, and a promise to take care of myself.

Much like my mother, I noticed that the pain in my hip and knees from arthritis worsened. My hip was especially bad, and I had the feeling that I was the next one to need a hip replacement. After the week was up, I felt relatively better about going home and was psyching myself up for the transition.

I was more open to it and excited that I would finally be able to hug my kids and tell them that I love them. I know they were happy that I was home; they wouldn't stop talking about it. The boys hated the psych unit and they were very uneasy about visiting. It was quite a shame because I wanted to show them off to my new friends, but that was the last thing they wanted.

I needed my life to be as normal as possible again. I still had my job that had to be done, I still had my house to maintain, and my mom was still very ill in the hospital. I wasn't able to go back to work just yet, the doctor said I should ease into it, and to take a few months to recover. I hadn't seen my mom in the hospital for a long while, so I decided that I would visit the next very day. It was just under two hours, door to door, so it was a bit of a time crunch, but it was the last of the fall colors and a nice drive. I was told to take everything slowly and not jump back into stuff, but I desperately needed normality in my life.

I was heartbroken every time I thought about my mom or visited her. I knew that it wasn't her time yet, she was far too young. She had the hip replacement so that she could live again, not so that she would die. Watching her fade away ever so slowly was one of the most difficult things I had to do. I knew it wasn't good for my mental health, but there was nothing I could do about it. I had to visit her and spend time talking to her. When I walked in that day, her face lit up when she saw me. I was so excited to see her, but she looked so frail. We didn't talk about my breakdown because she wasn't very coherent, and I wanted to talk about happy things, not sad memories. I didn't even know if she knew about it or not, but it wasn't important. What was important was that we spent our time together talking about the good times. It was fun to remember with her as my mom still had a fabulous memory and could recall details.

To watch my mother die was horrible. I hope for a little glimmer of life from her and if I saw it, I would hang on to it. I sat with her, and begged her to take a bite of yogurt. I held the spoon for her, and eventually, she would give in, have a bite and then put her hand up. She couldn't have anymore; she was full. She used to be such a major spark in my life, and now she was the complete opposite. It was frustrating how she was wasting away. It was even more heartbreaking to watch my dad try so hard to help her.

My dad sat there from morning till night and watched her. My mother, the happy, strong, determined woman who let nothing stand in her way, became this frail, sad woman who was a shell of her former self. She was so wasted away that her false teeth no longer fit inside her mouth. My father, the thoughtful man that he is, got her new teeth even though she would never need them.

On the days that I couldn't drive up to see my mom, I always made sure I called my dad so that I could talk to her. Our conversations weren't very long, but I just wanted to tell her that I loved her. My mom was my best friend; she was my rock. I felt that I could take any problem to her, and she and I would figure it out. She knew how to comfort me more than anybody did. She was my support system from the start, and even though she was so frail now, she didn't ever stop.

I had been out of the hospital for a while now and things were getting back to normal for me. I tried so hard not to think much about it, but my mental illness affected me deeply. I couldn't let it bother me as I was too consumed with my mom and her situation rather than with my mental illness. Did it bother me? Yes, absolutely, it changed me as a person, I struggled with everything emotionally. Some days I felt robotic just going through the motions, and that's when it struck me that I might never be the same. That I had this dark cloud over me that was just stuck there. The joy was gone, the happiness was gone, and the stress was building.

When I saw my mom, there were so many times that I wanted to talk about my mental illness. I wanted her to reassure me that it would be okay, that I would eventually get back to my former self. But she wouldn't understand it, and even if she did, it would hurt her too much. So I kept silent with my pain. She smiled a lot, and her head drooped a lot; I felt that it was way too heavy for her to handle. I didn't even ask my dad if he told her, I just assumed that he didn't. It was evident that her time was too short, and we needed to talk about happy things.

I guess, in our own way, we were preparing for the worst to come. I tried my damndest to remember some of the great times that we had, but it was just so difficult to do. It hurt to think about my mom, healthier during the better times, but we had to do it for her sake.

It was getting close to Christmas, and my mom was not short of visitors, that was for sure. I didn't know what to do this Christmas. Usually, my parents joined us, and my brother Jeff and his family would come. However, his family was growing, and I didn't think they would be joining us this year. Mom was not going anywhere, and my dad just wanted to be with her.

I understood, of course. But this was the first Christmas without them all, and it just felt odd. Dad didn't want to celebrate Christmas, and I felt the same way. However, in my case, I still had kids. I know they would have understood if I wanted to cancel it altogether, but I couldn't do that to them.

Jack's brother and sister-in-law and his dad were coming for dinner. I told my dad that I would come on Christmas day and bring them dinner. The kids would understand my absence, and Morgan and Jack could entertain Jack's family. Everything was planned out, and everyone was cooperative and in agreement.

I went to see my mom on December 23rd and was able to have some alone time with her. I kept looking at the lines on my dad's face. He looked so tired, but he insisted on being with Mom as long as the hospital would allow it. We had a good visit, and I tried to keep it as normal as I could. We laughed, we talked about when I was little, we talked about Mom bringing her students home for the weekend, our family camping trips, picnics by the river, my mother often having forty people for Christmas dinner, our trip to Hawaii, the neighborhood kids constantly hanging out at our home, and lots of other stuff.

The rush of memories was a good kind of nostalgia to live through but a painful one as well. I told Mom I would be back later on Christmas Day with Christmas dinner for her, and I expected her to eat it. She smiled, not the bright smile she always had, but the small, faint smile she struggled to put on her face. It was enough to tell me she'd heard what I'd said. I kissed her goodbye and told her that I loved her. I also told her that I would be forever grateful to her and then I left.

The next day, Morgan and I finished some casseroles. I wrapped gifts and put them under the tree and got ready to go to church that night. I felt out of place; the year truly had done its part in breaking our spirits. We went to the 4:30 p.m. service and then it was a tradition in our family to go out for Chinese dinner every Christmas Eve. Morgan had made reservations, and we were to meet her and Bryan there. I liked how there was still a little bit of normality left in the tradition. It was a beautiful church service, and I made sure that I said a special prayer for my mom. Little did I know, the year had one last heartbreak in store for us. Just as we were walking to our car, my phone rang, and when I picked it up, it was my aunt.

I could tell by her voice that something was wrong, and I sensed all the eyes on me. My aunt said that my mom's time had come and we needed to get to the hospital right away to say our goodbyes. The worst had come, and one look told Jack and the kids just what they needed to know.

Even though it was an oddly bright day, I felt as though everything was getting dark. There was a light that was fading from the world around us. We rushed home, grabbed an overnight bag, and raced down the highway to the hospital, each lost in our memories of Mom.

When we arrived, there were a lot of people there, mostly family. There was some family that I hadn't seen in years, and they had all come to say goodbye. I made my way past them, and they let us all through. I couldn't stop my tears the moment I saw her. There was a part of me that was ripping away.

I stood closest to my mom, with my dad by my side. My mom's eyes were already closed, and she was sitting upright in her bed. My dad had placed a little stuffed reindeer on her chest that moved up and down with every breath she took. He told me that when the reindeer stopped moving up and down, that would be how he could tell she was gone. I took his hand and tightened my lips shut as I heard the crack in his voice.

My aunt called my brothers Jeff and Tom so they could say goodbye, and then she called my mom's brothers, Barry and Brian and her sister Dereka.

It's rather odd to watch somebody die that has already closed their eyes. There is no place to look; you can't look in their eyes, so you study their nose and mouth. You watch the breathing go up and down. That's what I did before I felt a tug behind me.

My boys stepped up, and I made my way. I watched my boys say goodbye to their grandmother, whom they cherished. Then Jack said his goodbye. Then it was my turn. I had to ask my cousin to leave because I wanted to be alone with my mom.

Once they all filed out, I was alone. For the first time, I didn't know what to say to her. I didn't know if she could hear me. What should your last words to your mom be? I never thought about that, I never practiced it. I felt awkward all of a sudden. I felt like there was a certain way I was supposed to be, but also that there were no expectations of me.

Mom was lying there, and my heart grew heavy to the point that I could feel it exploding with emotions. In the end, I told her she was an amazing mother and that I would be strong for her. I told her that I would keep our family together since she was worried it would fall apart when she died. There was ease I felt when I said it, and the tears that escaped my eyes as I thought of my life without her.

Slowly, I bent and kissed my mother on the cheek one last time and said goodbye. I said goodbye for all the happiness she gave me, for all the pointless fights we had, for all the laughter we shared, and for all the times she was there for me. I wished so hard that I could turn back time to when I was younger and be with her again. I didn't want to leave her. I just wanted to crawl into her arms and lay there. But I pulled myself away and watched her as I walked out of the room.

When I went into the waiting room where everyone else was, my husband said that he thought we should go. We were staying at the cabin that night, and he said he didn't think I should be there when she finally left. With everything that had happened recently, I knew he was right. It was still so tough. I thought about it and agreed that the boys needed to get some rest. Morgan and Bryan were going to stay with my dad.

Once I got into bed, I just lay there. It wasn't long before my phone rang. The tune had never before sounded so ominous. I was told the reindeer had stopped moving up and down, and it was then I realized that Heaven had received a new angel. My mother had passed away in the early morning of Christmas Day, her favorite day of the year, and now Christmas would never be the same.

Chapter Fourteen

After the depressing phone call, I quietly laid in bed. Memories of my mother were circling in my mind on repeat. Insomnia overcame me. As I kept reminiscing about all the times we had spent together, tears started to stream down my cheeks. She was my best friend, in a motherly figure. I could tell her anything, and she always knew how to make me feel better. When she was sick these past few months, I couldn't tell her that I had lost my mind. I didn't want her to remember me like someone who could lose her mind. I wanted her to remember me as her child that she nurtured. I tried to remember our conversations close to the end, and I remembered one in particular: She wanted me to try and keep her family together. She was scared that once she was gone, her family would fall apart. She was talking about both her immediate family and her extended family. I made a promise to her that I knew I probably couldn't keep.

There was so much animosity between the family that I didn't know if it could be salvaged. After suffering a mental breakdown, I didn't know if I could do it. If I had the strength to handle the rejection or the phoniness that sometimes carries delusive contentment to make amends, pretending that nothing happened when in fact, a lot happened. We used to be a very close family. We used to get together for family dinner every Sunday and go on picnics. Christmas always consisted of three dinners that were held for the family: Christmas Day, Boxing Day, and New Year's. It was always fun to get together. I have many happy memories of those times. I have some amazing aunts, uncles, and brothers whom I want my kids to get to know. It is a shame what happens to families. It's hurtful that the younger generation misses out on what could be great times together. I made a promise to my mother, but I have yet to fulfill it. I was just getting to the point mentally where I considered trying to bring this family back together, but it might be too late.

My workplace was understanding of my condition. Though I felt fortunate to be able to take what turned out to be almost a year off from work, I was deeply encumbered by guilt about it, even after my mother's passing. However, my psychiatrist explained to me that my brain needed rest. It needed time to recoup from the trauma that I underwent, and it would be a slow recovery. I was asked to take care of myself because my body needed rest. However, I was oblivious to the term "self-care." I always put myself last, and by the time I had to take care of myself, I was too exhausted, though it's probably just an excuse. That was how I became so overweight, which was humiliating and destroyed my self-esteem. When you are overweight, you feel like a loser. You feel inferior to others like you just don't have it going on. I needed to exercise, and I hated that idea because of the pain that roared in my joints because of arthritis. My psychiatrist suggested that I try aquacise, a way to exercise that is easy on your joints, so I decided to give it a try. I researched and found a class three times a week close to my home, so away I went. It turned out to be very fun and I enjoyed it immensely. I promised myself to commit to it.

So, here I am, overweight, have had some challenging times with my children, more so than most, have chronic pain, and now I am mentally ill. How do you continue to face people with that resume?

The recovery was tough. I felt all alone, and I desperately wished to talk to my mom. I didn't want to burden my kids by talking to them, and my friends didn't understand the hellfire that roared inside me. Thank God Tammy was always there for me, except for my therapist and my psychiatrist, whom I saw weekly; she was the only person I felt comfortable talking with. It was hard for me to describe what I went through that not-so-fateful night. What kind of mother has thoughts of killing her children that she brought into this cruel world? Every time I thought of it, I cringed and felt sick to my stomach. I remembered those days in the psych ward, and I didn't want to go back. I was ready to work damn hard to get better. I had to!

Mental illness is hard on the person that it happens to, but believe me, it is doubly hard on the family, especially the children. With time, I became familiar with the new person I had become. I struggled with laughter, feeling joy, being the parent that I always prided myself on being, and trying to get back to the old me. I needed to learn to forgive myself, to realize that what happened was not my fault, but it was hard. I struggled to understand how it could have happened to me—a person so sane and sorted? I wondered if I was capable of hurting my own children. I couldn't get past that. I was a strong woman, and I should have been able to handle everything that was handed to me. Why couldn't I do that? Why did I go crazy?

I had one of the greatest psychiatrists, whom I totally trusted and who tried to explain things to me many times, but I refused to accept his professional explanations. The brain is such a complicated organ, and there are so many whys attached to it. It is hard for even the professionals to come up with answers to the questions that I couldn't articulate. I hoped somebody could give me something that was tried and effective. That someone needed to assure me that this was not going to happen again. However, I got that from no one. I was kept under a spell of turmoil that made it almost infeasible for me to process as a normal human. I didn't want to see anyone and wished to be at home, but I knew I had responsibilities and commitments.

It was about the third week in May when I finally decided to go back to work. It wasn't full-time at the start, it was about three half days a week, and once I felt that I could conquer that, we would move closer to full-time. That was the agreement. It felt so good to be back at work and doing something productive. Our staff was amazing in welcoming me back, and for the first time in a long time, I was finally somewhat happy. Jack was happy and relieved that I was back. He was very worried about me, but he wasn't the type to show his concern. He always masked his emotions. I just felt lucky to have him, as he was keeping the kids in check and the business running. Jack and I had always conquered our problems and challenges together. We talked things out in detail and usually came up with a solution together. However, this time was different. There were no solutions! This wasn't going to be an easy fix, and it wasn't something that I wanted to talk to him about. I remember telling Tammy how lucky I felt to have him because he was so even-keeled that nothing fazed him. He definitely was my soul mate, and at times I didn't feel worthy of his love.

It didn't take me long to get back into a routine. I was happy to get up in the morning and get ready for work. I was thrilled to be back at work, putting together spreadsheets, running budgets, and solving problems. But the business was not going so well. Our partner, Kerry, was the sales manager and bloomed with pessimism. He paid me daily visits to my office to have a chat. He would always exclaim that it was tough out there. His perseverance kept us in business, but we had to be realistic and eventually let some of our staff go. We just didn't have enough work for them. It was always tough to let good employees go.

After being at the office for a few months, I could feel the stress of the business looming once again. One day, I was in my office and Jack took off early that morning to work in our northern office. I was doing payroll when one of our employees came in and requested that I do something unethical in regards to his paycheck. I immediately told him that I would do no such thing, that's not how I operated. He seemed rather disappointed and upset. I just continued on with what I was doing and watched him come and go during the course of the morning. This worried me and I could feel my anxiety creeping in.

This particular employee had been with us for over a year, and he was a good worker. There was absolutely no reason that I should have felt threatened by him, but I did. I was starting to get scared. I didn't know what to do, and then I started to wonder if he had a firearm in his car. Oh my god, you hear about that all the time. You hear about disgruntled employees who come in and kill their employers. I wished Jack was here, so I could talk to him about it. I was getting very nervous and edgy. I decided to go home and spend the rest of the day there. I had previously made arrangements for our accountant to meet me at the office to go over some documents. So, I decided to call him and tell him to meet me at home.

I told our secretary that I was sick and was leaving early today, assuring her she could call me if something urgent came up. As I was driving, I looked in the rear view mirror and realized I was being followed. I immediately concluded in my mind that it was our employee. I had to get somewhere safe, somewhere to get rid of him, so he could not kill me. First, I thought I could lose him and aspired to get to the yellow light as soon as possible. Boom, I did, the light turned red as I drove through it, and he was gone. He would never be able to find me because I went down some side roads. I thought I better visit some places where I felt safe, so I went to the police station parking lot and sat there for a while. I thought about going to my best friend, Tammy's, but then I didn't want to put her life in jeopardy, too.

After the police station, I went to Walmart and sat in that parking lot for a while until I regained the courage to go back home. Jack and I had never given out our address to any of our employees, so I knew the employee didn't have it. I knew I would be safe there. I pulled up to my driveway and saw our accountant standing there. He came up to the car, looked at me, and asked me if I was okay. He immediately knew that something was terribly wrong. He started asking questions, and I was totally honest with him. I told him that someone was trying to kill me, that I was in danger. After a few more questions, he asked me if I thought I should go to the hospital. I didn't even need to think about it. I couldn't believe it was happening to me once again. I replied with tearful eyes, "Yes, I think I should go."

The accountant took me to the hospital. He waited and calmed me down until I was called in. He said he would contact Jack and let him know where I was as they escorted me back to that horrific place—the emergency psych ward. There were four separate cells (is what I call them), and each cell had a plastic bed with a one-inch mattress and a small plastic table.

Usually, you are there with homeless people. There is one bathroom, and everyone pees all over the floor and toilet. When you have to go, you are required to ask the security guard outside your door. It is probably the coldest place that I have been, and all I wished was to get out of there as soon as possible. This time, I wasn't as sick as I was before. One of my employees was trying to kill me, simple as that. It wasn't me who had killed someone (in my head). At least I was in a safe place right now. When Jack came home, he could get to the bottom of it and have the employee arrested. It would all be okay, and I would be fine. I'm not really crazy right now. I just needed a safe space to be in for the next little while until they decided what they were going to do with that employee.

Soon enough, I was put in a room in Unit 49. It felt very familiar, and I was embarrassed to see my old nurses again, some of which remembered me and said, "Hi."

In the next few days, word had gotten out, and a few of my friends stopped by to check up on me. I always felt special when that happened as there were so many patients who never got any visitors. I thanked God for blessing me with friends who cared for me. I was once again put on another anti psychotic medication and started to realize that I was wrong. Stress caused me to have these delusional thoughts. Once again, it was embarrassing when people asked me what had happened.

My daughter, Morgan, came to visit every second day. Even

though she now lived and worked in the mountains, and it was quite a drive for her, she made an effort. I was grateful she came. I could see how hard it was for her and her brother to see their mother like this. It was really taking its toll on them. Morgan shared what she had overheard from Jack Michael, who was about ten at the time. His best bud, Bodie, asked him, "So, what's wrong with your mother?"

Jack Michael replied, "It is like a camera, you know when the memory stick gets full?"

Bodie replied, "Yeah?"

"My mom's brain is like that. Her memory stick in her brain is full."

Bodie asked, "Oh, so they just gotta wipe her memory?"

"Yeah, that sounds right."

"Oh, that's simple."

If only that was the case. I appreciated their candor and innocence, though. Jack Michael was only ten years old and still very much a little boy who needed his mom.

If only my mental illness was that unambiguous, we would all live in a much better world. But it was way more complicated than that. I have no recollection of my time in the psych ward, except for when I was watching that MASH movie. Other than that, the first two and a half weeks of being in there have been entirely wiped out from my memory. I remember nothing. I asked my daughter and son if they would share with me how I was behaving, what did I say, what I did do, but they both refused, "No, it's too painful. This is our story, too, Mom, not just yours. And what we went through was hell, and we don't want to remember it. Please don't ask us to." I had to respect their decision. They had been through enough. It wasn't fair for me to ask them to remember those traumatic events.

The psych ward was very different this time because I didn't want to be there. I wanted to go home. However, I knew the drill. You had to stay quarantined for a few days. If you behaved yourself, you were allowed to go out of the locked doors, whether it was outside or to the chapel, or just to get a coffee in the hospital, but only for fifteen minutes. After you proved that you could be trusted, you were allowed thirty minutes, then you climbed all the way up to one hour. The psych ward overlooked the reservoir and had one of the most beautiful views in Calgary. It was peaceful to sit there and enjoy the view. The first time I was admitted, I took up smoking and once again, I found myself smoking again. It helped me relieve the stress and permitted me to breathe freely.

I made friends in the unit, and it was the one thing I could look forward to while I was there. Once you returned to the unit, you had to give your cigarettes back to the nurses, and they locked them up. There were so many patients there who smoked but couldn't afford them, so I asked the nurses to give them some of mine. I was happy to share.

I was very confused when I first arrived. I kept thinking to myself, why do they keep paging Morgan and Tammy as they must be in there, and why haven't they come to see me? I heard the page a few times before I spoke with Morgan about it. She put me straight and told me that it was not for them but for somebody else. We had a little laugh about it.

My dad paid me a visit once on a beautiful day during those trying times. We sat on the benches in front of the reservoir and had a little chat. We talked about many things, specifically my mom. We teared up a few times, but we held each other's hands and sat there in silence. Still, for the most part, we just enjoyed each other's company.

The very same night, Jack came and paid me a visit. Normally, we just sat and stared at the walls and didn't talk much, but tonight, I thought our visit was unusual. Jack probably would disagree, but he kept teasing me that he was going to spring me. It was good to laugh with him because I knew that he hated that place more than I did. I would love it if he kidnapped me, but they had security guards, and they did a patient check every 15 minutes to ensure that all patients were accounted for. I shared with Jack that, for a fleeting moment, I thought about ending my life, but I knew it was a cowardly move.

We talked about a family we knew where the mother

committed suicide and its consequences, especially on the children. He shared with me that he too had thought about it and realized that if he did die that I would be three million dollars richer. At that moment, when I kept looking him in the eye, I didn't struggle to articulate any words in my mouth. Instantly, I replied, "No amount of money in this world can replace you, and I cannot bear to lose you." He hugged me and told me the same thing. If everyone could be as lucky as we are, life would be so much better. Jack is an amazing man, and we have amazing chemistry. I knew that we would get through this one way or another. I took this intimate moment as an opportunity to talk about our business. We were in rough shape, we were flogging a dead horse, and it was time to look at an exit strategy. Jack continued to be optimistic, and I was hoping that he would finally realize that it was time to let go. I felt sorry for him as we had worked really hard at making the company a success and, at one time, we were very successful. But the recession this time was bad. We also talked about selling our house and the cabin. The cabin was getting hard to maintain. There was so much work that my dad used to do out there, but he was getting older and couldn't do it anymore. And Jack didn't want to do it. The house was way too big, but he was scared to have our son move schools, and I understood that.

While I was in the hospital, I got a very nice letter from one of my girlfriends, who talked about birds that she saw out her window while working. It was odd! She talked about someone named Terry, and I had no idea who that was. I asked Morgan about it when she came to visit that night, and she said that Terry was her son, whom I had met numerous times and even gone on vacation with. Apparently, I was sicker than I thought I was.

Tammy came quite often, and I really enjoyed her visits. She is certainly my best friend, and I do love her as a friend, even like a sister. Once when she was visiting, I gave her a big goodbye hug and told her I loved her. Jack was there at the time. When she left, he shook his head and said, "That's weird." I realized what he was thinking and had to set him straight that Tammy and I were only good friends; we were not gay! Sometimes, that man just doesn't friggin' get it.

At some point, and I don't know why my privileges were taken away from me. I was not allowed to leave the unit, no phone calls, and only family was allowed to visit. However, I was happy because they didn't take my clothes away. My nurses encouraged me not to worry about our business and encouraged me to utilize this time and get well. I had a very wise nurse who told me, "Come from the heart, not the ego. Ego can get in the way of your recovery. You have to be your own best friend, become your own best friend." So, if I lead with my heart, it would get me through the storm raging toward me, and this was one helluva storm. If I go with my ego, its job is to protect me and look at the worst-case scenario. It really resonated with me because I didn't like myself. I wasn't comfortable in my own skin. I thought it was a good idea, however, I knew that it was going to take a lot of work. They said a good exercise to practice was to ask yourself what you know for sure. So, every day, when I felt like challenging my mental ability, I would ask myself this question.

I got moved to a room with two other people. One was a young girl who stole my sunglasses, but I figured she needed them more than I did, so I didn't say anything. She just sat on her bed all day and moaned, and finally, I asked her if I could read her a story. She just nodded in agreement. I read her a Stuart McLean story, and she enjoyed it. It felt good to be kind to others. The other woman in the room was Indian. She dressed beautifully, however, she slept on the floor. It broke my heart to see her like that. Even though I asked her many times to try the bed, she always shook her head in silent disagreement.

Over time, I started to become friends with a lot of other patients. At that time, I didn't realize the consequences of being too nice and kind, and I made a mistake by making their problems my problems. I was warned about this and so had to tread lightly. They always tell you in the psych ward not to become friends with other patients, and they are quite strict about it. Even my husband warned me to stay away from other people. I disdained this rule. There were so many amazing people in the unit, and it was very hard not to make friends with them. But it's also challenging not to get sucked into their problems.

My psychiatrist told me that everyone was there for a reason, and so you need to maintain boundaries. I constantly told myself that, but if you don't socialize with people there, it is totally boring unless you enjoy doing puzzles. There was nothing else to do except write in your journal. I really needed to get my privileges back, so I could go outside and enjoy the beautiful view of the reservoir.

I had a revelation one day that I caused a recent flood in our home that caused a lot of damage. I apologized to Jack for causing the flood, and he told me that it wasn't me that caused it. It was our cleaning lady. I really had a hard time believing that because I was sure that I had caused the flood.

I finally got my privileges back. Once again, I was allowed to go outside and grab a good cup of coffee. I don't think I ever enjoyed a cup of coffee with a cigarette that much before. I liked going out in the sunshine, sitting on the bench that overlooked the reservoir, to just think about stuff. It was so nice to see families and people ride their bikes past. It was funny, some people would make eye contact and say a polite hello, and others just looked away because they were too uncomfortable. People are afraid of mentally challenged individuals; it is just that simple. But I think we are all the same, just going through some issues.

One bright sunny day, I was walking past the nurse's station, and I stopped to talk to one of my favorites, Kevin. Suddenly, I couldn't speak, and when I did speak, I stuttered very badly. I tried my damndest to talk normally, but I just couldn't. Kevin told my psychiatrist about my condition, and the next thing you know, a neurologist was examining me. It was somewhat embarrassing because he was a neighbor and we had many mutual friends. Nobody could figure out what was wrong, and it was months before it went away.

At one point during my stay in the hospital, there was a discussion between my family and doctors about going into long-term care in a mental health institution. There were only three in Alberta, and they were all far from Calgary. When I heard that, I was devastated and knew that I just wanted to go home. Right now, home for me was Unit 49, and to my surprise, I was comfortable there. When I was granted a pass to go home on the weekend, it was uncomfortable, and all I wanted was to go back to the hospital. When that was my wish, I knew that I was still unwell. I still needed treatment.

Until one Monday, when I was on my way back to the hospital, I started crying. I didn't want to go back there again. I wanted to be at home. To me, that was a sign that I was getting well, and it was not much longer before I got discharged. What a glorious day! I felt strong, and I felt happy. I was looking forward to being a mom again, to being with my kids and my husband. They had been through a lot, and they just needed to be themselves and not worry about me. I was going to be fine because I was going to put this illness behind me. I was on some strong drugs, and I was confident I would have no more psychotic moments.

However, being at home was an adjustment. Again, I struggled with acceptance of myself, but I tried hard not to be transparent about it. I just wanted to be there for my kids and my husband. I wanted so bad for the old me to be there for them. Still, I didn't know how to make that happen. I had been through a life-changing event and not for good. Even though I had masked my suffering and started to pretend that I was okay, deep down, I was still screaming, "Let me out of this hell." Tears brimmed in my eyes whenever I was alone. Nevertheless, I put on my brave mask whenever my husband and kids were around because that is what and who they needed.

I read a quote in the journal that I was writing in at the time: "Isn't it nice to know that today is a new day with no mistakes in it yet?" I thought if you got up every morning with that thought, wouldn't the world be a better place for you? It was funny, when I was sick, I felt no pain, yet I had severe arthritis in my hips and my knees. When I wasn't ill, it was very painful. I wondered why that was. Maybe, God figured, when you lose your mind, you suffer enough pain.

I was lucky to get a few months off work again. I still stuttered, and it was very annoying. It went on for about six months after I got out of the hospital. Occasionally, I suffered panic attacks when I struggled with breathing. In fact, I had a couple of them in my therapist's office.

Zach's high school graduation came and went. He had his heart set on traveling to Asia with his best friend, Bella. He was going to work for a few months, and then the plan was to leave in November for three months. I was worried about Zach. He was so terribly shy and introverted, but an amazing person. He is kind, thoughtful, and wouldn't hurt a flea. I hoped and prayed that this trip would let him spread his wings and help him realize what he wanted in life.

The day came for Zach and Bella to begin their adventure. I was very excited. Zach was a little hesitant about the 14-hour flight because he is 6'5", and those seats are really compact. I gave him a final hug and started to cry when I had to let him go. He looked at me and said, "I'll be back, Mom, before you know it. I'll be with you in spirit." That made me cry even harder. I was going to miss him so much. It was just like when Brooklyn left; I felt so hollow.

The months rolled on, and I was missing Zach terribly. I was hoping he was doing well and having a good time. I knew Zach wasn't a partier and didn't care to drink, so I wasn't sure how it was going.

One evening, I was going through his iPad, which I did quite often, when my own iPad ran out of battery. I clicked on Twitter, even though I didn't know how it worked, but I aspired to learn. I saw a message there, and being that I was very snoopy, I decided to check it out. It was from a male to Zach. They were talking to each other about how hot they were. I realized at that moment that my son was gay. It took a while to process it, but I can't say that I was surprised.

Zach had a few girlfriends when he was younger, but not

recently. I was a bit worried because life is hard for everybody. If you're gay, it can be a lot more challenging, and it can be a cruel world out there. I wondered how he was going to meet someone to love; what about having a child? I knew he always wanted children. My husband was also homophobic—how was he going to react? He would be devastated. I had so many questions, but I knew in my heart that I had to wait until Zach came to me when he was comfortable enough to tell me. I would support him to the ends of the earth and make sure he knew how much he was loved, and nothing could change that. Actually, when I really thought about it, I was quite excited. I would get to go to a gay wedding, and I wouldn't have a bitchy daughter-in-law!

Chapter Fifteen

Although it came as a surprise, I was getting used to the idea of Zach being gay. Often at night, my eyes and mind were pensively burdened by inevitable insomnia that could be comprehended in my worrisome eyes. During these times, I kept wondering how I was going to tell his father. Jack was very close to Zach and this was going to kill him. I thought I needed to tell him before Zach came home to manage his emotions beforehand. In my heart, I knew he was going to struggle with it. Zach wasn't flamboyant, so nobody could tell that he was gay. However, I prayed about it. I prayed that God would change Jack's mentality about homosexuality and for him to accept Zach for who he was, as he was an amazing young man.

I thought it would be a blessing if Zach became true to himself as that was more crucial than those around him judging him for the person he was. I knew Jack would eventually come around. He would not love Zach any less by no means, it would just take him longer to process it than usual. Jack used to get very uncomfortable when male gay couples were intimate on television, and I knew that he would be devastated once he found out.

One day, Jack and I were having a conversation about our

kids, reflecting on what we had been through, and he remarked, "We went through some tough stuff with both girls. What do you think Zach has in store for us?" I took that as my cue to share what I had found out and said, "Funny you should ask as Zach is gay. I didn't hear it from him, though. I saw some comments on his iPad, and I hope that when he comes home, he will feel comfortable enough to tell us himself. I would also hope that you would be supportive and loving, just as a father should. I know you are probably quite upset, but he will need our support and acceptance more than anything now. You and I both know how introverted and shy he is, and what he needs to know is that you —out of all the people who love him unconditionally—would accept him. In fact, he probably won't tell you at first. You will probably be the last person he tells, but I want you to promise me that you will support him."

Jack was stunned, and his response to this was, "I don't believe you." So, I got the iPad out and showed him the comments I had seen. However, he still refused to believe me.

"You can keep your head in the sand for a long time. However, it is the truth, and you better get used to it and change the way you think about gay men. Your son is keeping a huge secret from us, and I can only imagine how challenging it is to live with us while he has a whole other life out there. It's not fair to him, and it's not fair to us. As parents, we need to be there for him. These are tough times for him, and I don't want him to have to go on like this," I told Jack.

Jack went once again, "Until I hear it from him, I am not going to believe what my ears have just heard."

At this point, I started to get mad. I reminded Jack that Zach has always been a little different. "Zach, as a child, loved Youth Singers and would have given his left foot to be part of that group growing up, yet because he was your first son, you wanted him to play hockey. Yes, he liked hockey, but imagine how he could have shone while singing and dancing in that choir? You saw what it did for our girls. It gave them an opportunity. Zach probably wouldn't have been as introverted and extremely shy as he is today if you had just let him join the choir. He is an incredible young man, Jack, and you should be proud of how you raised him. However, it's not your fault that Zach is gay. It's not something that he chooses. He was born that way, and you must embrace it because it's not going to change."

Zach finally came home a month and a half later. I got very emotional at the busy airport. My spirits soared high when my eyes that longed to see his shadow finally detected him in the crowd. I gave him the biggest hug ever. I didn't want to let him go. And, the hug that I got in return seemed to be as equally demanding as mine was. For the next little while, I made use of every chance I got to talk to him, hoping that he would open up to me, but he never did. Deep down in my heart, I knew he would tell me when he was ready and felt comfortable in his skin.

At that time, many thoughts were saturating my mind. I imagined Zach being very anxious about his dad's reaction toward his sexuality. Jack often asked me, "So, did Zach tell you he is gay yet?" I always shook my head in dissent. Jack's attitude hadn't seemed to improve. It was frustrating, and I continued to pray that he would become accepting.

Then one day, when Zach and I were talking, we got onto the subject of gay people. The next thing you know, he finally came out of the closet. "Mom, I am gay," he told me. I could tell it was tough for him to tell me that. However, he got emotional after he told me, as did I. When the truth was finally articulated from his lips, I didn't know what to do or what to say. I just sat there and held him as tears streamed down my cheeks. We talked about how difficult life is for straight people, and it's just that much more difficult for a gay person. I consoled him and told him that he was a good individual, and that is what mattered the most.

We talked about how it's vital to be true to yourself and the considerable weight that he was bearing on his shoulders all this time had been lifted. We talked about how I loved him more than ever, now that he told me. We also talked about his siblings' and father's reactions. We both knew that his brother and sisters would have no problem with it, as most of the younger generation does not. Still, we also knew it was going to be challenging for his dad.

Nevertheless, I suggested we talk to him together whenever Zach was ready. For some reason, my instincts were convinced that Zach would never be ready, and he never was. Zach never actually came out and told his dad that he was gay. I explained to Jack that he told me, and eventually, we started talking about it openly in front of his father. And it was just assumed from then on in. I don't believe they have ever talked about it. It was funny, whenever we were with friends, I would tell them that Zach was gay. You could see Jack cringe, but I was the opposite. I couldn't wait to share with the world that my son was gay, as I was one very proud mother.

* * *

Our work continued to be a challenge. The onset of another recession was happening, and it looked to be a terrible one. Kerry came to my office daily, and he talked about how bad it was out there. Oil prices were dropping drastically, and the pipelines were not getting approved. The oil companies were reducing their capital spending, and the oil industry overall was in rough shape.

It was not good news for us. We needed new wells drilled, and the drilling forecast was not very positive. It was scary and depressing, and I just kept revising budgets and trying to figure out cost measures. Jack was trying to sell another rig down south as he hoped to get an influx of cash to continue running our business. On the other hand, Kerry agreed with me and aspired to shut things down before getting really bad.

Jack and I finally decided to sell the cabin at the end of the summer season. It would be a tough one for Jack to let go because he loved that place and everything it stood for. However, it was not going to be as hard for me as I loved it, too. We had so many good memories that we cherished out there, but it was also a lot of work—constant cooking, grocery shopping, changing sheets, and cleaning. Jack loved to have company, and I did, too. Still, I was the one who had to do all the cooking, prepping, and cleaning. It was exhausting. Jack handled boating and water sports, and I was grateful to him for that, but he did little else. The cabin also didn't have the same vibe after my mom died. I missed her presence out there so much. When we were there, I always felt it. And it didn't matter where I looked; I could always picture her there.

I had been spending some time with my Aunt Dereka. She was my mom's youngest sister, and we went swimming every Wednesday night. We really enjoyed each other's company and caught up on the latest gossip. We were close to Dereka and her family and often went on vacations with them. When I was in the hospital, Dereka often came to visit. It meant a lot to me, and I appreciated that gesture. Dereka had three great kids. They were all about the same age as Brooklyn and Morgan. They were all incredibly bright. Erin had a psych degree, John was doing his Ph.D. in virology, and Ben had a law degree from Harvard.

It was getting close to Mother's Day, and Dereka invited us for dinner on a Saturday night, which I happily accepted. We agreed that I would bring dessert. On Saturday morning, I was busily preparing the cheesecake I would take when the phone rang. It was Dereka's husband. As soon as I heard his voice, I understood something was terribly wrong. Their 33-year-old son John had collapsed and died that morning. John had been through a lot in his lifetime. He was diagnosed with cyclical neutropenia when he was only fifteen and came very close to death at that time. His one leg stopped growing when he was young. However, the rest of his body developed well. He was a pretty tall guy for someone who faced so many health issues. He walked with a limp, requiring him to have a hip replacement at a very young age. At one point, they also took out his spleen. He was hospitalized many times for numerous problems. Yet John was a trooper. Zach once wrote a tribute to him, hailing him as Zach's hero. In his twenties, John was diagnosed with leukemia and lived with that until his death. The university where he studied named a lab after John and presented his family with a posthumous Ph.D. John was one of the good guys whose values and integrity were often noticed and stood out.

The same afternoon, I got a call from Dereka, who was sobbing hysterically and had a hard time getting words out. At first, all she could blurt out was, "Leianne, he's gone!" My heart broke for her and for everyone whose lives were touched by John's passing. She asked me if I would inform the rest of the family. "Yes, definitely! Take care of yourself now and know that I will always love you," I told her and hung up the phone.

At first, I went and laid down to try and make sense of what had happened. I couldn't cope with this devastating news. John was a stellar young man with an incredibly bright future; life was so unfair. I thought of John's beautiful wife, who he had only married two years prior. I thought of his dad, his siblings, and then I thought of his mother. I couldn't get John out of my head. With every thought I had of him, a tear rolled down my cheek. "How would Dereka ever get through this?" I wondered. I did not know how I was going to support her. I was well cognizant that my mental health was not stable and I didn't know if I was capable of even finding the words to comfort her.

Even though I wanted to, I knew I couldn't do a slideshow for John's funeral. I felt immense guilt for not being able to do that for my beloved cousin. How could you begin to describe such an incredible young man? There would be so much to tell about John, and I knew I wouldn't be able to express it myself. I was no longer creative. I had nothing, I felt like I was empty, and I was just a hollow shell. I needed to get a grip. The last thing I needed was to be hospitalized again.

I missed my mom so much. I thought she would know what to do. My mom and Dereka were very close, and she would know how to comfort Dereka and be there for her. I just couldn't imagine the pain one must feel when losing a child. It shouldn't be that way. Parents aren't supposed to lose children. Dereka would never get over this. I didn't know how to tell her how sorry I was. John was an exceptional young man who endured a lot in his short life, and he will live on in the hearts of the people who had the pleasure of knowing and loving him.

* * *

It was a weird summer. With the warm summer gusts, I was still learning to get over John's passing. All the memories and the time we spent together were as clear as the blue sky in my mind.

We knew this was our last summer at the cabin as we were putting it up for sale in September. We knew the first person who saw it would want it. It was a sad summer with many unfortunate events for us. Jack's dad was also not doing well. He went down often to see him, and when Brooklyn and Brad were here, they tagged along to visit their grandfather. He did not look well, and you could tell that he was sad. August 13th was the mournful morning that I feared: Grandpa Jerry passed away. Jack and his brother were with him when it happened. He was a wonderful, humble man who possessed an evergreen aura. People loved him and used to give examples of the way he nurtured his two amazing sons. The funeral for Jack's father was well attended with many guests coming from Calgary. Brooklyn did the slideshow because I just couldn't pull it together. I could tell I was getting stressed with this series of unfortunate events that were lining up, right when I started to think that my life was getting better.

I had to clean the cabin by the end of the summer, and I knew that it was going to be hard on me. I went through all kinds of stuff that I had put away. It included funny hats, noisemakers, fake noses, and glasses. They were all for when I hosted my annual family car rally or when a bunch of friends gathered around the table for a poker night. There were a lot of beautiful memories that were attached to that cabin. It was going to be difficult to say goodbye.

My mom's ashes were spread there as it was her happy place. God, I was going to miss it. I held back the tears that were brimming in my eyes when I was packing up. At one point, I just sat in silence and reflected on all the things I was thankful for. I knew I wasn't doing well. I was trying hard to be strong, trying to remember and practice everything I learned in the hospital, but it was difficult. I couldn't remember anything, and on the long trip home, I rode in silence.

When we got home, I had some stuff to put away. Suddenly, I started to get confused. I couldn't remember where my closet was and other little things. I literally had to walk around my house to find anything. Eventually, I was successful. I then proceeded to put some clothes away. With all that work and responsibility on my shoulders, I started to feel sick again. For some reason, my mind was not at peace. I decided to take a break. I did not want to go back to the hospital. I hated that place.

Eventually, I fell asleep, and when I woke up, I told Jack that I wasn't feeling well and was going to stay home that day. I managed to get out of the bed and maneuvered my way into the shower. Strangely, I found myself in a perplexed state. I didn't know which bottle was the conditioner and which was the shampoo. Similarly, when I went to get dressed, I had to open all the drawers to find my underwear because I couldn't remember where I kept them. I can still envision how I pulled out a shirt and wondered, "When did I get this?" Until I found the one that I liked the most.

I finally got dressed and made my way back to the kitchen, which I still had to clean. Suddenly, I realized that I had forgotten to put on my bra. I was disgusted at myself. I then started emptying the dishwasher—usually a simple, quick task. However, it was a nightmare as I couldn't figure it out. I thought I was losing my mind. I didn't know what was happening to me. I would open up the cupboard and reach out for the item that I already had in my hands. The chores that usually took me five minutes took twenty. I was exhausted, so I went to lie down. Eventually, I fell asleep. I was happy that my house was nice and clean. Oh, how I loved a clean house!

I don't know how or when I got there, but once again, I started to find myself in familiar territories. I was in Unit 49 at the hospital, and before realizing where I was, I had no recollection again of how it happened, but I knew that I was sick again.

Things had changed a bit since the last time I was there two years ago. The most significant change was they had an outdoor courtyard accessible only from the psych ward. It was nicely laid out with a couple of picnic benches, chairs, and planters. When you were in the lockdown phase on Unit 49, you now had an opportunity to go outside and enjoy the sun. I wandered out there soon after I was admitted and made some new friends. Adam was a very handsome young man who seemed to come from a wealthy family. He was a very good musician and singer, and he wanted more than anything to make a name for himself in the business. However, his father was very disappointed and wanted Adam to follow in his footsteps and go to business school. Adam disdained his father because he was the reason he was stuck here. Adam was a very sane and sorted person. He often sang for us when we were in the courtyard, which was a treat for us.

Sue was a tall, dark, and beautiful woman who paced quite regularly with her head held straight and her eyes looking forward like a zombie. At times, Sue would approach and ask me if she was pregnant. I would say, "No, you're not; you're just sick." Sue often accused me of stealing her dinner or medication. And when I gently told her I didn't do that, she would just reply, "Oh." Sue had two little boys and she often talked about them. However, they couldn't come to visit her. I knew she missed them terribly and felt sorry for her. I got Morgan to buy her a teddy bear so that she could hug it when she was missing her boys. When she was coherent, we had some very good visits. However, Sue wasn't well most of the time, and I was very sad for her. I could tell that she was a nice person and someone that I would like to be friends with.

In the psych ward, I was instructed to wash my own clothes. I was running out, and I hated asking Jack to bring me clean ones, even though he would have no problem doing so. The washer was on a first-come/first-serve basis, so I went to check and see if it was free. I had to ask my friend to show me where it was because I couldn't remember. It was free, so I went back to my room and gathered up my dirty laundry. I put them in the washer, and I sat there quietly and stared at the dials. I didn't know which one to push or turn. I didn't have soap, so I just stood there and I felt incompetent. I'm sure it was an easy task to turn the dial to wash, but not for me. Suddenly, I started to cry, which eventually turned into sobs. Next thing you know, my friend Adam came along and hugged me. Hugs weren't allowed in the psych ward, but it was the one thing I needed at that moment. I was shivering and sobbing, and it was hard for me to breathe. He told me to look directly into his eyes and breathe slowly and deeply. He had the most incredible, piercing blue eyes. And so I looked him in the eyes and took deep breaths as he instructed me to. Soon enough, I was calm, and I could tell him what had happened. He showed me how to turn on the washer and went to get soap for me from the nurses' station. I was going to have clean clothes, after all.

I went back to my room and wrote in my journal, "You are feeling so low right now. You are in the depths of despair. You are desperate; you were trying to prove you could do laundry, a simple task is what it is, but when you are ill, not so much. And you are very ill right now, remember, one step at a time, don't beat yourself up. If you do things one step at a time, you will eventually get well. But it's not going to happen overnight." After that, I decided to write about what I needed and what I knew for sure.

I needed to get up. I knew for sure I could do that.

I needed to shower and brush my teeth. I knew for sure I could do that.

I needed to finish my laundry. I didn't know for sure if I could accomplish that.

I needed love. I didn't know if I was still loved by my family.

This was my third mental breakdown, and I wondered how many times it could happen before my family said, "Enough is enough." I hoped they would understand that this was not my fault. I found this hospital to be the cruelest place on earth. People could go crazy being in here.

I awoke from my sleep, and for some reason, I felt happy.

My mom came and visited me last night. It was the first time she had visited me. She visits my dad and Zach, but she never stopped by my dreams until last night. Maybe, she came because I'm so very sad, and nothing makes me happy anymore or brings me joy. This is such a cruel, unforgiving disease and I find myself asking God, "Why me? Why do you need to take the joy out of my life, to constantly wish that I was normal again?" I just felt like a lump of unhappiness, and maybe, she knew that I needed her then. I wanted the old me back so bad that it started to hurt.

I wanted people to want to be around me. To hang out with me like we used to! Being with my family and friends brought me incomprehensible joy that I missed. I was fortunate. I had a fantastic family, and I had some great friends. I was feeling so worthless like I was not contributing. I was so desperate then, but I couldn't fathom what for. I needed to get the old "me" back. I didn't like the new "me." I wanted to laugh again, but I was stuck in a place that was very, very dark, a place I wouldn't wish on anybody.

I told myself, "Stop feeling sorry for yourself, for God's sake. You are fortunate, so count your blessings. Be grateful that you are still here. You have family and friends who love you, and they aren't going to stop because you have changed. You are a kind person, you are kind to everyone else, you are kind to strangers, you are kind to your friends, and now it's time to be kind to yourself. What you are going through is not your fault! Take this time in the hospital and be kind to yourself. Give yourself a break. Your illness is not who you are supposed to be. It's keeping you from who you are supposed to be." The pain that I felt was unbearable and I just wanted it to stop.

For the sixth time on a sunny day, I tried to get the kettle to boil water. I saw everyone else come up and turn the kettle on with no issues. But do you think I could have done it? No way! So, I finally asked someone because I did not believe that I was so crazy that I couldn't get a fucking kettle to boil water. My nurse came over and told me, "The kettle is broken, and you have to have it set a certain way to get it to work." I was happy to hear the articulated words. It convinced me that I wasn't crazy.

That same day, I chose to go outside. It was nice and sunny outside. However, I chose a spot on a bench in the shade. I was not comfortable wearing shorts because of all the weight I had put on, and that's why I avoided the sun. So, instead of sitting in the sun and sweating like a bloody pig, I chose the shade. Right after I sat down, my friend Myra jumped up and abruptly left. She slunk back and asked me, "Have you seen a red pouch?" I replied, "I haven't, but I can help you look for it." Myra left again after I told her it wasn't here. However, she eventually returned. This time there were tears in her eyes. "My name is Leianne," I told her.

She asked, "Oh, you're Leianne?"

I thought Myra knew I was a nice person with no hidden agenda. She blew her nose in her shirt, and I offered her a couple of tissues, which she happily accepted. We sat together in silence, and I felt that we could see each other's pain. This was when I realized that everyone here has a story and is here for a reason. Myra talked about a court case coming up because her doctor can't, won't, or doesn't think that she is stable enough to be her children's mom. I thanked God that was not something I had to deal with.

I felt sorry for Myra. She seemed like a nice person, but she was very broken. When she was leaving, I stopped her and said, "You seem like a good person," and smiled at her. She smiled back at me and replied, "You too, Leianne."

Sometimes in the hospital, that is the best that you are going to get. I'm not crazy today, just happy that maybe I made Myra feel good about herself, even if it was for just a moment. And now she's gone, I sit here alone again and am thankful that she didn't drop her tissue for me to pick up because I have a weak stomach and get really grossed out by things like that.

I never minded the food in here; actually, sometimes I thought it was pretty good. But after having been in here for a while, when you realize the food is really crappy, that's when you know you are getting better. You also learn to eat with your head down, otherwise, you see things like Myra scratching her crotch to all beat hell and then touching her food . . . GROSS. Not only does she touch her food, but she goes through all the food trays that haven't been picked up yet and grabs people's fruit, muffins, and whatever she can get her hands on. Then she grabs her crotch again, scratching like crazy. It kind of takes your appetite away, so that's why you eat with your head looking down. I figure if I'm in here for a couple of months, I might drop 40 pounds.

I have made twenty-five new friends during my stay here. I can remember all their names, I say hi to them, I buy the sad ones gifts or chocolate bars or give them cigarettes. I like to sit with some and make conversation. Some are still my friends, but I avoid them when I'm back home because I know they will ask me for money and my family gets upset with me if I give it away.

I do love making new friends. One day I chose to sit beside Holly. She seems like a nice person, rather normal like me. I start talking to her and I like her, I really do. And then, out of the blue, she lets out the loudest BURP in my face. I could smell it, and then she burps again—no excuse me, no nothing—one new friend down.

On a not-so-good day, I'm feeling weird. I asked Kevin, my nurse, if I should go off green—green is the color you get if you are good and allowed to go off the unit by yourself. I like to go to the lobby and watch the people come and go as they visit loved ones in the hospital. Everyone knows you're from the psych ward because you have a hospital bracelet yet are wearing regular clothing. It's funny because even when the hospital staff notices you, some of them are very uncomfortable.

Kevin said. "No." I told him, "I feel out of control again." I told him I was scared I would get lost if I left the unit. He told me to stay on the unit today and to come to him if things got worse. Kevin is an exceptional nurse and one of my favorites.

I'm acting weird again. The nurses keep saying it's my medication but what scares me is that I am going to lose all my friends here. They are going to get better and leave me. I need my friends here as my other friends don't come and visit very often. It's prob-

ably a good thing because I say crazy things to them. My friend
Allison came once, and she lost her husband last year in a plane
crash. It was very tragic, but I told her that I got to have lunch
with him every day because he was in here with me. I must have
hurt her feelings because she never came back.

My cousin Shirl comes faithfully and we have some good
talks, it's so comfortable having her visit and a lot of the time, we
just sit and listen. Often, we will go to the chapel and she will pray
with me. I pray hard, I beg God for his forgiveness and to stop
making me sick. My aunt Dereka doesn't come anymore because
she is grieving her son John and she told me that she wasn't strong
enough and I can understand that. My brother Tom called once
to come and take me for lunch before he flew back home, but I
was on red and I couldn't leave the unit.

My best friend, Tammy, comes to visit, but it's weird, she acts
differently, just like my husband does and I can't explain it and I
don't understand it. I asked Jack to kiss me goodbye once, we
were at the front desk and some of the patients were watching our
interaction and I kind of wanted to make them realize that my
husband really loved me, but he refused. That hurt me badly, and
maybe he was uncomfortable showing some PDA. Morgan comes
as often as she can, but she has to drive a long way and I know it's
hard on her to see her mom in here again. My friend Karen comes
once in a while and we usually go and grab a coffee as they only
have instant in the unit, so a good cup of coffee is a real treat. And
Zach and Jack come, but they hate this place, so they don't come
very often.

So I need my friends in here, or I need a pass to get out of
here, the more I stay here, the crazier I become. My legs are
wobbly, I am groggy, I keep tripping over my feet, I can't
remember things like where my room is. It's an uneasy feeling. It's
a feeling that I don't wish upon anyone. I have to get better, I have
to concentrate on getting better, what that means, I have no
fucking idea, I just know that I hate this place, I hate that I have a
label now, that people will identify me that I am the one that went
crazy. I hate that I struggle with the fact that I am crazy, that I

might never be the same person that I was. How do I get that person back? Where do I start?

Kevin and my doctor came into my room one day to talk about long-term care for me. That means putting me in a mental institution for God knows how long, if not forever. That scared the shit out of me and I couldn't imagine having to go somewhere, however, if I didn't get well, it could be a very strong possibility. I needed to get well, I had people who needed me, who needed the old me, not the pathetic, sick person that I had become. I have to remember: one step at a time, don't look back. Be your own best friend, be kind to yourself. Your doctor told you not to live in the "what if" but rather ask yourself, "What's next?" He has said that "what if" destroys you and prevents you from moving on. You need to move, if you get stuck here, you will be hospitalized maybe forever.

I received a pass for the weekend and so far, I'm having a good weekend. I have had a few bad hours, but I haven't had to take the anxiety medicine the doctor gave me, so that is good. Saturday night, I felt totally normal, it was awesome—I worked until one in the morning and could really focus on things. That is something that I have to work on, pacing myself, but I couldn't believe how it felt so normal.

I didn't sleep at all on Friday night and Jack was forcing me to go to sleep, so I did "fake sleep"... that is what crazy people do! I didn't do drugs growing up, and when I got to stop "fake sleeping" I think my behavior mimicked what it was like being on speed. I was cleaning cupboards... emptying the dishwasher, then I would forget I was cleaning a cupboard...then I tried making coffee... then I started to organize those photos I've had for 22 years... the coffee took 45 minutes to make... I would grind the beans... try and find the mail... clean more cupboards... put the water in the coffee pot... remember that I was emptying the dishwasher... and finally, I realized I had to turn it on.

After I finished making coffee, I forgot to drink it because I thought I should try and finish that scrapbooking that I started three years ago... So, I think by the time I actually did have a cup

of coffee, it tasted like it had been sitting there for three hours...
Oh, DUH MOMENT...it had. You should have seen the flippin'
mess I had made when Kathleen arrived to clean house. There was
stuff everywhere...

Kathleen stayed with me for the day and helped me organize
the cupboards that I started, and she ended up taking most of the
stuff home. So if I keep this up, I won't have any more clutter or
dishes. God only knows what I gave her, but I'm feeling good
today, so apparently, Jack thinks cleaning house was good also!

I know I have to go back to the hospital and it makes me sad,
but I will stay in that hellhole as long as it takes me to get well.
Oh, pardon me, I refer to it now as my "exclusive all-inclusive
resort." I don't want to get out too soon, I never, ever want to go
back there in the future... and talk about when I was in here in
2011, and remember the time in 2013... oh, and then again in
2014—because then I will get a reputation of being crazy!

I would rather stay in there and sleep beside my new roommate, who arrived in the middle of the night, than go back and be
worse off. But that's okay because my new roomie is a total crack
addict and shared that she used to be a hooker, so she does
provide a little comic relief. Deep down in my heart, I feel sorry
for her and want to help.

Chapter Sixteen

After being in the hospital again for 2 ½ months, it was time to go home. I was happy to get out of there and get back to my normal life, even though I had no idea anymore what that was or how it looked. I knew that I had to take things slow. I knew that I should only try to make simple meals for my family. My doctor told me that making a meal could be one of the most challenging things I attempted because there is so much going on at one time. I wasn't a very good cook at the best of times, so for me to try and simplify things was going to be relatively easy.

I really wanted to get back to work, as the last thing I wanted was to sit around the house trying to find ways to fill my time. I started back as soon as I was capable again. It felt good to be back, although things at work were very stressful. Kerry saw no light at the end of this dark tunnel that was affecting the oil and gas industry in this city. I could tell he was anxious, and again, he would come into my office every morning and we would talk. I felt sorry for him, for he had no one. He was a single man, very tall and handsome, the early sixties with impeccable manners and, man, was he stylish. He was also very well versed in current events and quite often wrote a letter to the editor about something that he was passionate about. I enjoyed talking to him and valued our friendship, and I knew that Kerry valued and respected what I did for the company.

I never understood why he never married, as he was a very good man, very easy to talk to and very thoughtful. Jack and I couldn't have asked for a better partner. He used to be close to his two brothers, but his older brother conned him once and opened a credit card in his name. He then racked it up to the limit and Kerry had to pay it off. Like we used to, Kerry had a beautiful property on a lake in Manitoba where he would spend some time in the summer.

Kerry could read people the right way, and he had the class and diplomacy it took to be an excellent salesman. His passions were art, exercise, and wine. One time he came into my office with a gift for me and I was thrilled. When I opened it, it was a Cartier Luxury Pen. I had never had such an expensive pen before and I didn't want to lose it, so I put it back in its box and saved it.

It's funny, ever since I got sick, I have done things that I am not aware of. I read my journals and I can't believe that I was that crazy. I lost my first journal, I have a feeling I destroyed it to protect myself. After my mother passed away, my dad gave me her ring. It was a beautiful ring with three fairly large diamonds set on top of each other. My father had invested in the diamonds and had the ring custom-made for my mom. She wore it proudly and so did I after she died. One day, I was sitting in the hockey arena watching Jack's game and I felt the ring fall off my hand. I looked down and the ring had split right in half on two sides. That was just before I ended up in the hospital the last time and while I was in there, Jack took the ring to a jeweller and had it repaired. He brought it to me in the hospital and I was so happy to get it back, it brought me comfort knowing that my mom had worn it. After I got out of the hospital, I was having coffee with my aunt Dereka and I was telling her how it had broke and I went to show her that it had been repaired and it wasn't on my finger. I didn't know what had happened to it, and when I got home, I searched every-where for it, with no results. I was devastated, hoping that someday it would show up. I never took that ring off my finger and it fit snuggly, so there was no way that it could have fallen off. If I was to guess, in my ill state, I did something with the ring, thinking that I wasn't deserving enough to wear it. I have no other explanation, just like the disappearance of my first journal. All my other journals were in one place, but not that one. The mind is a very powerful thing and it does crazy things. I look back and can't believe the things that I thought I did or the thoughts that I had.

I loved my job, but it was very stressful. I was constantly doing cash flow analysis and revised budgets and amending them weekly and it was never good news. Jack, Kerry and I decided that we would defer our monthly wage just so we could keep our current staff. Kerry came back to the office every day and the news was always so depressing, I could see that this was affecting him deeply. The work just wasn't coming in; companies were cutting back drastically, including layoffs. It was a very scary time and we had a very bleak outlook.

Usually, January, February and March were very busy months for us, as companies were gearing up for spring break. We had always prided ourselves on not laying our field staff off during that time, even though it was typically dead for a couple of months.

Kerry would still come into my office every morning, and I could tell that he wasn't doing well mentally. I had a sixth sense for this kind of thing now since I had been around it so much while I was hospitalized. He had something wrong with his foot and had not been able to go to the gym or run, which was something he loved to do. He had decided to book a hospital in Montana to have his foot operated on. I knew what it was like to live in pain; my knees and my hips were in rough shape and every day, I struggled with chronic pain, sometimes, it was unbearable.

Kerry had his surgery and unfortunately, it didn't work, he was still unable to go to the gym or exercise. He soon became very depressed and I encouraged him to get an appointment with a psychiatrist and get on some anti-depressants. I was very worried about him as he was all alone, all he had was Jack and myself. I told Jack how worried I was, and he too, had noticed how down

Kerry had been. We remarked how lucky we were to have him as a partner as he had the same values as we did. It was tough though, as Jack was adamant about not shutting the company down, he was prepared to do whatever it took to keep it running, including financing it with our own savings. Years ago, when there was an apparent boom in our industry, our company was valued at more than 8 million dollars. Now it was only worth the heavy equipment—and that's if you could sell it. It was supposed to be our retirement fund, some retirement fund!

That Spring, knowing that work was slow, Jack and I and the boys went to Brooklyn's for Easter. We had a great time, it was so much fun to spend time with the grandkids. The boys loved it also. We only get to see Brooklyn's family a couple of times a year, so the time we spend hanging out with them is precious.

We were driving home after our visit and Jack got a phone call from Kerry. It didn't last very long, but when he got off the phone, he commented that the phone call was kind of weird. I asked, "How so?" He said that Kerry sounded like he was drunk and told Jack that he wasn't sure if he was going to come to work the next day. I thought that it was odd, as Kerry rarely missed work. Kerry had confidentially told me that he was taking antidepressants, but he wasn't sure that they were helping. I was hoping that they would, but sometimes when you are so down, it takes a lot to boost your mood.

The next day, I stayed at home in the morning to put everything away and Jack called and told me that Kerry did not show up at work and that he had not answered his phone. Both Jack and I thought that was very unusual and I suggested that maybe Jack should go over to his house and check on him, considering what he had been going through. And Kerry never did not answer his phone, it was tied to his hip as Jack's was.

In the meantime, my friend Tammy came over for a visit. It was so good to see her, we had been gone just about a week, so we had lots of catching up to do. While Tammy and I were having coffee, Jack called again and said that he was in front of Kerry's house and Kerry's car was out front. He said he felt uneasy about it and I told him not to go in. I told him to call Kerry's brother and have his brother come over. I ended the call by telling him to let me know how Kerry was and, if need be, I would go over and see him.

The next call that I got was not one that I expected. After answering hello, all I heard Jack say was "He's dead, he shot himself."

Jack has always gotten straight to the point, and this time it was no different. Hearing this news, I was speechless. I couldn't believe it, tears welled up and I started to sob. I knew Kerry was in rough shape, I knew he was suffering from depression, I just had no idea how bad it was. The more I thought about it, the more I realized how alone he was. He had no one except for Jack and myself and I struggled to understand that because he was such a great guy. I could understand why he had nothing to do with his older brother, as when his big brother told Jack that he had found him dead, his next words were to Jack, "I guess we will be meeting about the business right away."

I also knew that he was an integral part of our business and we wouldn't survive without him. Jack would try his damnedest to become a salesman, but he just didn't have what Kerry had. Jack too was well-liked and well respected in the business, but with the looming recession and sales dropping dramatically, it was going to be a tough go. All I wanted to do was shut it down and let it go, but I knew I was going to be in for a battle with Jack. It was all he knew, he had run the business since he was 18 years old. He was very good at it, but companies were shutting down, and the price of oil had dropped dramatically, not to mention the price of natural gas. People were losing their jobs, a lot of them were his contacts, we couldn't compete with the larger companies. The next few months were challenging to say the least. When Kerry passed away, we got a fairly large insurance payout that we had to share with his brothers. Sadly, that money had been spent and we were no further ahead. Jack was now researching a loan, which would be secured against our personal savings. I couldn't see any kind of light at the end of the tunnel, but I knew that it would destroy Jack to let it go. I was also at the point where I couldn't argue with him anymore, it was too stressful and I had to be careful of my mental health. Initially, I said, "No way," but he was so distraught about it that I finally caved.

We were able to carry on and that is what we did. Our personal lives were busy with hockey as Jack Michael had made the AA team, which was five to six days a week and Jack was loving that. He was so proud of Jack Michael and thoroughly enjoyed watching his games. It was quite a remarkable feat for Jack Michael as he had never played on the number one team, yet he made the team and kids that played above him did not. I don't think I had ever seen my husband so proud.

Tammy spent a lot of time with us, and when we decided to go to Hawaii, I felt sorry for her, so I invited her along. She willingly accepted as we would provide the accommodations and all she would have to pay for was her flight. We had a great trip, she and Jack would get up early every morning and walk on the beach. Unfortunately, it was too painful for me to do that because of my hip and knees.

Life went on, it was apparent that there was a definite void where Kerry's role was in our company. It was very stressful to watch our company die a slow death and I kept telling Jack that he was beating a dead horse, but he didn't care to listen. The work just wasn't coming in. Jack was making phone calls and people were not optimistic that it was going to pick up anytime soon, if ever. I wasn't going into the office full-time anymore, as I was trying to take care of things at home and it was hard to be around Jack as he was very grumpy. He kept pretending that things were going to get better and every time I heard the phone ring, my heart skipped a beat, hoping that it was work coming in. It did not look good, but I was trying so hard not to get depressed by it.

During the summers, it was hard not to miss the cabin, however, I made a point of renting a summer cabin for a week, so the kids could get some boating in. It wasn't like having your own, but it was still fun as Brooklyn and the kids would join us.

Morgan and Bryan were getting married the second week in

August. They were having a very small wedding, just immediate family and a few close friends. It was what they wanted, although I would have preferred to have more family. I rented a house in Fairmont for all of us, including Tammy, for two nights. In typical Tammy fashion, she did not offer to pay for her share, which is one thing about her that really annoys me.

The wedding was beautiful, very simple, with no bridesmaids or groomsmen, only about twenty people and a beautiful dinner in a greenhouse. Morgan's girlfriends decorated it and it was very rustic but beautiful. Morgan and Bryan seemed over the moon in love and I couldn't have been happier for them. I knew what it was like to have a soul mate, someone who you could count on to be there, someone who loved you unconditionally, whatever the circumstances were, and I know Morgan had found one in Bryan, just as Brooklyn had in Brad.

I was doing well, very stable, and was getting back to my normal self, though without the sense of humor or laughter that once filled my heart. I was so grateful as things were stressful financially because of work.

On one particular late August summer day, my brother Jeff was here on a visit. I went out to get some steaks for the barbecue and I found my freezer had quit. I frantically called Tammy to see if she had room in her freezer for my groceries and she said to come on over and she would make room. I was very thankful and she told me that I could use her freezer, as she had to move out that weekend and had no room for it in her new place. I was so lucky to have such a good friend.

Jack seemed pleased at the offer as we were really trying to watch our budget, not knowing what the outcome of our business would be.

The next day, Zach and I were on our way into the city and he said, "Mom, I think Lowes has a sale on freezers, we should go and look." I told him that Tammy had kindly offered me her freezer so I didn't need to get one. He said, "I don't think that's a good idea, Mom, you need to buy your own." And I replied, "But why, Zach? Why shouldn't I use Tammy's?" He replied that in a year, I wouldn't want to use her freezer and started to sob. This wasn't the first time that this had happened, but he had never told me why he was so angry at Tammy. At one point, she was one of his best friends and Morgan's. In the past, I had confronted Morgan and asked why she hated Tammy. All Morgan had told me was, "She is not a good friend and I'm sorry Mom, but it's not my story to tell." I had asked Zach a couple of times what happened and he usually ended up in tears but wouldn't say anything.

I was curious, and I had no idea whatsoever why they disliked her. She was my best friend, I told her everything, she was my go-to person, I adored her kids as if they were my own. I thought it probably was because Zach had told her he was gay before he told me. I had asked Tammy numerous times and she always replied that she had no idea.

I pulled the car off to the side of the road, held Zach's hands and looked into his eyes. I said, "Zach, tell me what's going on. It's okay, I can handle it, whatever it is. Trust me. "

At that point, as my heart was breaking for my son, he told me through his sobs that Tammy and Jack had had sex. Then he said, "I'm so sorry, Mom, you don't deserve this." I held him because he needed it and I did too. I was in utter disbelief and I was shaking so bad, trying to keep the tears at bay and be strong for Zach. I didn't think in a million years that it was possible. No . . . no way, neither one of them would do that to me, would hurt me like that. It wasn't possible, my best friend and my soul mate, NO WAY. Yet, Zach wouldn't lie. He told me that four years ago, when I was in the hospital, he came home and heard them. Jack called him all kinds of names and denied the whole thing, even though Zach had caught them red-handed. Zach had finally accepted that maybe he was wrong, that maybe he had made a mistake. Then, just recently, they had gone to a concert together and had sex again and the texts between them somehow ended up on Zach's phone. I felt sick to my stomach, I had a hard time seeing, I was in such shock. I didn't know what I was going to do. We went straight home as I couldn't even function.

When we got home, I called my girlfriend Karen and asked her to come over. I wanted her there when I confronted Jack so I had someone to hold my hand. She was on my doorstep in minutes and I told her what had happened. She too, couldn't believe it. She remarked how she noticed how much Jack loved me, as did many of my friends. I didn't cry; I was numb and still in shock. I dialed Jack's number, all the while holding my breath, and when he answered, I just came right out and asked if it was true. He didn't deny anything, he didn't say it was a mistake, he didn't say he was sorry, all he said was that yes, it was true, he was tired of lying and he wasn't coming home.

* * *

I felt like my world had shattered. I didn't know what to think, but I was determined not to let it destroy me. I slept at Morgan's that night, I needed time to figure out what I was going to do. Morgan made an appointment with my psychiatrist for the next day and both Karen and Morgan came with me. When I told him, I knew he was shocked as he had always remarked what a good guy Jack was and how supportive he was. There weren't many husbands who attended their wives' psychiatrist's appointments and went to the hospital every day that they were hospitalized.

After seeing my psychiatrist, I called Jack and asked him to come home so that we could talk. When he came home, I told him that if he was willing to go to counselling, I would like to try and work things out. I would try and forgive him for what he had done and, for the time being, he could stay in our home in the upstairs loft. He agreed to that and once he did, I wasn't sure how I felt about it. I started thinking about Jack and how incredibly lazy he was, how he never did anything around the house except make the kids the odd breakfast and help with dishes once in a while. How all he did was watch television and sports, how he liked to spend money and couldn't budget. How lately, he had been very moody, and we had rarely seen a smile. How he couldn't relate to Zach, and I started questioning my offer. Then I thought about what an awesome dad and grandfather he was. He was a good guy, people admired him and respected him and his children adored him. When I realized all of this, I also realized that it was Jack, who had saved me from my first marriage, at which point I vowed to forgive him. I would never forget what he did, but I needed peace and the only way that I could get that would be to forgive, and I was willing to do that.

We continued therapy for the next few months, but it wasn't going well. Jack had yet to apologize and I honestly didn't know what to complain about, as we always got along, so I had little to say. Jack, however, talked about how I was such a different person since I became mentally ill. He didn't like the new me. I didn't either, but I struggled to find a way to get back to who I once was. Jack didn't seem to want to make it work and I had to rethink my position also. I couldn't help but think of our vows, for better or for worse, in sickness and in health, and how he was breaking them. I was sick, yet it wasn't my fault. Jack was always grumpy and he wasn't the person that I once knew either—he became the glass-half-empty kind of guy.

It was weird not having Tammy in my life anymore. I missed her, despite what she did to me. I missed our talks and the way she supported me throughout my illness. By about our sixth visit to the therapist, I knew we were flogging a dead horse. I knew he didn't love me anymore and I also knew that I didn't want to be with someone that didn't care about me. We had decided that we would continue to live under the same roof for financial purposes, but we would be legally separated. I also told him that under no circumstances was I going to throw a whole bunch of money to a lawyer to settle this. I knew we were both adults and that we could figure it out between the two of us.

We continued to live under the same roof for months, and at one point, Tammy did come over. It was the middle of the night and Jack Michael was at her house hanging out with a few kids and he pulled a butcher knife from the block and threatened to harm himself. It was a scary moment and I realized then how it must be so difficult for him to accept his father's relationship with his best friend's mother. The next day, I was able to get him into a psychologist for some counselling. I also spoke to the school guidance counsellor just so she could keep tabs on him at school. After a few sessions, the psychologist told me that Jack Michael was good to go, so that was good news, but I was always on my toes with him. I knew he wasn't one to open up about his true feelings. I needed to protect him, I needed him to know that it was okay for him to be friends with Bodie, that I was okay with it and that I didn't hold any ill regard for Tammy. I needed him to know that I was going to be okay, and in no way did I ever blame him for this. Jack and Tammy were adults and made adult decisions, and it was not his fault and he had to believe that. He seemed much more relaxed after that and every time he went over, I asked how everyone was doing so he knew and understood that I wasn't in any way resentful.

The next summer was rolling around and I was in rough shape. It was terribly uncomfortable living under the same roof with Jack, pretending that things were somewhat normal. I hated it, and I began to dislike Jack also. I was starting to feel overwhelmed, I felt fat, I felt ugly, I felt incompetent and hopeless. The feelings engulfed me and I just couldn't pull myself out of it. I had never felt so worthless and hopeless to the point that I started to think of ways to kill myself. I googled it and I thought I had enough pills that maybe I could do it, but then I thought maybe not, the last thing I wanted was to fail. I would become the laughing stock of the neighborhood. Oh, I thought about my son's friend whose mother had committed suicide a year ago and how it devastated him. I thought I couldn't do that to my kids, that's the cowardly way out. I knew it wouldn't affect my husband, he would be happy as he could collect a hefty insurance policy. And part of me wanted him to be happy once again.

I'd go to bed thinking of different ways to do it, and I also couldn't stop thinking that I was being selfish and not thinking of my kids. What kind of mother would do that to her own children? I was mostly worried about Zach and how he would ever be able to get over it. But the pain that I was in was overshadowing the consequences. I was hurting, I was hurting so bad and it didn't matter what I did, I couldn't feel better. So I came up with a plan and, all of a sudden, I started feeling freer, realizing I could make the pain stop. I was going to start the car and let it run for a few hours to make sure the garage was full of CO_2 and then I would get into it, hopefully not having to sit there for a long time. I didn't want to have to sit because what if I changed my mind? I wanted it to be done pretty much without delay.

My plan was to be carried out in two weeks. I had to make sure that Morgan was with her husband and Brooklyn was with her husband when they found out. I was going to arrange a skeet-shooting event for Jack, the two boys and Jack's brother. After the event, the boys were to go to visit my dad, since they were halfway there, and Jack and his brother would come home and find me. I would put the dog in the basement in a far bedroom with the windows open. I had it all figured out, that Sunday, I even went to church and asked about funeral arrangements, pretending that I was planning one for my mom. I started writing my goodbye letters, spending hours on them. I had one for each of my kids and then I composed one for my good friends. I would write and then come back and write some more, making sure I forgot about nothing. I needed them to know how much I loved them.

The pain worsened every day to the point where I could barely get out of bed. I would finally get up and look at the calendar first thing, counting down the days when the pain would stop. I tried so hard not to think of the guilt that I was experiencing about leaving my children behind. On Friday, I emailed our security company asking that they cut off our service immediately as it had a CO_2 detector and my plan was happening on Sunday. Two days, two more days, and then you will be at peace, no more of this unbearable pain, no more embarrassment of the person you have become. It was all I could think about until Jack came home and looked at me and asked what the hell I was doing by cutting off the security system? I replied through tears that I didn't know, and then I crumpled to the floor, devastated that my plan had failed. I didn't know how I was going to survive, how could I get rid of this pain?

Unbeknownst to me, if I had asked Jack whether he turned it back on, I wouldn't be here today, as I just assumed that he did and my plan was terminated. I knew I was defeated and instead of feeling sorry for myself, I decided that I had to get a grip and start living again the way life was meant to be lived. Sure, I was unhappy with the way that I looked, but God gave me this body and this face and there was nothing that I could do about it, so quit dwelling on it and move on. I realized that he also blessed me with four incredible children who needed me. It took me about a week, but after that, I was okay, I wanted to once again be a mother to my kids, to figure out my life. I look back on those days and understandably, I was in a lot of pain, but I am also ashamed of having such extensive and inclusive thoughts of suicide. It would have destroyed my kids and they didn't deserve that. They've already been through so much in their young lives and were struggling as it was. I was not going to let this illness define me, it wasn't going to beat me, I would learn as much as I could about it and fight back to make sure that I stayed sane. I wanted to figure out a way that I could be happy again.

My good friend Tracy moved to San Diego a couple of years back and, thank God for her, because I talked to her on a daily basis. Tracy and I became friends years ago when we lived in the same neighborhood and we both had older children and babies at the same time. We were also the same age and she too had experienced a marriage breakdown due to infidelity, so we had a lot in common and a lot to talk about. I told her how unbearable it was, having Jack in the house living with us, knowing that it wasn't going to work out. Jack had changed dramatically, but he continued to pretend that nothing was wrong. Zach could barely look at him as he had yet to apologize to Zach for making him live a lie for four years.

The next few months were a blur—I was existing, I was trying to work, even though there was nothing to do. I tried to convince Jack to shut things down before we had to declare bankruptcy, but he just wouldn't listen. He wanted to keep flogging a dead horse and we were getting more in debt with the company. I continued my weekly visits with my psychiatrist and therapist.

I was finding the therapy tough as I was going back in time to my first marriage. On one of my visits to my psychiatrist, I discovered what a flashback was. I was standing on the top of the hospital garage after my doctor's appointment, taking in the beauty of the fall colors against the reservoir. It was hard to believe that such an incredible coveted piece of city property had a parkade on it. I looked down and there was the picnic table where I sat with my dad the day that he came to visit me. I had thought my dad didn't come to visit me, but he did and we sat at that table. I don't remember what we talked about, I just remember feeling special that he came to visit me. I remember a strange man sitting with us, I don't know if we talked to him, I just remember that he was scary-looking and staring at us. I remembered then that my dad had come to visit me when I was in the hospital and we had some pretty in-depth and heartfelt conversations.

Looking down also reminded me of the times when I finally got to go outside and have a smoke, I would sit there and watch the families ride their bikes around the reservoir, and few people would look back, but every once in a while, someone would give you a little wave. There was a very nice elderly man who walked his beautiful golden retriever, Gus, every day and he would stop and talk. He wasn't scared of us patients and he was very friendly. I looked forward to seeing him every day and chatting with him.

I saw the picnic table where I spent many hours visiting with friends—both kinds of friends, my friends from the hospital and my friends from home. I saw where my aunts Dereka, Marilyn, and Marian came to see me . . . where we cried together, where they so kindly listened to my funny stories and laughed with me, even as I knew they were worried about me.

Oh, and there's the picnic table where Morgan brought her friends and we all had a picnic one day. I had felt pretty special. Another time my friend Deb brought lunch for me, my favorite salad from Earls, and we sat there and talked and ate. Deb had saved my butt a few times, she was a good friend whom I knew if I needed anything I could count on. It was risky having friends come and see you when you're hospitalized because you aren't in your right mind and who knows what you would say. I don't remember what I said, but I know that some things were probably said that shouldn't have been said.

There is a lot of pain in those tables, in those moments, and I know there are a lot of realization and painful moments and memories I too have to relive. I also know that there are memories that I don't want to relive, and my doctor says this is my brain's way of protecting me, as those things are not meant to be remembered. I don't look forward to flashbacks. I look forward to just being me—whatever that may be—and I hope that my family still sees the "me" that they love. I hope that I can be a better me for them and a better me for me.

Chapter Seventeen

It was extremely painful having Jack living at home, to have to look at him every day and be reminded of what he did to me, reminded of who he once was and who he had become. I felt that I didn't know him anymore. We still sat every night at the dinner table and tried to pretend that things were normal. Yet they were far from normal. I was aware of Zach's contempt for his father. Jack Michael, on the other hand, seemed more forgiving, which I was so grateful for. I was hoping that this incident wouldn't change their relationship, as they were very close to their father. It was so uncomfortable having to eat dinner with him every night and make small talk.

Jack Michael continued to play hockey on the AA team, but this year it was very awkward as his best friend, Bodie, also made the team and Tammy was present at all the games. It was a thing for the parents to drop off the players about an hour and a half before the game and then go out to a pub and drink until game time. I was uneasy knowing that both Jack and Tammy were part of that crowd. When I arrived at the games, it was always awkward trying to find a place to sit that wasn't close to her. I felt bad when

I would see her young daughter looking at me, wondering why I wasn't sitting with her mother.

I didn't attend the parent parties, but I did make a couple of very good friends at the games, some of whom I shared what had happened between Tammy and my husband. One particular day, I was not having a good one; I was in a lot of pain with my hip and my knees. The game ended and I was on my way out of the arena when I ran into an old friend from a previous team. She asked me how I was doing, and my eyes welled up. I was really trying hard to control my emotions, but instead of being intrusive, she just gave me a big hug. That hug created sobs from my body that were uncontrollable. She guided me to a chair, where I sat and sobbed uncontrollably for all to see. I found myself sharing through the sobs that my best friend had sex with my husband and that I didn't know what I had done to deserve it. I was crying so hard and not realizing that a small group of people had gathered around me and had heard everything. I was very embarrassed and ashamed. People didn't know what to say, I felt their pity, but I also knew I had to be stronger. I barely cried when I was alone, why on earth would I cry in front of a bunch of people? I was angry with myself and knew that I had to move on.

On my way home, I knew that I was getting sick again, I couldn't remember how to get home, I didn't want to call my kids because they were stressed enough as it was, so I called my friend Robert. He was so kind and offered to come and get me, then he guided me to the highway, where I, through my sobs, came too close to a pylon and ended up hitting it. Robert asked if I wanted to come over for a cup of tea, but I just wanted to get home and crawl into bed. I felt so very blessed to have such good friends as Robert and his wife, Jane. I remember the first time I went into the hospital, Robert came and met my psychiatrist. He actually talked about my illness with him. He really cared, and it ended up being a very cool day, as Jane came too, and my good friends Cal and Jessica were there and Jack showed up. All six decided to go to the cafeteria so we could visit together. I was the only one who had dinner, everyone else had a bottle of water. This same group had gone on two fabulous vacations, once to Napa Valley, and once to Chicago, where the experiences we had were second to none and where we made memories that would always be cherished.

The six of us sat at a round table and I remarked that the last time we had sat at a round table was a few years ago, when we all went toNapa Valley together and were lucky enough to get reservations at the best restaurant in the world at the time, The French Laundry. It was the most expensive dinner I think I had ever eaten, but it was also one of the most memorable because of the company that I was with. This was a very different time—a hospital cafeteria, with a bare table and uncomfortable chairs, surrounded by medical personnel—but I felt so blessed to have such incredible friends who would come and visit me in such a dreary place. Conversation wasn't as animated as it was when we experienced our dinner at the French Laundry, it was somewhat guarded, but I could understand that, after all, what do people talk about when a crazy person is in their midst? I still felt special, I still felt like people cared about me and, when you're in the psych ward, you don't get to experience that a lot. There are so many people in there who have ruined their relationships with their family and friends, through no fault of their own, and I didn't want to be one of them. Regardless, of the circumstances, I shall never forget that meal at that table.

Soon Jack Michael's 16th birthday was upon us, and I looked back on the years and wondered where had the time gone? He was a great kid and I was so proud of him. He was handsome, smart, had a good personality, and very close to his big brother, which was a blessing. I know that he could tell Zach just about anything and Zach was there for him. We had planned on going out to dinner, at his favorite restaurant, and I invited his Dad and Jack Michael's girlfriend, and it was a nice evening.

When we arrived home, I was sitting in my bedroom and Jack came in and thanked me for including him in Jack's birthday celebration. He then remarked that it would probably be the last time we celebrated a birthday together. After he left, I burst into tears.

I don't know what was wrong with me, as lately I have been crying a lot. I knew that I wasn't well, I knew that I needed to be back in the hospital. I was getting very confused and I struggled to complete simple tasks like brushing my teeth. I struggled with finding my medication, turning out the lights and just moving throughout the house. I knew that I had to go back because I needed help. I was devastated by this, but I couldn't continue on. I was incapable of making my bed, or making something to eat, and I was sick again.

The next morning, I got out of bed and packed my things. I needed someone to drive me to the hospital. I didn't want to ask Jack as I didn't want to ask him anything anymore. I phoned my aunt, but I couldn't get a hold of her, so I decided to call my friend Michelle. Michelle had been a friend of mine for a few years, she and her husband were amazing people and they had come out to our cabin a couple of times with their three boys. Michelle was a beautiful Japanese woman who had raised three amazing young men and her husband, Jim, was a towering successful businessman and also a good friend. I nicknamed him Jim-Bob from the beginning and he really didn't seem to care! Jim-Bob had given Morgan an incredible job a few years ago and, as a couple, they were a lot of fun to be with.

After I called Michelle, she came right away and helped me pack and get dressed. She knew that I wasn't well as I was very confused. I asked her if I could have a cup of coffee before we went, as it would be my last decent cup of coffee for a while. I could tell she was worried about me, she had never seen me this vulnerable and I was struggling with even walking. I had made an appointment to see Dr. Tanguay. I got in right away to see him and he asked me a couple of questions, called Unit 49 and then, along with Michelle's help, he escorted me to the psych ward. Once again, I was greeted by the familiar faces of the nurses, all of whom were very kind, but again the memories of that place brought tears to my eyes. I was so sad, but I felt somewhat relieved when I was taken to my room. My bag was placed on the floor and I crawled into the bed. Michelle sat on the edge, rubbed my back and asked me if I wanted her to stay, which I replied, "No, it's okay, I'll be okay."

I didn't know how I was going to be okay, but I knew I was in the right place at that time. I knew my doctor was going to help me get better, become stronger, and more independent. I also knew that I needed time alone, to organize my thoughts so they didn't become delusional, although I didn't know how I was going to be able to do that. They were racing, I didn't know how I was going to go on, I felt helpless and absolutely hopeless and so very sad. I didn't want people to know I was in here again, what a failure I was, what a loser I was. What would people think of me, I once again was crazy, but I didn't know how to prevent that from happening to me. I also had to figure out how to stop caring what people thought of me and focus on myself, and being in the moment. I remembered talking to my dad about it once, and he said to me, "People don't normally care and those who do aren't worthy of your friendship." I knew that I had to practice self-love and acceptance of myself, but that was going to be really difficult. However, if I was going to be happy again, it was very important.

I don't have any idea how long I lied there. I had a window looking out at the parkade, and I stared at it while quietly weeping. I think I was feeling sorry for myself, sorry for my kids that once again, I was putting them through this. My nurse came in and asked if I would like to go for dinner, she said it would be a good idea if I got out of bed. I thought about it and agreed that I would go out to the dining room for my evening meal. I made my way out there, found my meal and chose a table that looked like it had some nice people sitting at it.

I sat with two men, an older gentleman named Ken and a younger man named Jonas. They were both very kind and while eating, we shared why we were there. Both men were severe alcoholics, drinking up to 40 ounces a day of hard liquor. Jonas was a handsome young man, about thirty-seven, who had been a successful worker in the oil patch and had recently split with his wife, who lived with their thirteen-year-old son. A few months back, his son shot and killed his grandmother and now was facing a jail term. It had destroyed Jonas and he started drinking heavily.

Both Jonas and Ken were smokers and I could hardly wait until my doctor put me on green so that I too, could go outside to smoke. When our meal was done, I started back to my room and looked up at the patient board, and what do you know, I was on green! I had freedom and all of a sudden, my mood was boosted, I felt better. I asked my nurse for my cigarettes and went out and enjoyed the sunshine along with a smoke. It wasn't a long walk, but I was in so much pain that it was a real struggle for me. I had to hold onto the hall banisters, as there were times when I was not sure I was going to make it.

The unit seemed to have a lot of characters in it this time. There were a lot more men than women, and I started to make friends. I met Wilf, a 65-year-old gruff man who bragged about his handyman skills. That is what he did for a living, so I asked him if he would make me something, and he was more than happy to oblige. Sitting with Wilf was an older, stout little gentleman with a cute round face named Kryz. Kryz seemed a little challenged, but he was cute and he made me laugh. Wilf started to brag that he had visited a sex shop that afternoon and he was quite proud to say that he had purchased a male vibrator for himself. He went on to tell us that it needed batteries and he had purchased those also and was quite excited about his evening. Kryz was captivated by this whole conversation and inquired as to whether he could get one. Wilf told him absolutely, and then Kryz asked if they took rechargeable batteries as that would be what he would prefer so he didn't have to buy new ones all the time. Wilf said, "Yup, they do. I'll pick one up for you if you like." Kryz replied sheepishly, "No, it's okay, I have an electric razor that vibrates!" I just about died laughing.

I was totally charmed by Kryz and his doings at times. He was a very likeable, little man. The next day, he was walking in front of me with a young girl who had a beautiful braid in her hair finished off with a lovely ribbon and I commented that I liked her hair. Kryz turned around with a big smile on his face and he said,

"Thank you." Kryz was balding, so it made the whole situation even more comical.

Then there was George, a young Hutterite from a colony about a hundred miles away. He told me all about the colony and their culture, it was fascinating, and then he invited my family and me out there in the summer to have lunch with everyone. I asked when I come, what can I bring as gifts? He said for the women, chocolate and for the men, whiskey. He told me that the women didn't like when the men sat around and drank whiskey, but the men sure liked it. I laughed and thought about what an adventure that would be. I would take my kids, and my aunt Dereka and her family and my dad—they would all love it as it would be quite the experience going to a Hutterite colony, where they are known to all eat together in a dining hall and the women have reputations of being great cooks. I will take them all gifts and do up candy bags for the children. I got excited just thinking about it.

Clarice was a stunning young woman, about twenty years old, and the men couldn't keep their eyes off of her, and their gazes followed her as she walked. Clarice played the cello beautifully and would often perform for everyone. Clarice had a crush on a couple of the young men that were in there and was quite flirty with them.

I slept well that night; it's amazing what drugs can do. I got up the next morning and was able to shower and dress myself before heading down for breakfast. I always had oatmeal and looked forward to it. This morning I sat with a new young man, Nathan. Nathan had been in the unit for quite some time and was very familiar with all the patients. He seemed to be friends with everyone, including the nurses. Nathan looked to be in his late twenties, an animated skinny young man whom I took an immediate liking to. I was telling him how I would love to have a good cup of coffee to enjoy with my cigarette, but I could barely walk the halls and there was no way that I could get down to the coffee shop as it was just too far. He said that we would fix that, no problem, and after breakfast, he told me to follow him. We got to the locked doors, and he instructed me to wait there. Before I knew it, he had brought a wheelchair back. I sat down in the wheelchair and there was no place to put my feet, so he instructed me to lift them up and HANG ON!

Oh my god! He ran as fast as he could down the hallway, and took a right, I just about fell out, and he continued to race down towards the coffee shop. I couldn't help but laugh, I hadn't laughed like that in years, it felt so good and I'm not going to lie, it was fun! We entered the gift shop; apparently, they sell coffee there, and Nathan explained that the coffee shop's coffee was over four dollars a cup, whereas the gift shop coffee was only $1.85 a cup. It was a Keurig coffee maker and he proceeded to go through the flavors, asking me what kind I wanted, and I told him just a dark roast would be good, and he said he was going to try a different kind. He took a sip, but remarked that he didn't care for it, and poured it down the sink. I was shocked, I said to Nathan, "You have to pay for that." He replied, "No, you don't, they expect people to do that. I do it all the time."

He then said, "Here, I'll push you over here where you can look at all the pretty stuffed animals, and I will go pay for the coffees." I gave him $20.00 and told him that I would pay for his also. I sat there waiting for him and when he returned, he said, "I'm gonna keep the change because I might need to buy something later." I felt sorry for him, so I didn't argue. He told me to hang on and went to the far end where there were pocket-sized stuffed animals and proceeded to pick one out and put it in his pocket. I was dumbfounded, I couldn't believe it. Nathan gave me the coffee and proceeded to wheel me out of the gift shop, outside to the smoking area. I scanned the area and asked Nathan to stop at a couple of chairs that overlooked the reservoir and he proceeded to tell me that he was Jesus, the son of God, and he could do great things. He had a brilliant mind. For instance, Unit 45 was the less desirable psych unit in the hospital. 11+34=45. 1134 upside down spelled "hell." That was Unit 45.

We sat on the bench for a while, and soon enough Nathan spied a woman and yelled out, "Deb, I got an angel for you!" He pulled out the little bear that he stole and ran over to give it to her.

When he returned, I said "Nathan, stealing is bad, you can't steal, that's wrong." All of a sudden, Nathan turned and started yelling at me at the top of his lungs, "It's not wrong, if you are hungry, it's okay to steal a loaf of bread to eat, if your friend needs an angel, it's okay to take something that will make her happy. God says so. The bible says so."

All of a sudden, the woman he gave the bear to, came over and she and Nathan got into a shouting match. Debra was screaming at Nathan to stop yelling at me and Nathan was screaming back. A small crowd had developed and I turned and was trying to maneuver my wheelchair back to the hospital. Tears started streaming down my face and I looked up and saw a couple of my nurses coming out to save me. One grabbed the back of my wheelchair, and the other went over to Nathan and Debra to see what was happening. I experienced a lot of different emotions in that short time: euphoria, disbelief, despair and sadness.

My nurse saw me to my room and suggested that I crawl into bed. I was happy to do so. I felt mentally exhausted and sad. I hated this place, but I knew I had to be here. I needed support, I needed help and it was not fair of me to count on my kids for that. Morgan had moved eight hours away, Zach was stressed out in university, Brooklyn had her own young family, and Jack Michael was 16, not prepared yet to deal with his Mom's illness.

I haven't been there to pick up the pieces, my kids have had to, they are young people, and that is a lot of responsibility on them.

It is very hard to try and explain to your kids and family what you are going through. Not only for me but for lots of people who suffer from mental illness. It is a dark, debilitating disease that is not picky about who it attacks, including impoverished people, blessed people, rich people, and people who have lots of families to support them. But for the most part, a lot of people are in there for the fifth and sixth time and have no family who supports them anymore. This is what mental illness does, it breaks down families and destroys them. My heart goes out to those friends of mine who have no one. Maybe at one time they did, but no more. Mental illness is a disease that is misunderstood many times, it's a disease that a lot of people have no control over, it's a disease that causes agony, stress and distress amongst its victims, but it also causes that for the family members who are trying to support their loved one. Sometimes to the point that they can't do it anymore and they give up when their loved one needs them the most.

I know this for a fact because I lost some of my family: my brothers, my uncles, my aunts, cousins and my husband. I am thankful that I haven't lost my kids—maybe they have lost respect for me, but they have stood by me through thick and thin and I know it has been hell for them. It has probably been harder on them than on me. They have become the caregivers, and that's not fair. Can you imagine having to live with the thought that your mother is mentally ill and might never be the same? That is what they live with every day and I do wish that I could turn back time when things were different and I was not labeled mentally ill or crazy.

Russell, a retired dentist who seemed like a decent guy, was the new guy in the unit. I was excited to get to know him as I always liked making new friends. After meeting him, I discovered he wasn't married and I immediately started thinking about which of my friends I could introduce him to. He was suffering from depression, which is another very tough mental illness and probably the most common among us. Russell had moved out here to be with his brother so he could ski. He was an expert downhill skier, which he mentioned often. But he was a likeable guy and had become good friends with Ian, a younger, shorter man whom I immediately liked.

Neither Russell nor Ian smoked, so we didn't have that in common. One day I went out to have a cigarette with other friends, Sid, Shayla, and Keegan. I was becoming quite close with the latter two but didn't know much about Sid. On the way back in from the cold, Sid asked to hold my hand, I thought to myself, "What the hell?" and then took his hand in mine. It felt weird and then he said that it felt nice to hold a woman's hand. I was kind of freaking out inside and, thank goodness, was able to let go when I got to the locked doors. Upon returning to the unit, I told Ian and Russell what had happened and Ian promised me that he would go out with me from now on when I needed a cigarette. I was grateful to him for that. By this time, though, I was starting to harbor a secret crush on Russell. We were close to the same age, I knew he didn't have a lot of money, but I didn't care about that. I knew I couldn't ski with him, but I'm sure he didn't care about that.

One day, I was on my way out for a cigarette by myself and I didn't see Ian around, so I asked Russell if he wanted to join me, and he said he did. I was embarrassed to smoke in front of him, but I didn't care, we were going out together and it felt good. I hadn't felt that good in a long time. I was excited to be in the unit and I was finding that I really didn't want to go home and have to face what was there. No income was coming in, savings were depleting, and having to deal with Jack and his moodiness. I knew I would get through it, however, and I had to remain strong for my kids.

One day I was lucky when my friends from the church surprised me, and what a wonderful surprise it was. We went to the chapel and they prayed for me. I go there often to pray because I feel so alone and I am hoping that God can help me get better. I beg him, I always thank him for my blessings and then I tell him that I don't want to be crazy anymore. I know people make fun of me, they avoid me, my kids are embarrassed by me, that I might do something crazy. It's so hard to be in here, but after I go to the chapel, I somehow feel better that God listened to me because he's the only hope I have. I don't know how to pray properly and I feel bad that I don't pray when things are good, I forget to. But there are days when I feel so alone and desperate that I reach out to God to help me. My psychiatrist tells me to practice mindfulness and I try, but I just can't concentrate. My mind wanders and I try very hard to bring it back to the moment and I just can't.

Unit 45 proved to be a little exciting at times, including the time that Clarice was offering up blow jobs in her washroom. As far as I know, only two of the men took her up on that, and they were walking around all day with the biggest smiles on their faces.

I loved everyone on the unit and we decided that in the summer, we were all going to rent motorhomes and take a caravan across Canada. We tried to recruit some of the nurses to go with us, but they just laughed at us. We were going to show them, though, and really make this happen.

Then there was the time that we got a young man named Luke in the unit who played the guitar and sang amazingly. He was quite the character and the young women on the unit thought he was very easy on the eyes. He always wore an Indiana Jones–type hat and had his pant cuffs rolled up to reveal that he was wearing flip-flops. His style was very infectious and I liked him immediately.

Ian was off on a pass one weekend, and Luke went missing in action. When they were picked up at a local stripper bar a couple of days later, Ian shared that they had quite the adventure and Luke had the entire bar hopping!

It was a sad day when my friends Jonas and Ken left. The three of us had often gone out for a cigarette together and they were both being transferred to the addiction side of a Long-Term Alcohol Treatment Centre. I came out to say goodbye and saw that all Ken had was a white plastic bag to pack his measly clothes in it. I told him to wait, that I would be right back, and came back with my beloved leather duffle bag that someone had given me. I told Ken to put his clothes in that. If nothing else, Ken could now go to the treatment center with a bit of dignity.

After they left, I was sitting there commiserating with Kryz, who had also become close to them and seemed very sad to see them go. I mentioned to Kryz that once we were out of there, I would pick him up and the two of us could go and visit them. Kryz asked if he could drive my car, and I said, "Sure, you can drive." He then looked at me and said, "That's great because I don't like people driving me. But one problem, I don't know how to drive." I wasn't sure what to make of that, so I just said, "We will figure it out, Kryz."

While I was in the hospital, I spoke to Jack daily, begging him to shut the company down as it was losing money daily. With the help of a lawyer that I had found, he finally agreed to it. When I realized that our company was done, it was nothing short of heartbreaking. My stomach was in knots for days, and the grief that I experienced at the loss of it was enormous.

It was also made clear to me by my psychiatrist that I would not be able to go home while Jack was still there, so Jack had to find a new place to live. I felt so relieved that I wouldn't have to put up with his moodiness anymore.

One day out of the blue, I got a phone call from Jack Michael. He said he had been in an accident the night before, had rolled his truck and it was totaled. I was just thankful that he was okay and not hurt, but I know he was devastated about the truck. The next afternoon, I received a call from Zach, stating that Jack had slept over at Tammy's the night before and, in the middle of the night, Bodie and a friend of his had stolen Jack's truck and they were the ones who rolled it. Jack had been sleeping when they took it for a joy ride; neither of them had their licenses. Tammy had woken Jack up and told him that if he didn't lie to the police and tell them that he was driving, that the insurance would not cover it and he would lose everything. So that is what Jack did. But then he thought better of it at school and met with his guidance counselor and the principal and told them the truth. They, in turn, called in Zach and the police and Tammy was confronted. She continued to lie about it, but eventually, the truth came out, although to this day, it is still uncertain as to who was actually driving.

I couldn't believe that Tammy would be so bold as to blatantly lie to the police and I was sure that Jack wouldn't want to have anything to do with her anymore after putting our son through that. I was wrong, and at that moment, I decided that they deserved each other.

Eventually, I got to go home from Unit 45. I knew I couldn't go back there, but unless I did something about my situation, I knew it was inevitable. My speech was bad again, and I was stuttering quite often. I tried to use the techniques that I learned in the hospital, but I struggled with every one of them.

It was a lot nicer at home without Jack there, that was for sure. The kids were more relaxed and I found that I was too.

I visited my friends to tell them about our breakup and I also told them that I wasn't going to ever ask them to take sides as that wasn't fair to them. Secretly, I was hoping that they would still be my friends and most of them were, but I knew deep down inside, that it would never be the same. It would be awkward, and I also knew that Jack needed friends now too.

I found myself desperate for friends, so I boldly asked a woman who I had only met once if she wanted to be my friend through Facebook Messenger. I had made her a friend on Facebook, as she had been through a lot and she didn't respond, she actually stopped being my friend on Facebook. That was a real blow, I thought she was downright cruel. She was friends with Tammy, so I figured that was where her loyalties lay. My self-esteem had never been lower, so low that I was finding myself wanting to go back to the hospital.

Over the next couple of months, I watched Jack close the company down. I didn't have the mental or physical energy to help him, so he was on his own. He was lucky that his brother came to help, which I was grateful for. I felt guilty as hell not helping him, but I knew I would break down emotionally to watch the demise of our efforts of twenty-seven years finally die. It was a lot, it was heartbreaking, but we had some savings left after we paid off the loans and debts, yet it wasn't enough for us to retire.

I hadn't been up to see my dad for some time, so I made plans to spend a couple of days with him. I arrived one afternoon and he seemed rather grumpy. We started having a conversation about my mental illness, and I really don't know what happened, all I remember was I was in my car heading back to Calgary to go to the hospital. I knew that I wasn't well, I just wanted to be back in the hospital, where I would be safe and I didn't have to worry about things. I arrived at the hospital, saying that I was suicidal. I really wasn't, I was just tired, I was scared, I was alone and I wanted the safety of the hospital once again.

Unfortunately, they took me to the new hospital, South Health Campus, where I soon settled in. I was excited to meet two wonderful women there, Lori and Kathi, whom I immediately became fast friends with. Lori was a beautiful blond woman, who worshipped the lord, and had a husband who worshipped her. Kathi was just as attractive and also was blessed with a loving husband. I was Lori's roommate and I soon found out that we were going to be getting Electric Shock Treatments (ECT) to our brains. It was a standard procedure for patients suffering from depression, but I was still scared as hell as it could affect your short-term memory. The way I looked at it, though, if it could help me, regardless of how scared I was, I was willing to try it. I was upset because the walk to the smoking area was too far for me to make it without pain in my back, so I gave up smoking for the time being.

Lori and I became best friends and shared so much with each other. She was the proud mother of three children and her husband used to be a Pastor. I cherished her and our friendship.

Two months passed quickly and once again, I was on my way home. I was going to make it this time. I could do it, regardless of the stress, and I was determined. This time it was going to be different, I told myself. I couldn't do this to my kids anymore, I had to get well, I had to stabilize myself. I struggled to understand why this kept happening to me.

I thought I was doing well, however, when I am ill, I think I am doing okay. If I am hallucinating, I think everyone sees the same things and I am quite normal. I don't appear to be ill. I honestly don't remember the next month or what I was doing, but all of a sudden, one day in November, Jack Michael came running into my bedroom and said, "You have to pack now, I am taking you back to the hospital." I was dumbfounded, I didn't know why I was going, but I didn't argue and went with him.

Unit 49. I don't remember a lot about arriving there, however, I do vaguely remember discovering that Russell was in this unit and being very excited—so excited, in fact, that as soon as he was alone in his room, I brazenly walked in. He was resting on his bed. I walked over and planted a great big kiss right on his lips. He quickly brushed it off and jumped up, exclaiming, "What the hell?" I was so embarrassed, mortified, to say the least, having read his feelings for me totally wrong. He never spoke to me the entire two months that I was in there and I wasn't a part of the "group," which hurt like hell. I wanted to play cards, go out with them, but I was totally ostracized by the group.

He hung out with a great big guy whose name totally escapes me, but I quite liked him. He was like a big teddy bear that I wanted to get to know better as a friend. He also hung out with a young woman, Sarah, also a dentist whom I became quite good friends with outside of the hospital. The only other memory that I have is the numerous ECT treatments that I had to have and the fact that this was a very different stay in the hospital as I made no new friends. That's my number one priority: to make friends, to make the stay bearable. I scope out the group, trying to find people that look nice and friendly and then I move in. But this time, it didn't work out for me and it was a horrible stay in Unit 45. That's all I've got from Unit 45, another chapter done and one that I wish was forgotten.

I was released on December 21st that year and Jack Michael and I decided to go to Brooklyn's and spend Christmas with her and her family. I was quite looking forward to it, and I would write about it if I could, however, the only thing that I remember about that Christmas is sitting on the island eating Christmas dinner. I have racked my brain to see if I could come up with something else, but I have nothing and I find that distressing. Your life is made up of memories, good and bad, and I know that the ones I would have made that Christmas would have been good so I feel like this illness has once again robbed me of something I could have cherished forever.

Chapter Eighteen

The next few months were some of the most stressful months that I have ever gone through. A friend of mine introduced me to a man who had a great investment opportunity. He was going to export equipment from Canada to Malaysia, where they had supply problems. It would take a few months to get there and we would triple our money. My friend, who was a very successful businesswoman, kept assuring me that this was a legit deal and at the presentation, there were many successful businessmen there, so I thought this was a great opportunity for Jack and me. I initially gave him one hundred and fifty thousand dollars. What happened next was not expected, he needed more money for unforeseen circumstances, it seemed like the list was endless and so was the money that I had to give him. He kept telling us that if we didn't give him the additional monies, our entire investment would be lost. I was given promissory notes in return, thinking that would protect my investment. He then needed more money, as the investors he thought he had didn't come through. Once again, he said we would lose our money if we didn't pony up, so I had no choice but to give him more.

I was devastated and totally sick to my stomach. I was taking money against our line of credit and then Jack finally had enough and told me to stop. I was throwing good money after bad and I had no idea when I was going to get my money back. The shipment finally arrived in Malaysia and then we were hit with tariff fees. We had to pay if we wanted our money back, otherwise, the equipment would just sit there and get rusty, which would deem it no good.

Besides the stress of this, I had to mentally prepare for my upcoming hip replacement. I was so nervous about it, but was looking forward to not having any pain there anymore. My cousin Shirl told me that she was going to come and take care of me. I couldn't believe it, how was I going to repay her for something like that? I was excited about not having to use a walker, but still, I worried about my knees and my other hip.

The stress of the money continued to increase, the most stressful part was Jack kept asking me where our return was. I tried to explain it to him, but I didn't know what to say, all I had were the promissory notes that apparently were no good. I was devastated and stressed to the max and I knew that Jack would never forgive me. Jack was still grieving his business and he seemed to think that he was worthless without money, yet if he was careful, he would still have enough to retire. But he wasn't careful and bought himself a luxury truck.

The hip replacement went off without a hitch. Dr. Tanguay came and saw me again in the hospital and I felt honored that he was there. It had been a year since I last saw him. Usually, they keep you in the hospital for a couple of days, but for some reason, they kept me in for a week.

When I came home, it was heavenly having Shirl there. She cooked and tidied up and the boys enjoyed her homestyle cooking. She was an excellent cook and also an excellent caregiver. I still tried to think of ways that I could repay her, although I knew she wouldn't want anything in return. She was such a kind and giving person, I was very lucky to have her in my life and more than anything, I wanted to show her that.

. . .

The stress of the money I lost was mounting and I had to consider cashing in some of my Retirement funds to see if I could get my money back, and before I knew it, I was into this venture for more than a million dollars. I continued to correspond with the man whom I had invested with and then he stopped corresponding all together. Did he scam me, or was he embarrassed and under so much stress himself that he couldn't do it anymore?

Jack hated me now, and that hurt. I didn't love him anymore, I had forgiven him, yet I would never forget what he did to me. However, he thought this was worse. That is how much emphasis he put on money. I agreed life would be so much simpler had he forgiven me and let it go, but I knew that he never would be able to. At that point, I vowed to pay him back every penny when I could. I didn't know how I was going to do it, but I was determined that it was going to happen.

My kids were amazing, however, and stood by my side without judgement. I was so very lucky to have them as they were incredibly understanding. They all said, it's only money, Mom, it could be so much worse. That made me feel better, but the sleepless nights and the gnawing in my stomach never went away.

My hip healed well, and it was so nice not to have that pain anymore, yet my other hip was really bothering me and my knees were all eventually going to need to be replaced. I was also experiencing major pain in my back when I walked or stood for more than about eight minutes. I could get relief if I sat down, but going shopping, cooking, cleaning the house, and walking were out of the question. Oh, I could still cook, but I would just have to sit down every few minutes and hope that dinner wouldn't burn. I finally decided to get a wheelchair, so I could do things if someone would agree to push me. I have only ventured out a handful of times in the wheelchair, however, as I hate it. I hate people staring, I feel sorry for the person pushing me because I am so heavy. But it was nice to be able to go with my friends and family to some Christmas Markets and out for walks along the river.

A girlfriend of mine had introduced me to a new doctor who

was a pain specialist. He specialized in injections and I started seeing him about three times a week, hoping that it would help. Unfortunately, it didn't, but I continued to go see him. He was an incredible doctor, very kind and caring and I was grateful to my friend for setting me up with him. I also started seeing a physiotherapist, a massage therapist, doing Prolotherapy by a Naturopath and more. The costs of my medical bills were overwhelming, as was the cost of the medication I was on. It just added to my stress level.

Then the pandemic hit, and everything changed for everyone. It was so hard to believe that the entire world was affected by something so horrible. People were dying, losing their jobs, their livelihoods, kids no longer had to go to school, it was devastating to see what was happening around us and it affected me deeply. I was trying to be very careful and stay home as much as I possibly could, as I really didn't want to get that virus. I was also conscious of counting my blessings as there were so many people in distress because of it.

I got an alarming call from Brooklyn one day, and she told me that her father, Gord, had died of a fentanyl overdose. I felt nothing when I heard the news, except for feeling sorry for his latest wife or relief, depending on how he treated her. Brooklyn was going to get his truck, which was nice for her and I was happy for her in that respect, but I also felt bad as she was struggling with the fact that her father had died of a drug overdose. Apparently, he never cleaned up his act. Brooklyn came out later and we went to visit his wife. It did come out that she too was beaten, actually thrown down the stairs with her mouth duct-taped. I knew what she had gone through and we bonded because of that. She was a Filipino woman, younger than Brooklyn, and she was very sweet. She didn't deserve what he did to her either. I planned to keep in touch with her as I felt sorry for her and it would be my honor to be her friend.

I value my friendships, I used to work hard at them, but after I got sick, I struggled to do so, I don't have the mental energy anymore. I'm embarrassed and humiliated by things I have done, I have no filters or boundaries when I am ill and I have lost some incredible friends and family members whom I miss very much. I don't blame them for not wanting to associate with me anymore. I'm okay with that, I accept it and just have to move on without them, but to say that I don't miss them would be a lie. It's a sad reality of what this illness does to people, where friendships are often on the line. When you are trying to get well, and you discuss your illness with friends, you are not looking for sympathy, you're past that, you are looking for empathy, but it's difficult for them to offer that because they don't understand. They don't understand what it's like to go through this hell, and believe me, they don't want to. To have to experience it again and again, is disturbing and upsetting and maybe they are a little bit scared. That is why my friends from the hospital are so important because they know, they understand and they are easy to talk to about it. The truth about this illness is that it is life-altering, your personality changes, you can even suffer from PTSD because of it. It's a sad reality, but it is the truth and I can't begin to tell you how much it hurts.

Chapter Nineteen

I t was a chilly but sunny morning. I loved mornings now, I was so excited about getting started with my day. It had been a rough couple of weeks, I felt myself showing signs of psychosis and I had made my Psychiatrist aware of them, which we were monitoring closely. I was experiencing forgetfulness, I would go to a cupboard for tea and forget what I went for, forget to brush my teeth, and showering was a daunting task if I remembered to shower at all. I wasn't sleeping well, I was having a hard time concentrating or carrying on a decent conversation, and I was somewhat scatterbrained. I would start a task and move on to two more before I finished anything. The biggest issue was that paranoia was setting in—I was worried about so many things and no matter how hard I tried, I couldn't refocus to stop worrying.

I think I was taking on too much. I was working on a photo book for my dad that had more than a thousand photos in it, and it was hard seeing all those photos of my mom. I saw photos of my brothers when we were a family and photos of family gatherings that I couldn't go to because I was too ill or because I didn't get invited. It would be nine years since my mom left us and I missed her more than ever. If I could just have one more conversation with her, I would be over the moon. I could tell her about what I was going through and she wouldn't judge me and she would call every day to make sure I was okay. I needed that so much.

In my dad's book, I also made a special page spread for my cousin John, as I had many photos of him and I wanted my dad to have a tribute to him. There was one particular one of John and my mom on the Seadoo that I always loved. As always, creating the book was a very emotional experience, and these flashbacks added another dimension to it, but I loved doing it, I just hoped that my dad would like it.

Besides the scrapbook, I was working on a new project. I was setting up an e-commerce store selling various trending products and it was a lot of fun to figure out what to buy. I had to put my other idea of a clothing business on hold until we got this other store up and running. I was still channeling ideas for it and I made sure I wrote every one of them down, as this was a passion that I was not going to forget about and I really wanted to make it happen.

My memoirs had been coming along well, and I was nearing the end. I was thinking long and hard about how I was going to end it. I was getting to some stuff where my memory had failed me, but then things slowly started to come back and the flashbacks were coming on strong. For some reason, I often went back to that bench where I sat with my dad the very first time I was in the hospital and the only time that he came to visit me. I kept seeing that bench and our conversation and then, all of a sudden, a flashback that I chose to forget long ago returned. I remember that I was molested by a family friend when I was four years old. He was about 16 or 17, it was very scary, very painful, and I would often dream about that time. It probably explained a lot of my problems. I just wish it would go away, but even though I was little, I will never forget it, how I didn't understand why, and how I knew I could never tell anyone. It's funny how something so terrifying sticks with you, how it's hard to deal with, hard to forget. I actually brought it up to my psychiatrist during our next visit and he wanted to talk about it, however I did not.

Even though I was experiencing some flashbacks that I didn't want to remember, I was having some really good days. I didn't remember a recent time when I had been so happy, even though the pandemic was happening and we weren't allowed to socialize at Christmas, Brooklyn was still planning on coming out. She was going through a rough time, I was struggling and I talked to a few people about it, knowing that a gathering was wrong, and my good friend Dean remarked, "Leianne, here is Covid, lowering his hand to his waist and here is family, raising his hand to his shoulder. What you have to understand is Family trumps Covid and you need to do what is right for your family." I had to agree with him, as it would do no good to have two of us in the hospital over this. The kids had to come out and pick up Gord's truck, and my grandkids were really excited about coming for Christmas. They were struggling with the decision to come also, knowing that we would be breaking the pandemic travel rules, but after many back and forths, they decided to come. Because they were so isolated, there were very few cases where they lived and they decided that the only reason they would stop while travelling would be for gas.

I was over the moon with the excitement of their arrival and being able to work again, however, I was aware that I wasn't doing well, physically or mentally. I was very forgetful, scatterbrained, slightly paranoid, would not eat, and struggled with sleep, all signs of pending psychosis.

When Brooklyn and her family came to visit, it was all a blur. Christmas was a blur, I remember bits and pieces but very little. The only thing I remember about Christmas dinner is Zach and Brooklyn carving the turkey and us cheering with our Santa cups. I couldn't function, I couldn't sit at the table with my grandchildren and do a craft, I was totally incapable. I had confessed to my Psychiatrist that I had been taking HEMP gummies for a couple of weeks now to help with the pain in my knees, back and hip. I hate complaining about that because I know it's my own damn fault. If I wasn't so overweight and exercised more, I wouldn't have this problem, I hate that I am in this condition. I had been told to stay away from marijuana-related products as it can cause psychotic episodes, but it was working, the pain was a lot more tolerable and I could get comfortable enough to sleep. It was so liberating not to be in so much pain. I told my dad that the HEMP gummies were helping and he sent me a bunch more, so I was taking them four at a time and found that they were helping a lot. I was able to sleep with very less pain, but I was so tired and I slept a lot. I knew I was in trouble as I was very scatterbrained, I would go to the cupboard and forget why I was there, I would start to make my bed, go look for my toothbrush, go into my closet and not know why I was there. I was eating very little, which I wish was my personality, but it's not.

Then on Christmas Eve, things started to go strange, I dropped Brooklyn off at her stepmother's so she could pick up her truck, and then I was to go to my friend Ian's to drop off some butter tarts for him. My GPS started taking me in a different direction and it was sending me weird messages. I finally got turned around and was heading in the right direction, but the GPS was sending weird messages like, "Go to the airport." It continued to show me funny little messages, which I don't recall, and then I figured it out, it was trying to figure out how crazy I was at that moment. It was sending me messages that I didn't understand or comprehend why it was talking to me like that.

I finally made it to Ian's, and I saw him only for a minute and then I was supposed to go pick up Brooklyn at Zach's place of work. I was going to be driving by our old office space, so I decided to stop just to say goodbye one last time. It was sad to be there, and I sat there for a few minutes, reflecting on the thousands of times I entered those doors to do a job that I loved. How every time someone entered the door, a little bell would ring. I remembered how Jack would always say, "Just me," and then usually come into my office to see how I was, how Kerry would always come in and make sure he greeted everyone before he started his day. Then there was the time that one of our employees accidentally let our new puppy out that we brought to work every day and he was run over. How our office manager, Rita, was such a great employee and I was so grateful to have her. That door held a lot of memories, but now they are gone, our business where we worked so hard was done. It was time to move on. The tears were rolling down my cheeks, remembering all those times and how painful it was to let that business go. That business was our livelihood, our future, our passion. I grieved the loss of it, but not half as much as Jack grieved it. I know, even though it was just about three years, he was still in pain. I felt so sorry for him.

I picked up Brooklyn at the dealership where Zach works, she had to drop her truck off there, and then we went to Costco so we could get some booze for Christmas. While at Costco, Zach showed up at my car, demanding to know what the hell I was doing there. I figured he had some sort of GPS on my car and was tracking me when he said, "What were you doing at the shop?" It was freaking me out, but I thought it was for my own safety and that they were trying to figure out how crazy I was.

Brooklyn got back in the car and we had one more stop at friends to give them some butter tarts and a Christmas ornament that I got for them.

When we got home, Brooklyn insisted that I go and lie down and I have no recollection of what happened the rest of the day or night, although I know it was important I get to church, as tomorrow was the anniversary of my mom's death. It's a very unsettling and sad feeling. Church didn't happen, probably because it was online, and I slept most of the rest of the day. I did get up for dinner and then I asked Brooklyn if she would put the boys' Christmas stockings together and she said she would and I just went to bed.

The next morning, Kaitlin was one of the first up, it was Christmas morning, and again I remember picking what chair to sit in. It was stocking time, everyone got a stocking and I did too. Brooklyn gave me a stocking that she and her siblings had put together. I hadn't gotten a stocking in a long time and to say I was excited would be an understatement. I was admiring each item in my stocking and then I came across some body wash, Vitabath, and I started to cry. Brooklyn asked me what the matter was and I told her that Vitabath was my mom's favorite and you could only get it from Avon. I had looked for it for years but have never been able to find it. Brooklyn said she found it at Shoppers in the small town that she lives in. I asked her what made her buy it out of the hundred or so body washes available and she said she had no idea and, even though I was shocked I remembered this particular body wash, I felt that it was a sign from my mom that she was going to be with me on this particular journey.

Brooklyn was handing out gifts and I remember the kids opening up a few, but not really. In our house, we open each gift separately so everyone can see what you got and ooh and ahh over it, and it takes forever, but I love it. I remember Jack opening up his Kobe Bryant Jersey and Zach opening his drill, and my grandson Tyler opening up his used iPhone that I had packaged up so nicely, yet he commented that he didn't need a phone, he was still too young, and I was so disappointed in his reaction. But I guess that's Tyler and that's okay.

After breakfast, I think everyone went skating on the pond out back, and I once again retired to bed. I was thinking to myself, I had better get a grip or I am going to end up in the hospital and this time, it might be long-term. Oh my god, I can't do long-term, I just can't.

Brooklyn could see I was upset and offered me my lottery tickets to scratch, so I did and it was weird, I could see the answers, I knew I was going to win, this was a plant, this was going to save me. I was going to win a million dollars, the money that I had lost, it was going to be okay. I would have to give some to Jack, but even so, seven hundred thousand was still a lot of money. I was very excited and kept scratching, but it apparently was going to be at the end of the tickets when I won, so I decided to let Jack Michael scratch the rest, as he likes to do that and he could acknowledge the win and get excited, so I put them away for later.

The rest of that day was totally lost to me. Once again, I had planned to make this Christmas so special, yet it was just another day that I had very little memory of.

The next couple of days and nights were a total blur again I have nothing... literally nothing about what we did, what we ate, games we played, conversations we had... nothing. Those particular Christmas memories are completely blank and I find that very upsetting. Later on Brooklyn told me that I woke up Boxing Day morning, came out to the living room and started to cry because someone had stolen all the Christmas gifts. I don't remember that at all and hopefully my grandchildren weren't around to witness it.

I know that Brooklyn and Brad left for home the next day and I said goodbye, but that's about it. I remember being very sad they had to leave and wishing they could have stayed a few days longer and also feeling depressed and guilty that I wasn't there for them and I didn't spend any time with them. I love when they come to visit and I just felt like I had let everyone down.

The morning they left, I was browsing through Facebook, which is usually what I do, and the first thing that popped up on my feed was a photo of my cousin John, who had passed away six years ago. At first, it shocked me, and as I started to look through, there were more pictures of him taken recently. Then there were messages popping up that said John was alive! I didn't know that God was listening to me, but I think a miracle happened, I don't know how this happened, but I think John is alive. I know he is, and then there was a picture of him and his beautiful wife, Terry, that kept popping up on my Facebook feed all the time.

I couldn't believe it, I started scrolling through and was in shock. I started to cry uncontrollably, I couldn't believe that after six years, John was actually alive, yes, John was alive. I was trying to process it, and I struggled with so many emotions. My aunt probably knew, and I was thrilled that she didn't have to be sad anymore, I was thrilled for his siblings, his dad and especially his beautiful wife. They were going to have the life that they deserved and wanted. I couldn't understand it, though. Throughout the day, I cried, sobbed at times, and then I finally called Brooklyn and told her that John was alive, I saw his photo, it was true, Brooklyn, it was a miracle. Then I asked her quietly if my mom was alive, please let it be so, but she told me no, and I started to cry again. I asked her if her dad and Tammy really had an affair, and she replied, "Yes," and I was relieved about that.

I knew that she realized that I had finally figured it out. This was a test for the sake of mental health. They had used me, as a guinea pig to see how my mind would react to trauma and tragedy. I had been tested for quite some time and I knew it was for research. The test set a precedent, the first time such a test was conducted. Wow, and on a global scale. But then I thought it was quite cruel to test me like that, and I struggled to understand it. I knew that if something came out of it, some good, some insight into the brain, helping sick people before they did something tragic, then I was okay with it. Every time I thought about John, I would cry, I saw a picture of his headstone and cried again in anticipation of when I would finally get to meet him. I was so excited that I could hardly contain myself. And, to think his family wouldn't have to grieve anymore, that was all the affirmation I needed.

I don't recall anything that was said or done for the rest of the day and night, I just remember waking up on the 29th, pouring myself a coffee and just being excited to see John—and then it happened, I knew everything I was thinking was true. All of a sudden, something was triggered inside me, and yet, I don't know what. I started to sob again, and it was uncontrollable. I said to myself, enough of this fucking shit, I am going to put an end to this once and for all. Something big was happening, something really, really, big. I poured my coffee into a cup for the car, went in and packed a bag, grabbed my coat and off I went in my car, wearing pajamas, hair uncombed, face not washed, no makeup—destination airport.

I had figured out in my mind that this façade was coming to an end, and before I started my life's work of helping people understand mental illness, Oprah had come to Calgary in her private plane and had gathered up my entire family and friends to take us on a vacation.

I could not stop sobbing because I was so excited to see John. Then I wasn't sure who would be there with their private plane, would it be Oprah? Or would it be some other billionaire mogul? Oh, wow, I was very excited when I got to the airport. I wasn't sure if I should drive around and find where the private planes were or go through Canflight? I decided to go through Canflight, they would know what I needed and where I was supposed to go. I struggled with where to park and then I thought, I'm going to be important, I can just leave my car here. Just then, it hit me again, if John's not dead, maybe my mom's really alive? Oh my god? Could it be, could she really be alive? Even though Brooklyn said she wasn't, I believed in miracles now and she might be waiting on the plane to surprise me. I was crying quite hysterically now and had to calm myself down before I went to the airport and made a fool of myself.

I started to realize how big this was—and then it hit me, this was the pandemic, oh my god, not Coronavirus, the pandemic was mental illness. Wow, this was big, this was really big. I struggled to believe that the entire world staged the pandemic in support of mental health. We're talking about a City of Calgary Citizen of the Year award—oh my God, what should I say, how should I react? I would need a speech, Robert could help me write a speech. The whole airport was pretty much shut down— just for me. Once again, I started sobbing and couldn't stop. Sure, there were a few actors milling about, but for the most part, it was just me. I couldn't get a grasp on it, how big this really was... that this might actually make a difference... that many lives could be saved. I knew that my friend Robert did it, he's the one that should get the credit as when I was in the hospital once, he approached my psychiatrist and said, hey, let's do something here, I know some influential people, let's put our heads together and see what we can do. And, boy, did they do something, I didn't have anything to do with it, except maybe be the poster girl for mental illness. This was very exciting, so much so that I was having a hard time breathing.

I was in awe, I didn't know what to do next? Two security

guards approached me. Aha, so this is how they are going to do it. I wondered where Oprah was? I wondered where Robert was? They will probably come out and guide me to the plane, where my whole family will be waiting to go to Mexico. They'll all have margaritas and tacos on the plane. Everyone will be there, green, red and white balloons will pave the way to the plane, along with Mexican dancers, a mariachi band, and maracas. Oh shit, I didn't pack for Mexico, what am I going to do? I packed for the hospital, why did I pack for the hospital? It's weird, my pain is gone, I can walk now, another miracle, no more pain. Thank you, God!

The security guards sat me down and asked me my name. I was shocked, wouldn't everyone know my name now? Like the Queen, Queen Elizabeth would know my name, I was about to get some sort of honor from her, and a Nobel prize, I would get that too. I should start planning my speech...

Wow, when I think of what people sacrificed, closing down their businesses, losing their jobs, just for mental illness, but I didn't understand it, I didn't get it, I was confused. Maybe not only Oprah, but a lot of billionaires are in on this: Warren Buffet, Bill Gates, Elon Musk, Jeff Bezos, all of them. Probably everyone in their life, one time or another, has been affected by this terrible disease, now we were all going to stand up and put some money behind it to see if we could get some insight into how the brain works. To see if we could prevent some of the horrible things that happen when you are stricken with this disease.

The security guard asked my name again, and I told them, then when they asked what I was doing at the airport, I calmly said, "I'm looking for my friend, Robert, you know Robert, the guy that does all the commercials for Canjet?" They asked, "Why do you need Robert?" And I replied very quietly, "Because Oprah's plane is waiting for me, my family is all waiting for me on that plane and I think she is taking us to Mexico." I said this with a big smile under my mask. One of the security guards left and the other sat there and we talked, we talked about who was going to be on the plane, why her plane was there, everything. Around a half an hour later, Zach showed up, what a surprise, I thought he would be on the plane by now, but no, he was here... to take me to the hospital. I slowly accompanied him back to my car and noticed Jack Michael's car behind me. I started to sob and begged him not to take me to the hospital. He should just take me to the plane and stop this nonsense of pretending. They were all waiting for me, all my family and friends, I didn't want them to wait any longer.

He called Jack and said we were going home first so he could pack me some clothes. "Please, Zach, don't take me back, please," I begged, "I made a mistake. Zach, did you know that John's not dead? Zach, it's a miracle. Who else isn't dead? Is Gord still dead? Zach, please don't tell me that this whole affair thing between your dad and Tammy was a farce, I don't want him back." Zach sadly replied, "No, Mom, it's all real." Then I quietly told him, "Zach, John's not dead, I saw him."

He looked at me with deep sadness in his eyes and he firmly replied, "No, Mom, he's not alive, and I don't want to hear about it again."

I couldn't figure out why he seemed to be hurting, why he looked like he was about to cry when we were all going to Mexico? I had a feeling that the surprise was waiting at home, there would be all kinds of cars lining the highway, ending at our house, and just thinking of that calmed me down. But that was not the case, the boys went in and packed me some clothes and then we were on our way again.

I'll bet Dr. Tanguay was going to be standing there when we arrived at the hospital to greet me and then he would tell me that he was coming with us to Mexico. I will be able to give him a hug now, something I have always wanted to do. Oh my gosh, it was going to be fun. I'm just going to go along with what's happening so I can act surprised. I didn't want to ruin the surprise after all, although I was getting a little agitated that we were going to such great lengths to pretend that I was crazy. We had to wait quite a while in the hospital and then they put me in the emergency in a very uncomfortable stretcher. I have now figured it out, I am supposed to be in ugly hospital garb, with my hair unkempt, and I was to go through the hospital yelling, "My name is Leianne McNair and I am mentally ill."

I did exactly that, except it backfired when I saw the two security guards approaching. When they reached me, I threatened to knee them in the balls if they came any closer—like I could get my knee-high enough to do that! Wrong thing to say, all of a sudden, they had my hands behind my back so fast and were dragging me back to where I came from, I didn't know what to think. They definitely hurt my wrists, when they threw me down on the stretcher, my face hit the desk and it hurt. I was getting hurt, what kind of nonsense is this? Why would they do that? I am about to change the way the world looks at mental illness, I deserve some respect! I can't believe that Oprah would allow this to happen to me. What the hell? And the fact that they have had this charade going on for nine years, mind blowing!

Once again, I was admitted to the psych ward and it was weeks before I started to realize that I was wrong. Covid was the pandemic, I was very obstinate in the hospital and refused to wear my mask until I realized that there was no parade, no Oprah, no billionaires, no friends and family proud of me. I still struggled and cried every time I thought of John and how he wasn't alive. I was unable to get a decent night's sleep. I thought Apple was controlling my iPad, as they had altered all my photos to see if I picked up on it. The lengths they were going to, to see if I was crazy were unbelievable.

After two days in the hospital, I was put in isolation for two weeks. They kept wanting to test me for COVID and the third time the nurse asked to test me, I told her that the only way I was going to get tested was if they allowed me to test her. Guess what, I didn't have to take the test!

I was still feeling like Apple was controlling my iPad, that there was a camera in my room. It was eerie and I didn't know what to think.

During isolation, all I was allowed to have was my iPad. Zach didn't allow me to have my phone and I was not allowed to go on any kind of social media. Zach had somehow become a techie and blacked everything out. However, he did not black out my credit card, so what I did to pass the time was shopping, and oh my, was it fun. I kept records of everything that I bought, and before you knew it I spent close to two thousand dollars. I had just finished purging my house and now I'm going to fill it with more crap. What the hell is wrong with me? I told myself I was buying it to see if I wanted to sell it through my business.

And then the humiliation and embarrassment of it all came to light and I couldn't get over it, it made me sick to my stomach. This was a tough one to get over and once again, I had to ask why? What have I done?

Once my week was done in isolation, I was very excited until a doctor came in and told me that I would have to do another week in isolation because I had been at the airport. I screamed at her that she was a fucking bitch and that she should never have become a fucking doctor. I did not know how in the hell I had to be in isolation when I had not been in contact with anyone and both of my tests came back negative. It was very frustrating, as I wanted to get out and make friends. I accepted my fate and continued to shop... .

Another week passed of solitude, a very hard week, but I was finally out in the unit and looking to meet friends. I was very excited. I was better now, except for dealing with the embarrassment of what I had done and what I had put my kids through again. It was nothing short of hell for them and it was again a tough pill to swallow. I was on some heavy medication, but it kept me stable and sane, so I didn't complain. I put my faith for my well-being in the doctors' hands and I trusted them, for I knew that they were smart, well-educated people and they knew what they were doing. I have been blessed to have so many wonderful, amazing professionals working with me in the past and it really annoys me to see patients complaining about them. I figure that these doctors, nurses and pharmacists are highly skilled and I am grateful for what they do for me.

Chapter Twenty

On the unit today, it was busy, patients were yelling that they were going to sue, that the system was fucked, that the medication they were on causes all kinds of side effects. Because we were all in quarantine and not allowed to leave the unit, we were told that sixteen laps of the hallways equaled one kilometer. We did armchair yoga and Walk a Mile on the spot to get in some exercise. Because my back hurt so much and I couldn't stand or walk for more than six minutes, I would sit and once again feel humiliated. Young men were still pacing the halls zombie-like, there was no animation to their step and their gaze was still as glass. It was sad to see, and there were a lot of them. Young women were in the same boat; I didn't know most of their stories, but the ones that I did broke my heart. So it was amazing to see one of them who had been like a zombie not so long ago become a person again, one who smiled behind the mask, who could carry on a bit of a conversation—to witness such progress made me happy, so very happy.

I imagined that, at one time, someone witnessed me make such progress and when I reflected on that, it didn't bring forth pain, it brought hope, hope that someday I wouldn't have to go through this again, that someday I would have the tools and support to be able to work through things and remain well. That was my hope, that was my wish, that was my prayer.

Once again, I met some extraordinary people in the unit, they were amazing actually, and some very strange ones, too, but I try not to judge. I feel sorry for them more than anything. The high observation units are always interesting to be around. I was sitting in the common room one day, when all of a sudden, I heard a big ruckus and looked up to see Norma running out of her glass room completely naked. A male nurse quickly tried to find a blanket that he could put around her and guided her back to her room.

Then there is Ethan, who just got his clothes back a couple of days ago. Ethan is a young, thin, blond man, twenty-two years old, extremely good-looking, and an unbelievable rapper, very talented and quite charming. I honestly believe, that if a producer heard him, they would sign him on the spot. He was rapping freestyle with whatever music he was hearing, and it was amazing the way that he could make his words rhyme. Ethan seems perfect, but when he is not rapping, he is pacing up and down the hallways, yanking on his privates with his ass crack hanging out. He gets to the end of the hallway and then drops down on the floor to do pushups. He is breathing so hard, he just about vomits, the whole thing is rather disturbing. When he raps, a lot of it is made up and there have been a couple of times when his lyrics were extremely crude and rude, yet he was a likeable young man. I considered him to be my friend.

There was one guy in high observation who screamed incessantly and banged on the door to get out as he needed to go to the washroom. The other night it went on for 30 minutes. Four security guards and two nurses gowned up—it took them about 8 minutes for everyone to get ready. When they finally let him out and into the washroom, he started laughing hysterically, shouting, "Suckers, I was just kidding, I don't have to go to take a piss!" He was hauled out of there quickly, only to turn around 10 minutes later, really needing to go to the bathroom.

Spence is an interesting man, a very handsome, thin, forty-something-year-old, with three small boys at home and a wife whom he adored. When Spence came in, he obviously had ADHD as he was fast-paced at everything and he seemed rather jittery. I had never seen someone like that before, but after introducing myself to him, I immediately liked him. My heart broke when I read him a passage in my book and he cried. He was very kind and thanked me for reading it to him and then asked if I could email it to him. It really touched me as I knew that Spence could relate to the passage. I discovered that Spence was a very bright man and interesting to talk to, and in our many visits, I never saw that vulnerability come through again. At the moment, even though it was painful, it made me feel validated for the first time since I started writing this book and for that, I shall be forever grateful to him. I had a feeling that Spence and I were going to be good friends.

I have made another very good friend, Melissa, the mother of three beautiful children and wife of a pilot who loved her very much. Melissa had beautiful blond hair, blue eyes, and an ivory face. She was quite a bit younger than I, and as soon as I met her, I immediately liked her. She was a very proud mom who spoke fondly of her family. A few days into our friendship, she shared why she was in the hospital. She was a nurse and had been taking medications from the hospital where she worked and was also an alcoholic. I didn't judge her, when she told me, I just told her that I was sorry and I truly meant that—my heart went out to her and I knew that the situation she was in could have happened to anyone. I just felt very lucky to have her as my roommate on this part of my journey.

My heart went out to Melissa as she had two major hurdles to overcome, mental illness *and* addiction. She was confident that she would be successful and I knew that I had someone else to pray for. I was proud of her as she had a long and difficult road ahead of her. Melissa and I were becoming the best of friends and would often stay up late at night, talking about our respective lives. Even though we were at different stages in our lives, we were able to talk about anything. Then Melissa started having some medical issues and, before we knew it, she was put into isolation. A lovely young girl was put in my room to take Melissa's place.

Because Melissa was in isolation, there were no longer any games between us, no sharing lunches together, and when I expressed how terribly sad I was and how I was missing our talks, she expressed the same sentiments. We were right next door to each other and made a little knock signal on the wall, so we knew when each other needed to talk.

One evening, I heard the knock and went over to have our evening visit. Because she was now in isolation, she had to stay in her room, and I stayed in the hallway, with a small bedside table between us. She sat down and with a devious little smile, looked at me and said, "I have a surprise for you." I couldn't imagine what it was, so I jokingly said, "I'll bet it's a vape," and she nodded yes. I just about died; my own kids would not sneak a vape in for me! I had quit smoking 9 months ago but had started vaping to take the edge off to try and maintain my stress level. I had suggested to my kids to put a vape in the McDonald's fries or under the burger, but oh no, that was wrong, what if I got caught?

With this news from Melissa, I had mixed feelings. I was so excited to have a puff, but it was wrong, and what if I got caught? I was curious how her husband snuck it into the hospital and she told me he bought a coffee-mate and put it inside the jar. He carefully peeled back the top, placed the vapes and the chargers in a Ziploc bag and buried them in the coffee-mate. He glued the top back on and we were set. I just laughed, this was a total drug-smuggling move.

I felt honored that they would go to such great lengths to put a smile on my face and was impressed with her husband, who was totally against doing what he did but did it for his wife, anyway, as he was the type of man who would do anything for his wife. That was love.

We had to overcome the hurdle of her passing it to me without being caught, there were mirrors and cameras everywhere and all of a sudden, I felt like all of the staff were watching us. Eventually, I would look left, I would look right, then pass. I felt like a criminal. Oh my gosh, I hoped I didn't get caught. I kept thinking of the irony of coffee-mate appearing like cocaine and it made me laugh. I didn't dare tell my family as they might think that I would get kicked out of the hospital. Every time I went into the bathroom, every time I hid the device in my bra, and every time I took a puff, I was terrified. It really wasn't worth it, but it gave this experience a bit of an edge that I had never experienced before. I felt like a total badass, yet I was so scared I was going to get caught.

There are times during a hospital stay when you meet some fascinating people like, for instance, Lisa. Lisa was a large woman with long stringy gray hair. She had a cute, cherub-like face and I liked her, even though she would get right in my face and growl because she thought that I was Lucifer and that I ate her sushi and chicken. I didn't understand that part, but it made me chuckle. Every once in a while, Lisa went on a rampage and would yell that Lucifer was in the building and watch out because he was going to get you. Lisa would often shout out, "Call Gordon Ramsey, get him to come and cook us dinner, I know you have his number!"

Then there was Nicholas, who seemed quite bright, but was annoying as hell. He went on and on about the doctors and how useless they were. When he spoke badly of Dr. Tanguay, I had to step in and tell him to stop, that Dr. Tanguay was an amazing doctor and incredibly intelligent. Enough was enough. The next few times when he went on about Dr.Tanguay, I just didn't have the energy to argue with him any longer. He knew my thoughts and I would just scowl at him, he made me so angry.

I once saw this quote, "Even in the word hopeless, you can still find hope." My prayer is that this is true for so many of these people. Sometimes, these experiences seem funny, but when I think back on them, all I feel is sadness and I hope that their loved ones realize that it's not their fault.

Mental-health patients include addicts as well, addicts who come in all shapes and sizes. An addict is not only the homeless guy that may come to mind when you think of an addict, but can also be a mother with a promising career as a lawyer and three small children at home, or a businessman, a roofer, a young adult just starting out, or my new friend Melissa. There is no discrimination against this disease. This is a long, tough road that has obstacles bigger than anyone's to overcome. You have to be committed, terrified, and determined to get through without the help of your drug of choice, whether it is alcohol, heroin, fentanyl, or meth. When it comes to drugs, sometimes it only takes one time to try it and you are hooked. I can't explain why someone would try it once and nor do I want to, but sometimes the outcome of that is addiction.

As a parent or spouse behind the addict, you soon realize that the drug is more powerful than you are. That you can't compete with its power, that you begin to resent it, that you struggle to understand the power it has over the power of love. How can that happen? There are a lot of people, mostly family members, who become tired of being lied to, tired of being beaten down, tired of giving money for food and seeing it go to drugs. Those people have not stopped loving the addict, they just can't do it anymore and have chosen to stop supporting before it destroys them and hoping if they don't fuel the addiction anymore, the addict will stop. Eventually, the addict may end up on the streets, in a shelter or, God forbid, dead. But, again, it's nobody's fault, the addict doesn't want to hurt his/her family, all they can think of is their next drink or fix. They try not to think of their family because it hurts too much, it tears them up inside what they are doing to them. And if they are a victim who the family has given up on, it hurts. They hurt, they are alone, except for their addicted friends and sometimes they end up totally homeless, yet they still can't see beyond the next bottle or drug. They can't see what life would be like without those things and the pull behind a bottle or behind a little pill is too strong. Yet, it's that pull that the loved ones don't get, and they have to make the incredibly difficult choice to give up.

I spent one morning with a gentleman whose son has been a victim of this terrible disease. This man has been broken down so many times by the lies and the deceit that he had to give up, he had no choice. In order to save the rest of his family, he had to let his son go. When he told me this, I could see the pain in his eyes, I could see that he wished for a different outcome and that he missed his son terribly. I feel for him, I can't imagine what he's going through, but I also know he tried his best and his heart is broken. Eventually, his son died of an overdose and it broke my friend, he couldn't forgive himself.

I applaud both patients and families who have been able to get through the very tough stuff and move on with their lives. It is a very rough journey to get to the point of sobriety, and it is a life-long commitment. These patients will always be tested and their strength will have to prevail. And their families will most likely walk on eggshells for the rest of their lives, but they still have each other and a life worth living has been saved.

Families feel helpless, you feel hopeless, you put the two together and you don't have a lot. What you have is a reliance on the system, but sometimes the system is flawed, and sometimes the system needs the families to back them so their loved ones can be supported through this system. Sometimes, these loved ones can't afford the medication or buck the system and stop their medication altogether, and this is what is frustrating for families and the professionals treating them.

* * *

She's crazy, the woman is crazy. My god, you were in a loony bin? I have sat many times and imagined people saying and asking that about me, and rightfully so, as I *was* crazy. My kid even called me crazy in an email and accidentally sent it to me, so I can only imagine what other people say about me, whether it's pity or they are taking the opportunity to make fun of me. If you suffer from mental health issues, you try to not think about what people are saying, you try to keep your head up, but it's fucking hard and it hurts, it hurts bad, but you pretend it doesn't. You pretend that you're a big enough person that you can join in on the laughter, you are okay with laughing at yourself, or the pity that comes your way is warranted and you bask in it. I have had people in my life whom I adored and loved but no longer want anything to do with me. I don't know why, I might have done something when I was ill, something that I had no control over, but I can't help but feel the loss. Either way, when it all comes down to it, I am crazy, I will always be crazy, even when I am well and that's a tough way to have to live and it wasn't my fault. I don't care what people think of me anymore, I may have been crazy but I'm a survivor and for that, I AM PROUD OF MYSELF.

I was sure that I had had enough and then, while in the hospital, I was diagnosed with spinal stenosis—a spinal disease that I'm hoping surgery can fix. I'm close to being destroyed, I just don't know how much more bad news I can take. Besides not being able to walk, this diagnosis means that I am still wheelchair-bound until I can get some medical help. I was relieved to finally have an explanation as to why I can't walk and I was excited that maybe someday I might be able to walk again.

I was released from the hospital just about two months after I had been admitted. I was doing very well and instead of being admitted into the long term, which was the original plan, I was sent home. The long-term facility had a COVID outbreak and everything was set back, so I was offered the option of an intensive day hospital program that I was hoping to get into. I would meet with a therapist and a psychiatrist on a regular basis and the rest of the time, I would be learning new skills to manage my illness. I hoped that I would be accepted as it was a very popular program with limited space.

I did pass the criteria and was admitted into the program. It ran for four weeks, every weekday from 9 a.m. to 3:30 p.m. I started the next week and was excited about going home, however,

I was also anxious about leaving the safety of the hospital, the lack of responsibility that it offered, and leaving my friends behind.

About six days after I got home, I was stricken with the flu bug, even though I had had my flu shot. I suffered severe vomiting and diarrhea for several days and had to miss some of the day programs because of it. There were crucial exercises that I was learning and I was hoping that I would be able to remember them.

I was doing well, I thought I was completely sane, and all of a sudden, weird things started happening again. Things I couldn't explain, every time I turned around, something bad was happening to me. Things were disappearing, things had been put in places they didn't belong. My orders had started coming in that I bought while I was in the hospital and they were either damaged, or they were crap. My blister pack's days were all mixed up and it was hard to tell which pills I had taken and which ones I hadn't.

One night we had a snow and hail storm, and there was a blizzard in my front yard but not in my backyard. I was totally perplexed and then I realized how it had happened—and it was George Lucas that did it. Yes, I know it's hard to believe, but once again, I thought that Oprah was behind it all and she asked George Lucas to create a blizzard over my house. In the middle of the night, his crew did their movie magic on my house! I took it all in stride, pretended I wasn't affected by it, but I was yet again excited. I didn't tell anyone about George Lucas, but I did tell my psychiatrist some of the things that were happening. I explained that I felt I had a computer virus, where nothing would go right. When he suggested going back to the hospital, I begged him not to send me. Instead, he increased my medication and kept a very close eye on me. The increase in my medication made me so hungry. I would eat dinner and then, without a word of a lie, I could eat another dinner. It was discouraging, as the last thing that I wanted to do was gain more weight, I was way too heavy as it was.

My delusional state lasted for a few weeks and then, one day, I woke up feeling depressed, sad, and disturbed by what had happened. I realized that it wasn't true, that Oprah could care less about me and that I was not going to be able to change the way people view mental illness. It was a very sad day for me, but I decided I shall not give up! I can't give up, giving up would mean the loss of me, the loss of my family, the loss of my life...I shall continue to fight and not give up!!!

Chapter Twenty-One

After leaving the hospital, I knew times were going to get rough. I was excited about working with my old psychiatrist, Dr. Mirok and my therapist Lyuda. I had a lot to talk about to both of them.

The house still hadn't sold and because we hadn't worked or collected any income for the past 5 years, the bank was moving in and they were about to take it. It was unbelievable how much it costs to maintain this large home and I was anxious to get rid of it. I also couldn't keep up with the interest payments and my ex had refused to help me out.

Dr. Mirok and I talked candidly about my medication as once the house sold, I was about to navigate through the most stressful time of my life, trying to move out of this big house, downsize, trying to find an affordable place to live. My retirement savings was depleting rapidly and I was worried. I was incapable of working, even though I loved to work, but my physical disabilities and mental capabilities stopped me from getting a job. One day, I decided that I would start an e-commerce store and diligently got to work building a website. It took me forever as I had to research everything on how it should be done, but eventually I completed it. I was very proud of what I had done, but now to move on to the next step...marketing, which required money. I had no idea what I was doing and was just not comfortable with putting it out there. Here I was, 60 years old and trying to re-invent myself, what a terrifying thought.

Surprisingly, considering how much stress I was under, I was mentally stable. My prayers continued every day, hoping that I could find an answer.

One day, while talking to my youngest son about my illness, I noticed that he was holding back tears until a few broke through and it broke my heart. I realized once again how painful my past was for my children and I also realized that I couldn't have them or myself go through another psychotic incident. Right then, I vowed to do something about it and made one of the hardest decisions I have ever had to make in my life. I was going to ask to go to a long-term mental institution with hopes of getting well, getting my life back, wanting to live again, and finding the joy in my life that had been destroyed by the demons that haunted me. I needed to rid myself of those demons once and for all and even though life would be difficult, I needed to find happiness in the small things that make life worth living. I knew that I was a good person, a nice person, yet I didn't like myself very much because I identified as mentally ill, which I was, but it became an obstacle that overwhelmed me and I couldn't move past it. Every time I thought I was moving past, it would creep up again and BAM, it would bite me in the ass big time with another psychotic episode!

As soon as I asked my psychiatric team if they would recommend me for the Mental Institution, they put in a request and it was immediately accepted. I knew I was lucky as there was a huge waiting list to get in.

While I was still on a waiting list, wouldn't you know it, my house sold. I had 60 days to get out. I was terrified, I didn't know where I was going to go, I was so immobile that I didn't know how I was going to manage packing up 20 years of our lives. The boys were both working, the girls lived out of town, I didn't know what I was going to do.

As soon as I told my cousin Shirl that I had to move, she came over and we immediately started selling stuff and packing up stuff that I would give away and keep. God had blessed me with this angel and I was so very thankful. Other friends came over, some spent the weekend and helped me and others were there for an afternoon. I was so lucky. The days were going by fast, and Shirl was there every weekend to help me out. She actually did most of the work while I sat on my walker and dictated. I couldn't believe how much stuff I was selling, it was crazy and I was making quite a bit of money.

I still had not found a place to live while I was waiting to be admitted and I was really starting to stress about it. Jack Michael was going to go to his Dad's, which he was not terribly happy about, but after I assured him that he would be fine and it would be good for his relationship with his father, he seemed okay with it. I was hoping it would repair their relationship somewhat, and Jack Michael was in therapy to help him through the rough spots.

One day, I was talking to my good friend, Bonnie in Red Deer, telling her how I was struggling with finding a place, and without hesitation, she offered to let me live at her place with her and her husband. I gratefully accepted and suddenly the stress of finding a place alleviated.

The moving day was extremely hard, my ex, Jack, came and helped with the garage and I knew it was hard on him also. The boys wanted the opportunity to go through the house one last time and I detected the sorrow that they felt. I had a lump in my stomach that just wouldn't go away and I struggled to keep the tears at bay. I knew this would never be our home again, and I couldn't help but remember all the good times. Then suddenly, I remembered the really difficult times, and I was okay to drive away and not look back. I just felt guilty about not being able to provide Jack Michael with a home, his home. Jack Michael and I had become quite close since it was just the two of us, and we had connected on a different level and I was going to miss that.

· · ·

Just before we moved out, I got a phone call stating that I had a surgery date to get my second hip replaced. April 19th, which was a little over 7 weeks away. I was excited but also nervous at the prospect of getting it done. I wasn't nervous about the operation itself, I was nervous about post-op. I knew the limitations that went with the surgery, but also, in the back of my head, I knew the pain would be gone. Moving in with Bonnie and Al was easy. They were incredibly accommodating and provided me with a beautiful room on the main floor close to the bathroom. I felt very lucky and it was going to be good to be close to my Dad. I also looked forward to reaching out to old school friends that I hadn't seen for years.

The day of the surgery arrived, Bonnie came with me, we had a wonderful evening out with my boys the night before. I had to be at the hospital by 6 am as my surgery was scheduled at 8:40. We arrived at the hospital, I was gowned up, and the intravenous was inserted. They came and checked my blood sugar and temperature. Just before I was to be wheeled to the operating room, the anesthesiologist came into my room and told me that the operation was cancelled as my blood sugar level was dangerously high and they were considering admitting me because of this. My blood sugar level was at 25 and it should be around 6.

I had been diagnosed as a type 2 diabetic a couple of years ago, and while in the hospital the last time, my glucose levels were monitored on a daily basis with a range from 6-10. I wasn't that concerned, I changed my eating habits, tried to cut out sugar and was lucky enough to lose another 60 pounds. I was still overweight, but I was way down from when I started. I have to admit that I was a sugar addict and continued to have a sugary treat once in a while, but I wasn't really watching my carb intake.

When I heard my surgery was postponed, I was devastated to say the least. I was so excited that the pain in my hip and groin would be gone, although I would still have substantial pain in my knees and back. It also meant that the other surgeries I needed would all be set back to only God knows when. I felt deflated, all I wanted to do was to be able to walk again without the aid of a wheelchair or a walker, to not have to limp so bad, to be able to run errands and go for walks. That's all I was asking and I knew it wasn't much.

Every time I thought about the surgery, all I could think about was I would have been close to full recovery. Now with the postponement, I did not know where I would be able to recover as I was sure that Claresholm wouldn't allow me to recover in their facility. My worries once again amped up and I started to stress. I started to do some research on a diabetic diet and things that I could do to reduce my blood sugar levels. I discovered that three of the drugs that I was on caused blood sugar levels to spike and I didn't understand why no one had picked up on this as I was continuously having blood work done. My dad and my friend Bonnie were also perplexed and my dad decided to get a lawyer involved so that we could get some answers. He wanted to be involved and attend Doctor's appointments with me and so he did. Because I lived in Red Deer, most of my appointments were held via Zoom or on the phone and my Dad and Bonnie were there for all of them, asking the tough questions that I didn't want to ask. My dad felt that I didn't advocate enough for myself, so he was going to advocate for me. I was okay with that as I knew the kind of person that I was, never questioning a doctor's advice.

* * *

The room is barren, decorated with corals and greens, the popular decorating scheme from the eighties. It is very much a hospital room with a window looking out at another part of the hospital. I had arrived at the mental institution, my friend Tracy brought me down and the only thing she was allowed to do was drop me off. I cried when I hugged her and tried to pull myself together. I was so nervous. I was told I had to be in total isolation for 15 days, and I struggled thinking that a person with mental illness should not have to go through such a horrible stay. I was not looking forward to being here, I didn't want to be here, the difference this time I was being hospitalized was that I was coming on my own merit, that I was stable now, not sick or in a psychotic mode as was usual.

The good thing was that they let me have my phone and my computer, but there was no Wi-fi. Morgan sent me some movies that I could watch on my computer. I would usually watch one or two a day, try to read a book that I had brought, and sleep the rest of the time. I would find myself getting excited for meal time or the three times the staff brought around snacks and drinks. I craved a conversation with someone, and I was lucky enough to get more than 2 minutes twice during my stay. She was a nurse and seemed interested in my story, I was so grateful for her company and I really liked her.

My days in isolation are coming to an end. It has been a tough go, with no Wi-Fi, not being able to read, and the only thing I have to look forward to is daily nurses and aides for that two-minute conversation that I get. I will be released from this hell hole in two days, thank god. I struggle to understand the reasoning behind such a sentence. If you are not already depressed when you get here, this will certainly send you into a tailspin. Two days.... the countdown is on, it seems like just yesterday that I arrived and if I said I was not nervous about the upcoming freedom, that would be a lie. I didn't know what to expect, this place was huge and I didn't know how I was going to manage to get around. I didn't know what to expect when it came to the programs offered, but I was intrigued. I was also excited at the prospect of meeting new people. Some of the most wonderful, amazing people in my life are those I have met while in the hospital. Would there be another special friend in my life again?

Today is the day that I get out of isolation. My freedom began with breakfast at 8:00. I got out of bed and got myself dressed, made my bed and tidied up. I liked to have a clean room, and I was so hoping that they would come by and vacuum today.

I ventured out of my room, trying so hard to make contact with whomever I ran into. Breakfast was either poached eggs and toast or cream of wheat. I opted for the cream of wheat. The eggs were poached hard and did not look terribly appetizing. The food here is something to be desired. I got my coffee, I do have to say, they serve good coffee here and I managed to maneuver myself with my tray perched on my walker to a table. I sat by myself, hoping that someone would join me, but it never happened.

I was supposed to get an orientation this morning and sign up for various groups, so I was looking forward to that. Looking around, I could see the little kitchen, the tv area and a sitting area.

I met a couple of people and started to feel a little bit better. I was trying to think of ways to strike up a conversation, and I came up with, "How long have you been here?" It seemed to be a good ice breaker, some would give me a curt reply, others would go on to tell me why they were there. For the most part, there were no happy stories, although the clients seemed comfortable in their surroundings and willing to talk about it. I knew once I made some friends, I would be okay.

I met with Lindsay today, the programmer who advises you on the different programs available. I chose swimming, arts and crafts, woodworking, social, and computers.

My dad and my aunt were coming to visit today and I was excited to see them, to be able to get outside and enjoy the nice weather, but when I was being wheeled down to meet them, all of a sudden, I was overcome with emotion and tears started streaming down my face. It was overwhelming. I didn't want the visit to be centered around how much I disliked it here and how homesick I was, but I didn't know how to spin the conversation any other way.

After they left, I felt empty and alone. I knew that they were going to take my phone and computer away, and that was going to be like cutting my right arm off. Those two things gave me purpose while in isolation.

Even though I hadn't been able to focus on a book for the last 10 years, I was determined that I was going to try and read a book so that somehow I would be able to pass the time while confined to my room. Success.....I had found myself a Sydney Sheldon novel, one of my favorite authors, and even though I had read it before, I didn't remember it and after 10 minutes, I found myself enjoying it. It gave a little spark to my day and I was actually looking forward to an evening without my phone, reading my book.

My first day of Vocational Recreational programming did not go well. I had forgotten to pack closed-toe shoes and I needed them for the woodshop. Yes, I was going to try out woodworking. They were going to let me do the first class with improper footwear, however, I would need proper footwear for the next class. The task given to me was hand sanding a project, my least favorite of anything. It did a number on my arthritis in my hands and I did not enjoy it at all.

Once I got back to my room, I ordered a pair of shoes off Amazon, hoping they would get here quickly, but little did I know that they would take over three weeks to arrive. During that time, while others were in programming, I spent my time working on a diamond dot that I planned to give my son. It was arduous and tedious work, placing each little square diamond in the correct spot and ensuring that it was placed straight so as not to screw up the other diamonds. It was also a very large piece that was somewhat overwhelming at times.

This was to be my existence until my shoes came. There was nothing to look forward to here except for mealtime, which was served cafeteria style and even then, that was a letdown most of the time. The food here was not very good and often tasteless and mechanical. I so craved a good, home-cooked meal or some fast food.

My shoes finally arrived and I was excited that they fit my foot also. I was ready to take on vocational rehab programming. My only hurdle was actually getting to class, this place was huge with very long hallways and it was becoming apparent to me that I was really struggling to walk even with my walker. So I compromised and found a way to sit on my walker and push myself with my feet to get around. The only problem was that hallway to the Voca-tional Rehab classes was slightly downhill and I found it a challenge to go down and then back up. It certainly gave my legs a workout and because I had to go backwards, I was constantly running into things. I was quite proud of myself for coming up with this method of transportation.

My other classes were Cognitive Behavior Therapy and Advanced Skills. Both classes required a lot of comprehension and attention and there was very challenging homework after each class. I was learning new skills on how to change my way of thinking that would last me a lifetime.

My other daily duties included getting my meds and getting my blood sugars checked three times a day. The nurses and aides here were fabulous and all very good, which made things a lot easier.

Most of the patients here were also incredible and I enjoyed getting to know each and every one of them.

Before I came, I had a lady make me up a pile of little tiny wooden "Fuck" words that I would give out, saying, " Don't ever say that I never give a fuck." It was always good for a laugh and people that I gave them to, would always get a charge out of it.

I honestly don't know how long I will be here, but I do know that right now, this is the best place for me. That I am building skills that will last me a lifetime and that I am learning a lot about myself. I also know that I am a good person and that I am going to beat this illness and not let it define me. I am in this mental institution because I want to be, I know that I never want to have another psychotic episode, as they are very painful to try and overcome, not only for me but for my family.

In a cancer patient's unit, when a patient has finished chemotherapy, a bell is rung, and everyone cheers, even though the outcome is still unknown. These patients have been through the worst and by no means do I mean to minimize what they have gone through, as I'm sure it is nothing short of hell. But it's too bad that when a psych ward patient is well enough to leave the hospital, they don't get a bell. Sometimes, they leave and you don't even get to say goodbye. You feel cheated, your friend is gone, someone, you will never get to see again, and you never even got to say goodbye. But if you're lucky, even though it's frowned upon, you might get a hug, and that is better than a bell any day.

I know that this can't be a popular train of thought, but I have envied cancer patients for a while now. They endure their treatments, which are probably nothing short of torture, and they either come out in remission, or they tragically die. Either way, the pain and suffering of their reality and heartbreak finally come to an end.

If they are in remission, their family is joyous and celebratory, and rightfully so, and it is unfair of me to compare myself to the horror and the physical pain they experienced. Yet, when I get out of the hospital, the question on my loved ones' minds is always, "I wonder how long before she goes back in?"

If I died, the pain from clearly losing my mind numerous times would finally be gone. My kids wouldn't have to hurt anymore or be embarrassed or frightened. And neither would I.

But there is no way I could die by suicide. Why can't God take us away like cancer patients and our obituary could read, "She lived a very brave life, having tackled this horrific illness. Her pain is no longer and she shall finally Rest In Peace without judgement."

When a person dies after having lived with mental illness, sometimes it's a relief to those who have become burdened or to those family members who gave up so long ago and now don't have to feel the guilt anymore. But to the one who suffered one of the many aspects of this horrible illness, she yells from the depths of her grave, "IT WASN'T MY FAULT... I BEG YOU TO FORGIVE ME FOR PUTTING YOU THROUGH THIS HELL." People who live with this horrific illness are actually amazing people, having endured some really rough times in their life and having lost loved ones through no fault of their own.

Don't get me wrong, I don't want to die, I want to live my life to the fullest. I want to be there for my kids' special celebrations, the birth of their children, to watch my grandchildren grow and thrive. I want to be able to listen to them for a long time, to be able to hug them whenever I can—but that's prevented by this fucking mental illness.

I want to be a survivor, more than anything in this world. I don't want to have that "crazy" label anymore. But I also want people to understand how this disease affects those who have it. How it can be so deadly either by suicide or by homicide. How the inner turmoil when you can't stop ruminating tears you up inside and starts to destroy you—and that is when you are in your sane moments. When you are very sick, you have no control over the things your mind tells you what to do and, if you're unlucky enough to remember them, it's devastating to your inner psyche, to your ego, to yourself. Mark Twain once said, "Of all the things I've lost, I miss my mind the most." It is such a true statement and if you lost your mind as I did, you could be suffering from effects like PTSD. I personally have grieved my illness and how it has affected my life these past eleven years, and it has been tough. It has been tough to accept it and it has been tough to grieve it because it's not tangible. I learned that the journey could be tough, but it can be worth it if you can accept it. I know I am capable now and I have the capacity to rebuild, I just need the strength to do so.

If you know someone affected by mental illness, reach out, listen, be compassionate and be kind, understand that they can't help it. Keep in mind that it's very hard for them to talk about it as a lot of people are terribly ashamed and embarrassed that they were stricken by this disease, in whatever capacity. Keep in mind that they might not be the same person they once were, but that doesn't mean that you can't still care about them or love them, but you can't judge them. They need that support more than anything now. There is nothing worse than losing people you truly care about when it's not your fault, but they fail to realize that. This disease can be life-altering, people that suffer from it sometimes have trouble finding joy in their lives anymore. Laughter doesn't exist. They may tell you they are okay, but it's possible they are not, as mental illness is such a hidden disease.

If you have a friend or family member afflicted with mental illness if you think they might be struggling, put your feelings aside, whether it's hurt, anger or frustration. Offer to pick your friend or family member up and go for a walk to listen to the sounds of nature, to walk beside them in silence, if need be. Take them for a drive in the country with some upbeat music playing and sing with them. Have a cup of coffee and laugh with them. Just be there for them, because if they know you are there if they know that you care enough that you will pick up the phone even if you don't want to, and just listen... you might be offering some hope or, more importantly, you might just be saving a life. And regardless of whether that person has a mental illness or an addiction problem, believe me, that life is worth saving.

Acknowledgments

There are so many people who have been on this journey with me, so many friends and family who chose not to judge me. Ones who chose to accept me the way I am, who chose to forgive me for mistakes I made that I don't remember and who continued to stand beside me when I was failing badly. There are also many friends and family who have stopped talking to me, who are embarrassed by me and who don't want to understand this illness, and for that, I am truly very sorry and I just want you to know that if you won't forgive me, I was honored to once have you in my life. Thank you.

I am forever grateful to the following people in my life: my Mom and Dad, who made me what I am. My cousin, Shirl, and my aunt Dereka I need to acknowledge my faithful and loyal friends, Bonnie & Al, Karen, Tracy, Cathy, CJ, & Richard, who helped me get through the roughest times and I knew they were there if I needed them. I thank the friends that I met while in the hospital, who understand what it is to go through this illness and aren't afraid to talk about it: my good friends Sue & Lori, Brett, Randy, Jasmine, Nathan, Natalie and of course Ian Grainger. (He wanted me to mention his last name!) I'd like to thank Jonas, who I also met in the hospital and who named my book, but who tragically didn't make it past his 38ᵗʰ year. I need to thank my ex-husband, Jack, who gave me a good run and some fabulous memories that I shall always cherish and who saved me from a life of misery. I have to acknowledge my brother Jeff who has been through hell but can still manage to make me laugh. To my brother Tom and his wife, Sandra, who were there for Brooklyn when she was all alone in Australia, I shall be forever indebted to them for the role they played in making sure that she was safe until someone was able to be with her. I am forever grateful to these friends and family, Brad, Bryan, Bella, Katie, Brooke, Bodie, Tamara, Korie, Lori, Kyla & Archie. You were all there for my kids when they were going through hell and saw and experienced things that kids shouldn't have to see.

You all played a role in the survival and happiness of my family, or you were there when we needed you the most, and I express my true thanks to all of you for that.

And I can't forget the many doctors in the Rockyview and the South Calgary Campus who were in charge of my care. Some of these doctors were very harsh with me, but they never talked over me, always respected me as a person and made sure I understood things. Some, I felt they could be my friends, even though they could be one tough son of a bitch, and did things that I didn't like, but I know that is what made them great doctors. And, then, there were nurses and student nurses who listened to me and sometimes shed a tear with me, and trust me, I shall never forget you. There are some good medical professionals and there are some great ones; the great ones know who they are and will always hold a special place in my heart.

I'm hoping to recover because of all of you, that I will have the capacity to rebuild, but whatever comes of me, good or bad, I shall be forever indebted to this amazing medical team.

To all those mentioned above, thank you from the bottom of my heart, I shall never forget you. Actually, that's not quite true, I don't have a good memory at all anymore, so I just might forget you. I actually thanked Cathy as one of my good friends and I have no idea who that is.

.

Manufactured by Amazon.ca
Bolton, ON

28814974R00152